H.H. Sedgwick

Spectrum of Ecstasy

Spectrum of Ecstasy

Embracing Emotions
as the Path of Inner Tantra

Ngakpa Chögyam
with Khandro Déchen

ARO BOOKS
New York & London
1997

Aro Books, inc.

PO Box 330
Ramsey, New Jersey 07446

Book design & typography by Shardröl Wangmo
Cover by Dorothy L. Mason
Ngak'chang Rinpoche & Khandro Déchen
Photograph by Jaye Ann Ito

First Edition

Printed in the United States of America

Library of Congress Catalog Number 97-072919
ISBN 0-9653948-0-8

This book is dedicated
to Khyungchen Aro Lingma,
and to the gö-kar-chang-lo'i-dé, and
the ngak'phang tradition of the Nyingma School.
May the non-celibate, non-liturgical, non-institutional
tradition of the eighty-four Mahasiddhas,
Padmasambhava & Yeshe Tsogyel
thrive in order that all beings
may realise the union of
spacious passion in passionate space!

If there is any value to be found in this book,
it is entirely due to the inspiration of
the Nyingma Lineage.
Any faults are entirely due to our own inadequacies.

Om A'a Hung Bendzra Guru Jnana Sagara
Bam Ha Ri Ni Sa Siddhi Hung

Om A'a Hung Bendzra Guru
Pema Siddhi Hung

Contents

ix   List of Illustrations

xi   Acknowledgements

xiii   Editor's Note

xvi   Foreword – *Kyabjé Chhi-'mèd Rig'dzin Rinpoche*

xvii   Introduction – *Phüntsog Tulku Rinpoche*

3   Opening

13   Chapter 1   *Rainbow of Liberated Energy*

27   Chapter 2   *Hall of Mirrors*

73   Chapter 3   *View, Meditation and Action*

83   Chapter 4   *Discovering Space*

105   Chapter 5   *Reading the Field of our Energies*

123   Chapter 6   *Yellow Khandro-Pawo Display*

135   Chapter 7   *White Khandro-Pawo Display*

149   Chapter 8   *Red Khandro-Pawo Display*

163   Chapter 9   *Green Khandro-Pawo Display*

183   Chapter 10   *Blue Khandro-Pawo Display*

195   Chapter 11   *Five-fold Display*

235   Chapter 12   *Method*

257   Chapter 13   *Dancing in the Space of the Earth and Sky*

277   Glossary

297   Appendix A   *Sky Signatures*

301   Appendix B   *The Confederate Sanghas of Aro*

307   Index

List of Illustrations

ii   *Déwa (bDe ba)* – Ecstasy

x   Ngak'chang Rinpoche and Khandro Déchen

2   *Ma kyé (ma sKye)* – Unoriginated

12   *Ja-lu ('ja' lus)* – Rainbow body

26   *É kha (e mKha')* – Primordial spatial expanse

72   *Gom (sGom)* – Meditation

82   *Namkha (nam mKha')* – Space / Sky

104   *Ying (dbYings)* – Open dimension of reality

122   *Sèr (ser)* – Yellow

134   *Chu (chu)* – Water

148   *Mar (dMar)* – Red

162   *Lung (rLung)* – Air / Wind

182   *Ngön (sNgon)* – Blue

194   *Chö (chos)* – As it is

234   *Nang tong (sNang sTong)* – Vividness / Empty appearances

256   *Long (kLong)* – Vastness

296   Ngak'chang Rinpoche executing a calligraphy

Ngak'chang Rinpoche & Khandro Déchen

Acknowledgements

We gratefully acknowledge all our Lamas, but especially: Kyabjé Dudjom Rinpoche; Kyabjé Dilgo Khyentsé Rinpoche; Kyabjé Kunzang Dorje Rinpoche; and, Kyabjé Chhi-'mèd Rig'dzin Rinpoche.

Heartfelt love and respect to our vajra sisters: Jetsunma Khandro Ten'dzin Drölkar and Khandro Ten'dzin Wangmo.

And to our vajra brothers: Ngak'chang La-kar Chö-kyi Wangchuk Rinpoche; Lama Tharchin Rinpoche; and Gyaltsen Rinpoche (Lama Sonam Sangpo).

We thank our vajra sangha of ordained ngak'phang disciples: Ngakma Nor'dzin Rang-jung Pamo; Ngakpa Rig'dzin Taklung Rolpa'i Dorje; Ngakpa 'ö-Dzin Tridral Nyima Dorje; Naljorpa Mingyür Lhundrüp Rolpa'i Dorje; Ngakma Shardröl Rang-tsal Ja'gyür Chhi-mèd Wangmo; Ngakma Yeshé Zér-tsal Wangmo; Naljorma Jig'mèd Khyungtsal Pamo; Ngakpa Traktung Wangdrak Rinchen Pawo; Naljorpa Rang-rig Long-tsal Dorje; Ngakpa Shérab Long-gyür Wangdrak Rig-tsal Dorje; and Naljorma 'ö-Sel Nyima Chèrdröl Khandro.

We thank our entire vajra family of apprentices and the apprentice vajra families of: Ngakpa Rig'dzin Taklung Rolpa'i Dorje; Naljorpa Mingyür Lhundrüp Rolpa'i Dorje; and, Ngakma Nor'dzin Rangjung Pamo & Ngakpa 'ö-Dzin Tridral Nyima Dorje.

xi

Acknowledgements

Finally, many thanks to all the Friends of the Confederate Sanghas of Aro – Sang-ngak-chö-dzong in Britain; Aro Gar in the U.S. and Canada; Aro Gesellschaft in Austria; Aro Gemeinschaft in Germany; and, Aro Stichting in Holland.

NGAK'CHANG CHÖGYAM ÖGYEN TOGDEN
KHANDRO DÉCHEN TSÉDRÜP ROLPA'I YESHÉ

Aro Taktsang
Penarth, South Glamorgan, Wales
Anniversary of the birth and passing into rainbow-body of
Jomo Pema 'ö-Zér, April 13th 1997

Editor's Note

A proportion of this material was previously published in 1986 by Element Books as *Rainbow of Liberated Energy*. The text has been completely revised and expanded by Ngak'chang Rinpoche, and Question and Answer Commentaries have been added. In these question and answer sessions, Rinpoche and his sang-yum, Khandro Déchen, present their responses as a teaching couple, which is their usual style of giving teachings. Often the questioners find themselves in the interesting position of answering their own questions in the act of asking them, and all that is needed is to have this pointed out to them. At other times, questioners are led to discover the answers to their questions through an extended dialogue with Rinpoche and Khandro Déchen, who may ask *them* questions in return. Sometimes questions will spark Rinpoche and Khandro Déchen to relate anecdotes from their personal lives to illustrate the answers. In editing, an attempt has been made to preserve the lively and often humorous quality of these exchanges. The questions and answers were compiled from a variety of different occasions, and include written questions submitted by the apprentices of Ngak'chang Rinpoche and Khandro Déchen during the writing of this book.

The following anecdote is taken from the original introduction to *Rainbow of Liberated Energy*, written by Dr. Stephen Glascoe. Since it was felt to give an interesting angle on the author, I have included it here:

At one time I persuaded the local hospital neurology department to perform an EEG or brain wave activity scan on Ngak'chang Rinpoche. This wasn't difficult as there were several people who were fascinated to see if years of committed mental training would have any noticeable effects on his EEG readout. To explain briefly, there are two main kinds of brain wave activity: beta waves, which have to do with conscious thought or concentration; and alpha waves, which are associated with relaxed or calm states. It is known that a number of factors influence alpha wave activity. Meditative states certainly do so; some drugs do to a lesser extent; even a hot curry will show a small effect. So I certainly expected to see some changes from the normal in Ngak'chang Rinpoche's readout.

As they attached the electrodes to his scalp, we watched the pen trace out the patterns of his cerebral activity in response to various instructions: "Just relax... okay now we've got some mental arithmetic questions for you..." Puzzlement turned to astonishment amongst the observers: what was happening? Was the thing connected up properly? The head of the department, who had remained in the background until now, shot Ngak'chang Rinpoche a quick, quizzical glance and leant over the EEG machine. She went through the instructions again, expertly fiddling with the array of dials. Her frown deepened as the pen steadily recorded the slow, even picture of complete relaxation. "It just doesn't *do* that," she said. "Eyes closed... now open!" This is normally guaranteed to demonstrate a flick from alpha to beta activity.

Editor's Note

I tried to appear cool outwardly, but inside I was dumbfounded. At last, with half the neurology department clustered round the readout, Ngak'chang Rinpoche was asked to 'be angry'. I think this fazed him for a moment; he certainly looked a little confused. Then I suggested he might try a Tantric visualisation of an 'angry manifestation' of one of the wrathful awareness-beings.

Suddenly the pen went berserk, skitting about all over the paper. There was a breathless feeling in the room as the electrodes were finally removed from his scalp. Relaxing afterwards, Ngak'chang Rinpoche was quite modest about the whole thing. "If he had wanted to," he said, "my teacher could have got that pen to write his name in Tibetan script".

I would like to thank all the people who helped with the preparation of this manuscript for publication: Dr. William Greenberg; Ngakpa Shérab Wangdrak Long-gyür Rig-tsal Dorje; Naljorma Jig'mèd Khyungtsal Pamo; Naljorpa Rang-rig Long-tsal Dorje; Leslie Kramer (Pema 'ö-Zér); and Zoot Khandro (A-tsal Sang-gyé Khandro). Many thanks also to Dorothy L. Mason (Chèrdröl Khandro); Mike Calloway; Alan C. Margulies; and to Ngakma Yeshé Zér-tsal Wangmo (Wendy Megerman), managing director of Aro Books. Special thanks to Richard Simon, without whose generosity this publication would not have been possible.

It has been an honour to work on this book, and it is my hope that everyone who reads it will gain great benefit from it.

ANDREA ANTONOFF
Editor

Foreword

I have great pleasure to write this Foreword Note for *Rainbow of Liberated Energy*, in its new revised and expanded edition called *Spectrum of Ecstasy*.

Ven. Ngakpa Chögyam Ögyen Togden has been my disciple since 1978. We have met each other on many occasions, especially in my every teaching tour of Europe. He has profusely studied the Tantric Buddhism of Tibet, and Meditation in the Nyingma Line.

I find great pleasure to have appointed him to give empowerments, especially of Khro-ma Nakmo in which he has experience of long practice and retreat.

Spectrum of Ecstasy is a work of Ven. Ngakpa Chögyam Ögyen Togden's adept knowledge in this field. I have no doubt about his success, and that the readers of this book will find themselves benefited.

May All The Beings Be Happy

Kyabjé Khordong gTérchen Tulku
Chhi-'mèd Rig'dzin Rinpoche

Introduction

This enlarged and revised edition of Ngak'chang Rinpoche's first book, *Rainbow of Liberated Energy,* provides further authentic glimpses of the vastness of the spatial dimension. The new text is particularly enhanced by the question and answer commentaries given by Ngak'chang Rinpoche and his sang-yum, Khandro Déchen. The end of the twentieth century finds many people helplessly submerged in narrow and stressful life situations – these direct question and answer communications act as an antidote. The personal vision and style that are characteristic of Ngak'chang Rinpoche and Khandro Déchen are very vivid and full of energy. Words can be judged by the energy with which they convey the essence of the teaching, and increasingly people want to get to the essence to solve their problems rather than taking up different cultural conventions.

I hope many people will avail themselves of the spatial vehicle of Ngak'chang Rinpoche and Khandro Déchen's words, and by doing so, reach the state of utter freedom and compassionate happiness. The instructions contained within this book are apparently simple, yet they are deep and meaningful. Through them, one can discover the nature of one's primordial Mind – the enlightenment or Buddhahood that is inherent in every sentient being. Relatively, through working with our emotions, we can liberate the raw energy of our neurotic fixations, function better in society, and lead a more meaningful life.

Ultimately, through embracing our emotions as the path, we can attain the most subtle level of the essence of the five elements — the luminous rainbow-body.

I extend my heart's wishes for this book and its author: Ngak'chang Rinpoche, lineage holder of the Aro gTér, my friend, and a pioneer of the Buddha Dharma in the West.

RINCHEN PHÜNTSOG TSA UK DORJE LHOKAR TULKU

Opening

Our being is a brilliant pattern of energies, a spectrum of possibilities. At every moment we have the capacity to experience the open dimension of what we are.

L iving as we do with alternating pleasure and irritation prompts us to evolve different styles of approaching life. Sometimes our living context voluptuates with seductive possibilities. Sometimes we experience the world as a series of confrontations and antagonisms. Sometimes our situation is confusing and we experience life as a scenario that merely generates bewilderment.

This alternating display of life circumstances can become intense, and if our lives appear to be lurching out of control, we might be tempted to take ourselves in hand by instigating a 'tyranny of the will'. If we experience some success in this endeavour, we may decide to take refuge in 'the will'; because suppression of emotion might seem to make life a little less chaotic. For anyone who has come to rely on such methods, the idea of embracing emotions *as* the path could appear quite horrific. If we find the vivid display of our feelings somewhat inconvenient, then the idea of opening ourselves to the free-flowing quality of our emotions may seem too dangerous – especially if the texture of our lives is rather raw.

We may not want to rip ourselves open just to experiment with what it feels like to be a gutted fish. If we were to do that, then anything could happen. We could put ourselves at risk in ways that might prove too hideous to bear. We could involve ourselves in areas of experience that might prove too explosive to handle. We might have to sacrifice certain comforts and securities that we have come to regard as indispensable. The whole idea could start to seem a trifle terrible. In the face of this, it might seem better to be 'sensible'.

For life to be as smooth and undisturbing as we might like it to be, we need to keep our feelings strictly under control. If we have spawned the conviction that freely experienced emotions are rather disagreeable, then being sensible could seem to be the safest option. This could be described as 'taking refuge in tepid safety'. But the problem with a tepid existence, is that it continues to cool – our relationships, and our interpersonal environment all become stiff and lifeless. This is the trade-off for feeling safe.

We may decide to dominate our emotions, and attempt to become some kind of 'will-powered athlete'. We can become quite devious in how we deal with our tightly-bound emotions. For example, we might indulge in the insulated pride of feeling that we will not burden others with our feelings. We find it necessary to exercise an emotional discipline that turns life into a tight-rope walk with a tight-lipped stoicism. We cannot sympathise with anyone because we expect the same constrictive behaviour from others. If this athletic wilfulness is taken to an extreme, we simply ossify. We may tell ourselves it is possible to make up for any lack of sparkle with our enhanced efficiency, but all we actually manage to accomplish is to wrap our life in cling-film. Suppression of emotion and deification of the will have distinct drawbacks.

We have undergone some kind of emotional lobotomy in which we have gained the dubious and vaguely arid comfort of 'feeling in control of the situation'. This is rather like saying: "I know that life is a bit limited now that I've decided to put myself in this wheelchair, but at least I'll never sprain my ankle again".

Using the same kind of nervous logic, we can come to believe that we should 'rise above' our emotions – as if human feelings were some sort of spiritual disability. From this fragile perspective we may attempt to reject our emotional personality in favour of a 'spiritual' calm – a state in which the pause button has been securely depressed, where there is no chance of feeling anything at all. But 'rising above' our emotions in this manner amounts to little more than attempting to vaccinate ourselves against life. By this means, we gain the dubious benefits of experiential impotence; or at best, some form of pseudo-spiritual emotional sterility.

We might become rarefied ætheric but slightly bloodless beings. It might seem preferable to be untouched by the dynamic earthiness of life, and to be oblivious to our loss – because, after all, who needs emotional depth in the stratosphere? From this neutered position we might well begin to find the body an encumbrance – we would prefer to fly away to some other realm where pastel-coloured beings are constantly smiling. . .

However, we could be conspicuously unattracted by the timidity and shallowness of this type of control. We might feel that living by whim and wild impetuosity are what life is really about. So we could abandon ourselves to our impulses, and see where that led. We could experience our lives as a series of juxtaposed extremes: pain and pleasure, agony and ecstasy, tragedy and comedy, boredom and obsession.

We could be said to be relating to life *through* intensity, as if intensity held some kind of meaning in itself. We might view the tangles of our emotions – the giddy highs and the heavy devastating lows – as 'the rich tapestry of life'. But this cliché is little more than a way of looking back at pain in order that it appears to have been to our advantage. When we are actually experiencing pain, our 'rich tapestry' more often reveals itself as mere flaccid verbiage.

When we abandon ourselves to impulse in search of intensity, life can become very earthy indeed. We may have experiences of the earth in which we collide with it a little too heavily. The more we throw ourselves at life in an attempt to feel real, the more pain we tend to inflict on ourselves. If we pursue this approach, we may find ourselves meeting the earth at terminal velocity. In seeking intensity, our contact with the world becomes explosive – the repercussions throw us off balance, and the ricochets whine alarmingly around our ears. Contacts become head-on collisions and we sustain repeated emotional injuries, often without understanding what is happening. We could become completely brutalised by our interaction with the earth element. In fact, our relationship with all the elements could become extreme – a truly rich assault on our sensory being. If you were strong enough you could feed on this bombardment. You could experience fire and water in direct conflict.

But with either extreme – controlling our emotions or abandoning ourselves to intensity – what we are avoiding is direct and naked confrontation with the real nature of our energy. With either extreme we never actually experience ourselves. We never *taste* the texture of our world. We never *touch* the qualities of our own being in their incredible fullness and variety.

We never make real contact with the totality of our being or our sphere of perception.

It is important to experience our emotional energies simply and directly. Our emotions are a spectrum of fluid and fluent energies, and experiencing their energy fields is the purpose of our exploration. This might seem a wild proposition, and you may feel that you do not have the right qualifications to embark upon a spiritual path. You may feel that you are not the right sort of person for this kind of enterprise. You could even imagine that 'spiritual people' are somehow intrinsically different, as if they had specialised spiritual organs that you lack. Ideas have proliferated in most societies that practices for realisation are for 'advanced beings'. Psychologists might say that only certain personality types are drawn to this kind of activity. Some people might consider themselves too pedestrian or down-to-earth to engage in spiritual practices.

These ideas miss the point completely. They fail to recognise the unique qualification of all human beings – that we are all beginninglessly enlightened. Whether we comprehend it or not, it is important to allow ourselves to be open to the idea that we could well have more potential than we ever dreamed. Our being is a brilliant pattern of energies, a spectrum of possibilities. At every moment we have the capacity to experience the open dimension of what we are. But somehow awakened Mind appears rather remote from where we find ourselves – confused and bewildered by the alternating patterns of pleasure and pain that form the landscape of our emotions. One of the most enlivening, exciting, and fulfilling discoveries we can make as human beings is finding that our emotions are actually reflections of our awakened enlightened potentialities. The complete unexpurgated range of what we feel is a spectrum of ecstasy.

Question and answer commentary

Q   I'm interested in what you said about how viewing the highs and lows as 'the rich tapestry of life' is a cliché.   Isn't it useful to be able to find something positive in whatever happens to you, no matter how painful?   Are you saying that this view is always a crutch of some sort, in order to make things seem meaningful?

Ngak'chang Rinpoche   Yes.   That's the short answer. . .
The longer answer is that it rather depends on whether you are *living the view* as a practitioner, or living in the best way you can as a regular citizen; as a real *mensch*. . .[1]   For someone who is not attempting to realise the non-dual state, I would say that the 'rich tapestry of life' idea can be quite useful – even though it might ring a bit hollow every once in a while. . . even though it doesn't actually cope with death very well. . . even though it could merely become a means of emotional repression.   It's not that it isn't useful for a human being to look at life that way – if it provides a more open context.   It's simply that it is not useful for a practitioner to look at life that way.   From the perspective of Tantra, any method of looking back at pain in a codified way in order that it appears to have been an advantage, is problematic.   We have to see things *as they are* – not as we would like them to be.   We have to *taste* bitterness and sweetness – totally – rather than entering into any kind of prosaic logic about what bitterness and sweetness may mean.

Q   What about the idea that one can also get great pleasure from seeking intensity, as well as great pain?   Is it a problem because you're imposing some kind of artificial pattern?

---

[1] *Mensch* (Yiddish): a reliable person who has honesty, integrity, and courage.

Khandro Déchen   That would seem to be the reason. Tantrikas
allow intensity – they don't reject it, but they don't cultivate it
either.   There is certainly some degree of intensity in living your
life to the fullest, but that's not what we're talking about.   Intensity
is a natural by-product of being *complete* in your actions, associations,
and participation – but actually *seeking* intensity is merely neurotic.
There is a subtle, yet quite enormous difference.

Q   When I first heard this idea of taking refuge in 'the will'
because emotional energy is inconvenient, I thought: 'That's
me!'   But I never connected that with suppression of emotions.
I always thought I was keeping them in their rightful place, not
giving in to superficial whims or childish desires for comfort.
I thought I was taking the more difficult path of 'maturity'.
Hearing this described as a way of hiding from pain, of avoiding
life, is startling!

KD   Yes, control is a great security, isn't it?

NR   You see. . . there are no formulæ that can be applied.
It's not that you should change and give in to superficial whims
or childish desires for comfort.   You can stay as you are – you just
need to let go of the *compulsion* to act in any particular way.   You
can exercise your will, and you can sometimes keep your emotions
in their 'rightful place', and sometimes allow your emotions to
sneak into unauthorised areas.

KD   The most important thing is that there is no rule apart
from awareness and kindness.   Any emotional rule you stick to just
becomes a reference point, a means of substantiating your identity.

Q   You mentioned that psychologists say that only certain
personality types are drawn to spirituality.   Is that something you
regard as worth considering?

NR   Why not?   It's worth considering everything.   We should not be cut off or closed-minded about psychological findings.
I think that some people *are* attracted to Buddhism as an escape from the modern world, but that is quite antithetical to the actual spirit of Buddhism.

Q   So you do feel that there's something to the idea of certain types of personalities being attracted to Buddhism, for example?

NR   Certainly.   Buddhism, like any other religion, serves social needs at the cultural level.   That's why it's important to be able to taste the essence of Buddhism through direct practice.   That's why there is no purpose in accepting Buddhism as just another belief system.   *The most important aspect of Buddhism is finding out for yourself.*   Entering into the practice of Buddhism as a belief system is quite unhelpful – especially for the integration of Buddhism into our own Western cultures.

Q   You mean that if we don't discover Buddhism to be true in our own experience we'd be likely to incorporate a lot of Tibetan culture?

KD   Yes, that is very likely.

Q   And are you saying that would be an encumbrance?

KD   Well. . . Tibetan culture can be very colourful and beautiful. I think it's simply a matter of knowing which is which.   Which is Buddhism and which is Tibetan culture.

NR   If you like some aspect of a foreign culture there's no problem in exploring it, and adopting what you find interesting or fulfilling.   But culture is not the same as spiritual method. Aspects of culture may be supportive to spiritual method, and when they are, that can be very useful.   But they *may* only be useful to those who are born into that particular culture.

Q   'Can' and 'may' make it sound pretty 'iffy'.

KD   Well, culture is relative.   So it's relatively helpful and unhelpful according to who is making use of the culture as a supportive method.

NR   It's not that aspects of other cultures are particularly 'iffy' – aspects of our own culture are also 'iffy'. We can feel free to explore any culture, but we need to have some awareness of what we're doing with regard to practice.

KD   As practitioners, Buddhism, in its essential nature, should be our culture.   Beyond that – we should integrate with the creative, positive, and humanitarian aspects of the culture of wherever we happen to be living.

NR   We don't have to give up opera in favour of Eastern folk music, just because we've given up varieties of twentieth-century Western neurosis in favour of a non-dual teaching from the East. That would be an act of terminal naïveté or just an adolescent rejection of parental cultural identity.

1

Rainbow of Liberated Energy

Emptiness is the essence of being. It is this emptiness which
allows us to manifest. Emptiness is the most salient
quality of what we are — it is the ground of being.
Energetic being arises from this emptiness as the
play of energy, and material being
arises from this energy as the play of form.

The five coloured lights that illuminate our being are
the quintessence of our emotions. They are also the
quintessence of the elements that comprise our materiality
and the substance of our world. These are very mysterious
sentences, but by the end of this chapter they will make sense
of themselves. The five coloured lights are the essence of earth,
water, fire, air and space. We will explore the qualities of these
five elements in order to arrive at some understanding of our
individuality — the personal dynamic of our being.

The psychology of Tibetan Tantra describes our world and our
being as perceivable in three recognisable ways. We will come
to know these as the 'three spheres of being'. It is important
to remember that although we are talking about a threefold
division of reality, the three spheres are actually indivisible.

They are divided only for the purpose of enabling us to comprehend the nature of our confusion and liberation. They are divided in order to analyse the paradox of our dual/non-dual situation because this kind of analysis resonates with our perceptual orientation as human beings. It is a method of helping us to relate to how we are, and to how we function.

It could be said that we are viewing the same reality through different lenses. When we look through the view-finder of a camera, we see things in their accustomed size. A wide-angle lens enables us to encompass much more than our eyes alone are able to see at any one time, but everything we see is smaller. At the other end of the scale, we can see what the world looks like through a telephoto lens. We lose our panoramic vision but we can home in on things; we become aware of more details. At either end of the scale we see both a lot more and a lot less. The reality is the same but our vision is different.

To make another analogy – we can slow the running speed of a film, or we can increase it. If we were to speed up a film of a dance performance, something interesting would happen. We would notice aspects of pattern in the dance that only become apparent when the passage of time, as we know it, has been condensed. We would become aware of spatial interrelationships and the patterns we saw would develop qualities of rhythm. We would experience some sense of the entire company as a unitary organism. If we were to shoot the same action in slow motion, the patterns of movement observed in terms of conventional time would cease to be apparent. But we would begin to become aware of the delicate subtleties in the articulation of individual limbs, the tensing and relaxation of muscles, and the rotation and oscillation of hips.

We could witness the gradual and delightful unfolding of movements. To extend the analogy further: we could zoom in for close-ups in the slow-motion sequences, and pull back into wide-angle for the high-speed footage. These different visions of reality would seem even less alike. But they are not separate realities. Every view and every method of understanding reality is simultaneously spontaneously present. There is no point at all at which one could say: "This is the *actual* reality, the others are distortions". All one can say is: "This is human vision according to my individual perception". One can say: "This is human perception as modified by my culture, class, age, gender, and life experience". It would seem there are as many different realities as there are perceivers of reality.

So when we examine the three spheres of being, we must begin with what is utterly fundamental: the sphere or space of origination. This individuated space of origination is the first of the three spheres of being: the *sphere of unconditioned potentiality*.[1] This is the primary sphere – which is empty, but from which the energetic and material aspects of being arise. Emptiness is the essence of being. It is this emptiness which allows us to manifest. Emptiness is the most salient quality of what we are – it is the *ground of being*. Energetic being arises from this emptiness as the *play of energy,* and material being arises from this energy as the *play of form*. It is not easy to understand emptiness as the direct and powerful source of endless manifestations. It is especially difficult for this understanding to be a lived experience – outside the emptiness discovered within the practice of *shi-nè* – silent sitting meditation. We need to realise this emptiness experientially as the ground of being before we can relate directly to the magical arising of phenomena.

[1] *Chö-ku* in Tibetan, *dharmakaya* in Sanskrit.

Shi-nè is a way of allowing ourselves the space to experience and actually know emptiness. There is something rather uncompromising about this.

At this point, intellect is totally out of its depth. We are left either with the experience of emptiness – or without it. There are no half-measures. In order to comprehend this vastness, we have to let go of the experiential agoraphobia that cripples the free dimension of our being. There is no dipping your toes in to see if the temperature is comfortable; because, from the point of view of duality, the temperature is never quite right. There is no shallow end in which to linger tentatively – this space demands immediate and total immersion. The *water* of the experience of emptiness is so startlingly brilliant, clear, and sparkling; that it demands our complete participation. If we relax, and let go completely, we find ourselves in the water having dived effortlessly. We will have dived with natural grace, and then we realise that this is our natural condition.

Because openness is our natural condition, it constantly nudges us. If we practise shi-nè, we encourage this openness. Shi-nè is the method of getting used to emptiness. With sustained practice of shi-nè it is impossible to avoid making a certain important discovery – duality has to commit suicide at some point. This is an odd sensation, because it was duality (at least in part) that talked us into Buddhist practice in the first place. This is when shi-nè becomes ever so slightly treacherous; but this is also when it becomes interesting. It is treacherous because we realise that duality wants to watch itself become enlightened. Dualism wants to get as close to the liberated state as possible without surrendering its dualistic position. Duality wants, in some way, to suspend itself millimetres above the surface of the glorious ocean of non-dual experience.

This becomes interesting as we realise that it is actually the *sparkling through* of our beginningless enlightenment that prompts us to practise.

When we realise that we cannot relate to emptiness through the process of duality, it becomes easier to consider letting go of our reluctance to dive into the ocean of direct experience. But if we try to dive without letting go of duality, the instant re-wind cuts in and we find ourselves back on the edge with some vague memory of wetness. From the point of view of duality, emptiness evokes terror. From the view of liberated-being, emptiness evokes delight.

Emptiness is the inexhaustible source of phenomena. It generates energy as its primary display, in the form of the five coloured lights. This display is known as the *sphere of intangible appearance,* the *sphere of energy*, the *visionary sphere.*[2] This is the sphere of primal creativity, the sphere of energy, of light and sound. This sphere of energy is the bridge between emptiness and form. This is the sphere of *magic*. This is the visionary dimension of Tantra.

Light and sound are the most subtle aspects of our perception, but we should not take the words 'light' and 'sound' too literally. Light and sound simply equate to a level of experience, and to a manifestation of energy that can be pointed at by those words. It is simply that our sense faculties of smell, taste, touch, and cognition are not adequate as vehicles to open up that realm of experience. Light and sound have a connection with space and time; and the knowledge that exists in their non-dual expression. This is the non-ordinary reality of the tantrika. The sphere of intangible appearance is where the Tantric practitioner engages in the alchemy of transmuting duality into liberated-being.

2 *Long-ku* in Tibetan, *sambhogakaya* in Sanskrit.

This sphere of energy is the essence of our materiality and the substance of our world.

The world that we know is the third sphere – either the *sphere of relative manifestation,* or the *sphere of realised manifestation.*[3] The sphere of relative manifestation is the dualistic version of the sphere of realised manifestation. The sphere of relative manifestation is the world we perceive through our dualistically-filtered sense fields: filtered seeing, filtered hearing, filtered smelling, filtered tasting, filtered touching, and filtered thinking. In Buddhist terms our faculty of cognition is a sense along with the others; but in the West, especially, we allow this sense field to override the others. It can be quite a breakthrough simply to grasp the idea that we 'ideate' the world as much as we sense it with our other sense fields. We *see, hear, smell, taste* and *touch* the phenomenal world and filter it all through our thinking.

The three spheres of being are subtle and crucial teachings in understanding Tantra. These three spheres are a symbolic [4] expression of the nature of being; they open up our cramped sense of what we are. The sphere of unconditioned potentiality is emptiness, or creative space. The sphere of intangible appearance is the primary display of energy, appearing as sound and light – as the symbolic images of the visionary world. The sphere of realised manifestation is the non-dual aspect of reality available to our unfiltered sense faculties. The sphere of realised manifestation is the self-perfected, evident, substance of the world.

---

[3] *Trül-ku* in Tibetan, *nirmanakaya* in Sanskrit.

[4] The words 'symbol', 'symbolic' and 'symbolism' are used in a specific way in this book. They all refer to the visionary sphere of the *long-ku* (*sambhogakaya* or sphere of intangible appearance). Symbols in this sense are always self-created out of the *chö-ku* (*dharmakaya* or sphere of unconditioned potentiality).

Symbols arise as compassionate communication from within the sphere of intangible appearance, and are expressed through Tantra as the sphere of realised manifestation. But symbolism is a deep and subtle subject, and one that cannot be approached through associating one thing with another, in the way that a pound note or a dollar bill represents the power to purchase. Real symbolism is not arbitrary. We cannot simply say: "This is a symbol for that" – there must be some real connection. Symbols are a spontaneous manifestation of what they symbolise, that arise within the being-space of realised masters. Realised Tantric masters discover symbols as a compassionate response to the unenlightenment of those who have connection with them. Discovery of a symbol is concomitant with direct awareness of 'that' which is symbolised, and contains the motivation to communicate it as a method of liberation. Symbols arise from the expanse of reality which is beyond symbol, but which is open to the enlightened recognition of those who are completely identified with the communicative quality of compassion. A symbol is a means of causing the compassionate expansiveness of reality to manifest at the level of vision. If we invent symbols through the process of intellect, they are not really symbols, as Tantra understands symbols. An invented symbol would have to be called something else – perhaps a logo, visual metaphor or corporate image. There is a fundamental difference between symbol and logo. The Tantric masters or *gTértöns*[5] work in one way, and graphic designers work in another.

[5] gTértöns are incarnations of the twenty-five disciples of Padmasambhava (or disciples of these disciples) who find the Hidden Spiritual Treasures that were concealed by Padmasambhava and Khandro Chenmo Yeshé Tsogyel. These Treasures (gTérma or gTér) are classified as *sa gTér* and *gong gTér*. Sa gTér are found as actual texts or objects. Gong gTér are concealed within the Mind-continuum of the twenty-five disciples, and are discovered through revelation. There is also a category known as *dag-ngang gTér* (gTér of pure vision), in which the symbolic material discovered springs from the nature of Mind itself. *See* Tulku Thöndup Rinpoche's *Hidden Teachings of Tibet* (Wisdom Publications, 1986).

The designer considers the relative meaning of certain phenomena and fabricates an image which conveys the meaning pictorially. Even if the designer is a Buddhist practitioner designing something for a Buddhist centre, the result is not a symbol. The enlightened Tantric master *discovers* symbols. True symbols are windows through which we can view the *essential nature of our being.*

The symbols we are about to explore are not exotic in any way. We are not going to be looking at something that is alien to our experience. We will not really be dealing with 'deep mysteries'. We will simply look at ourselves and at our surroundings. The symbols we will explore in the second part of this book are not the fantastic or elaborate geometric patterns known as *khyil-khor* (mandala or cosmogramme), and this could come as a disappointment to some. We will not even talk about the awareness-beings (the *yidams* – wisdom beings or meditational deities). However, we hope that what we have to discuss may actually prove to be more useful in terms of everyday life experience. You may even find it something of a relief to deal with what you already know. It may be a little more immediately practical than a detailed analysis of specific khyil-khors. Such studies would lead us into the complexity that often makes books on this subject comprehensible only to the specialist. These amazingly rich and incredibly detailed symbols exist in astonishing variety in the Tantric systems, but their essence is actually profoundly simple. It is the five elements: earth, water, fire, air and space.

So, here we will be looking at the essence, and what emerges from it which could be of use to us in our everyday lives. It is important to realise that symbols do not limit that which is symbolised. It is vital that we are able to relate personally to the symbols we explore.

As you become used to working in this manner you will find that the field of symbolism evolves in a way that is increasingly personal.   If you take your interest further, you will also find that the vivid complexity of Tantra speaks more directly when you are able to relate to its fundamental structure.   This fundamental structure emerges from the nature of the elements themselves. The elements are the basis of the buddha families.   The elements are the origin of the *khandros* and *pawos*.[6]   At the level of the Sutric teachings, they are also the basis of the purified skandhas. This is a fundamental and essential level of symbolism, something we can relate to immediately, as being integral to our experience. We are examining the elements that constitute our environment, our physical being, and their essence: the *rainbow of liberated energy*.

[6] *Khandro* and *pawo* are explained in detail in Chapter 13.

Question and answer commentary

Q You said that duality wants to watch itself becoming enlightened, that it wants to get as close to the enlightened state as possible without surrendering its dualistic position. Why is this?

Ngak'chang Rinpoche Because the enlightened state is terminally seductive.

Khandro Déchen Because we *are* beginninglessly enlightened, so our enlightened nature will continually sparkle through our neurotic condition.

NR That is unavoidable. Absolutely unavoidable... even though we may be hell bent on maintaining duality. When our enlightened nature sparkles through, there are three possible responses: attraction, aversion, or indifference. It's the attraction aspect of our neurotic state that wants to get close to the enlightened state, because we have the idea that it just might be the most fabulous reference point[7] in the universe. But it's also the enlightened state itself, the fact that we could be continually teetering on the edge of self-liberation, that actually provides the pull or draw. The aversion aspect of our neurotic state also wants to get close to enlightenment, but it wants to get close in terms of its inherent suicidal tendency. With indifference either option seems fraught, so we retract and hope that we will not remember the possibility that presented itself. It's very tricky stuff. It's incredibly sneaky – duality is alarmingly clever. Aversion wants to stay alive – which is also why it wants to commit suicide in enlightenment. Enlightenment beckons like some tremendous height from which we might fall.

7 Reference points are what we use to establish our existence as: solid, permanent, separate, continuous and defined.

There's a sense of vertigo. We're hypnotised by the interplay of mortality and immortality – of existence and non-existence. Attraction wants to dissolve into a subtle objectification of the enlightened state, in order to achieve immortality. Unfortunately, as soon as you start to engage with a dualistic approach to non-duality, the discussion becomes a trifle psychotic.

KD There's no way out of this paradoxical language problem, apart from abandoning the approach of obsessive form-orientated intellect. Silent sitting meditation is actually the only answer.

Q Are there any other ways of getting used to emptiness besides practising shi-nè?

KD The best and easiest answer is 'no'. There are other answers, which involve taking life experiences as *reflections of emptiness*. But viewing personality disintegration and other life-crises as a practice would involve extended discussion. And anyway, this practice, although quite a good idea, also requires experience of shi-nè meditation. So we come back to the same answer: no.

Q If 'seeing' and 'hearing' are sense fields, how is it that the sphere of energy isn't perceived through them, if it consists of sound and light? Does that mean that the Tantric visions are not actually visual?

KD Yes. What we consider to be 'visual' is only one aspect of 'vision'. The visionary aspects of Tantra that we see are symbolic of the vision of Tantra. The visual awareness-images we see, in Tantric iconography, are the *nirmanakaya* aspect of Tantra – the aspect that exists at the level of realised manifestation. Our visual and auditory sense fields then, are windows on sambhogakaya visionary experience.

Q   What did you mean by total commitment to emptiness?

NR   Yes, emptiness demands our total commitment.   There can be no wallflowers at this party.   You're either in there, with the experience, or you're outside in the rain.   We're continually invited to reciprocate the innate dignity of this ocean[8] by experiencing it fully – that is to say: the oceanic nature of existence continually beckons us by offering reflections of our own oceanic condition.

Q   Rinpoche, you said that the sphere of intangible appearance is where the Tantric practitioner engages in the alchemy of transmuting distracted-being into liberated-being.   Can you explain this process?

NR   This is something of a vast subject, so I can only answer briefly.   Basically, because we're essentially empty in nature – if we dissolve our experience of ourselves into the experience of emptiness, we can reappear in a different form.   We can step into the telephone box of emptiness and step out as Superman, or Superwoman;   or, as Padmasambhava or Yeshé Tsogyel.

KD   Transmutation is only possible because of the experience of emptiness.   I can't become Yeshé Tsogyel until I can let go of being whoever it is that I currently feel I might be.

Q   I was very interested in what you said about the process we have of filtering – the way we perceive through our dualistically-filtered sense fields.   Could you say more about this?

---

[8]   The reference to 'ocean' implies a sense of totality in terms of nothing being excluded or lacking.   Each ocean is characterised by the sameness of the water and the individuality of the waves and currents.   The waves and currents are indivisible from the body of the ocean, but nonetheless individual.   Buddhism is not nihilistic in terms of individual extinction.   Nor is there an implication of a monist non-duality in the sense of enlightenment as 'becoming a dew-drop that slips into the shining sea'.

KD   The process of filtering means that we vet all incoming information from the outside world. The outside world is full of suggestions that we could interact differently, but we spend most of our time ignoring them. The filtering system we've developed is fantastically elaborate, because it also has to vet itself – it can't filter out every sign of non-dual experience, or we'd die of boredom. You see, there's a lot of excitement connected with our inherent non-dual condition, and our filtering system has to allow some aspect of that through. That's both a problem, and our one great chance.

Q   Can we come to understand how the filtering system works and dismantle it?

KD   [laughs] No. That would be impossible. We'd have to try to use the filtering system to examine itself. . .   All we can do is sit. All we can do is sit and allow the filtering system to dismantle itself – then, as it's dismantling itself, we'll see what it is, and understand how it works.

2

Hall of Mirrors

Every thought, every feeling, every sensation or action
is enlightenment; but we do not realise it...
We are never separated from it. There is no need to look for
enlightenment in any other place than where we are.
It is there, unrecognised, in every moment.

In the language of Buddhism, to wake up means to realise that our painful or confused emotions are merely the nightmares of duality. To wake up, means to realise that our dreams, however pleasant they may seem, are only dreams. Whether dreams are enjoyable, fearful or instantly forgettable melodrama, they are not actually happening in the way in which we experience them within the dream state. Dreams, unless they are dreams of clarity,[1] seem very real in the moment of the dream, but often completely vacuous only moments later. However, our dreams do have some connection with our waking lives. In times of anxiety our daytime issues are reflected within the dream state. In a similar way, the style of our constricted energy is dynamically linked to the unrestricted display of our liberated energies.

---

[1] Dreams of clarity are the visionary dreams of yogis and yoginis, which reveal special teachings and methods of practice for the benefit of others.

Every state of being is open to liberation because every state of being is none other than liberation itself – in a distorted form.

This could be seen as our great hope as beings. Every mind-state[2] is connected with our beginningless enlightenment. Every state of mind, no matter how confused, in its free condition[3] is none other than the liberated state. 'Good' and 'evil' do not exist as separate fields of energy. This means that no one is either too good or too bad for spiritual practice. Anyone who is tickled by the possibility, can engage with their own condition at the level of practice. This is all that is initially required. You simply need to be curious – to be intrigued by the possibility that you are actually quite well qualified to make a radical shift. In the very moment that you allow this idea to stir you in some way, you stand at a doorway that opens on a tremendous panorama of potential. Every moment is an amazing possibility.

Every 'negative' state of mind contains something of the quality of our naturally liberated state. Every thought, every feeling, every sensation or action *is* enlightenment; but we do not realise it. When you sip a glass of Brunelo; savour a piece of dolcelate; wash the dishes; vacuum the carpet; take a shower; call on a friend; flirt with a new and tantalising person; cook food; make love; go shopping for a suede shirt or silk underwear; or, hit your thumb with a hammer – enlightenment is there. We are never separated from it. There is no need to look for enlightenment in any other place than where we are.

[2] 'Mind-state' refers to the little-'m' mind (Tib. *sem*). This is the condition of the conceptual mind, as distinct from the *nature of Mind* – the large-'M' Mind (Tib. *sem-nyid*). The nature of Mind is that from which mind-states arise.

[3] The 'free condition' is that in which patterns are either absent; or, present in a state of unconstrained flux. This is another way of describing the non–dual state, in which form is recognised as emptiness. The free condition is that in which there is no clinging to any kind of reference point; not even the reference point of emptiness.

It is there, unrecognised, in every moment. So, why do we constrict our energies? What prevents us from recognising our enlightenment if it is beginningless and ever-present? How do we discover the stillness of balance, and the vibrant creativity of openness within the same emotional state? In order to find the answers to these questions, we need to gain a deeper understanding of what we are and how we function.

When we suppress our emotions, clearly a quality of balance is being sought. When we risk abandonment to the heights and depths of our feelings, a quality of openness is clearly present.

This is definitely not a matter for intellectual speculation. Thinking does not help at all, in coming to a real understanding of emotions. The intellect is of little or no value in discovering what we are beyond the texture of what we feel. In order to understand what we are, in order to realise our unconditioned nature, we need to become simpler in our approach. We need to discover *space*.

Space is the quality of experience in which there is no clinging to the content of Mind through the process of attempting to establish reference points: 'this and that' are 'there', therefore 'I' am 'here', in distinction to 'this and that'. Space is the dimension of our existence in which there is no attempt to artificially divide 'self' and 'other'. But there is also no loss of presence into an experience of 'everything is one'.

As soon as the idea of space is discussed, paradox arises. This is unavoidable. However, there is no need to be too perplexed by extraordinary definitions. At this point it would be better to envisage space as 'lack of pressure' or 'absence of neurotic speed'. For the purposes of these initial chapters, all that is needed is the sense in which space is a quality that we have quite naturally.

It could be equated with a feeling of being completely relaxed in all aspects of our being; yet very awake and alive – a sense of having all the time and room we need to do or be anything in any moment, without fear or confusion. You could say that space was simply feeling natural and happy in your own skin.

We need to allow space for our experience to be precisely what it is. This may seem mystifying, unless we take the time to question the nature of our experience. But how can we do that, and what would we find if we did try to examine our own experience? Maybe this would be a good point to put this book down and experiment with experience.

exercise

just sit where you are / feel what it is like to be you / try not to put words to what you feel / just sit with what you feel, and see what happens / see if you can find what is there beyond the desire to attach words and ideas to what the feeling is like / see if you can see, hear, smell, taste or touch what you are / try everything you can in an attempt to sense yourself, apart from thinking about it

If you have tried to examine the nature of your experience in this way, you may have discovered something quite peculiar. You may have discovered that it is impossible to examine the nature of your experience, without the process of intellectual examination also becoming part of your experience. If we look for the nature of experience with the rational mind, we will never find it – we will only ever dwell within the limitations of the rational mind. The living quality of experience exists only in the present moment.

As soon as we analyse it, we become involved in historical research. We may as well have crept off to some chilly archive to examine pictures of sunny days – when all around us, there was a real sunny day to experience. Maybe there are gin and tonics available on the lawn and delightful parasols beneath which to sit. Maybe there is potted crab, or salmon and cucumber sandwiches with chilled Chablis. Or maybe there is champagne and orange juice. These things are not available in terms of archival research on emotions. That belongs to the tortuous technology of duality.

When we operate in this way, we artificially separate experience into two fields: 'perception' and 'field of perception'. The term 'perception' applies to the act of perceiving – the way in which we register the presence of the world through our sense faculties. The term 'field of perception' applies to the world that we perceive. Attempting to establish that our perception and the field of perception are independent creates monstrous confusion. With this divisive logic we distance ourselves analytically from direct experience. Perception and field of perception are *inseparable,* and when we attempt to separate experience into distinct fields, we lose our 'knowing' and end up 'knowing about'.

Ultimately there is no division between our perception and what we perceive. Our perception and field of perception are mutually self-creating. What we see incites a reaction which influences how we see it. How we view things changes how they are. Enlightened Mind is divisionless. Our perception and field of perception are completely and utterly interconnected, and this fundamental indivisibility is the real nature of experience. So this is the answer to our question: all we find when we attempt to examine the nature of our experience is our dualistically confused commentary on it.

In spite of our compulsion to distance ourselves from the texture of our experience, we do also value the qualities of immediacy and spontaneity. Most people can remember moments of magic in their lives; moments when their consciousness was naturally expansive. There will have been moments when there was a feeling of spaciousness – when everything unfolded with a sense of wonder and ease. This is possible when we have unguarded moments – moments when we forget to mix in our pre-structured concepts with what we perceive.

The first throes of being in love can have this effect. Everything seems to be happening effortlessly and a sense of 'natural perfection' holds sway. Our enlightenment is ever-present and sparkles through at the most unlikely junctures. It is not something that has to be artificially constructed – it is simply there to be discovered.

Every emotion is an open-ended opportunity. Every feeling or sensation we experience is an expression of enlightenment – a manifestation of our spectrum of radiant energies. Yet almost always, emotions manifest as distorted reflections of those energies. These distorted reflections arise as a result of the way in which we constrict the *natural display of the mirror of Mind* with our compulsive intellectual contrivances. But however the dualistic hall of mirrors distorts us; a connection with our intrinsic unmanifested enlightenment remains.

Realised experience is total. Realised experience is what it is. Realised experience is all-pervasive and immediate. It is infinite in nature. It cannot be added to, or subtracted from, without straying into falsification or indirect experience. So, as soon as we divide experience into 'perception' and 'field of perception' we separate ourselves from realised experience.

This separation is what is commonly known as 'ego'.[4]   Ego can
be said to be a condition of duality; a false sense of separateness.
But the words 'ego' and 'egolessness' have developed too many
connotations to be of any real use in a Buddhist context; so,
instead, we will use the term 'distracted-being' for 'ego'; and
'liberated-being' for the even more confusing term 'egolessness'.
The term 'distracted-being' carries the idea that our enlightenment
and 'unenlightenment' are not separate. They are not heaven and
hell. They are not God and Devil. We have never been separated
from enlightenment – we only seem to be separated. But this
apparent separation is what we ourselves have fabricated through
our dualistic perspective. It is this dualistic perspective which
causes us to generate obsessive attempts to divide our experience
into perception and field of perception. However, because it is
not possible to divide experience in this way, we put ourselves
in an impossible situation, in which we imagine that this division
occurs naturally. This is what is known as illusion or indirect
experience – living in a waking dream world that is loosely based
on direct experience.

The natural condition of the individual is characterised by
immediacy of presence within whatever is experienced. The rest is the
strange lurid or lyrical gossamer of delusion; yet, it is within this
complex self-created mirage that we happen to find ourselves,
running circles around our experience with our thoughts. We
have trapped ourselves in a web of concepts, and cling to our
trap as if our existence depended upon it.

[4] *Ego* is a Latin word. Freud invented this term, as it exists in modern usage, and used
it to refer to both a self and a set of functions of the mind. It is not useful for Buddhists
to appropriate this word to describe the dualistic state of the individual. This is
especially the case when addressing the fact that Western practitioners need 'healthily-
developed egos' in order to approach Tantra without merely entrenching themselves
further in a dysfunctional relationship with the world.

This is not to say that there is no place for intellect – it is a valuable capacity. Intellect functions brilliantly in its own sphere – this is not in question. The problem with intellect is that we use it to distract ourselves from direct experience. In this web of contrivances we use our intellect abusively to judge perception as good, bad or indifferent, and we become conditioned to this.

Although from the non-dual perspective, the mechanics of confusion are completely obvious, they are actually far from obvious when we are caught up in them, and occluded within these bizarre procedures. All freshness of experience is lost. It is a bit like living on week-old crusts and trying to enjoy them – unsatisfying. You can splash them with water, toast them; and maybe, with enough jam or honey, they might pass for food. But you know you would be better off eating fresh bread.

We contrive our perception according to habitual judgements; and it is therefore indirect. We see everything according to categories. We create versions of the world with stylised perception; and our response to them, is to assume that they are real. As a result of this, our reactions, interactions and relationships can become severely distorted. There is no real experience, no real perception, no real response, and no real world.

In order to allow space for experience to be precisely *what it is,* we need to stop grasping at the phenomena we perceive. We need to loosen our obsession with relating to phenomena as a series of possible reference points. We seem to have a driving compulsion to understand everything we perceive in terms of our working body of knowledge. We relate to everything in terms of categories. We see everything in terms of how it relates to something else that we feel we understand.

We always want to know how one thing relates to another, and how new phenomena can be fitted into our system. We understand the world in terms of our previous experience of the world. But our previous experience was based on prior knowledge. Our map of reality is based on an endless series of such impressions that are adjusted according to our current cultural concepts of what is open to question and what is solid and unquestionable. On the basis of previous experience, persons, objects and events gain 'meaning' by being grouped with other persons, objects, and events. Once reality has been organised in this way, we fondly imagine that we comprehend our world.

If we are not able to operate in this convoluted way, we feel insecure rather than relaxed; and that is irony on a grand scale. We feel the need to be confident about our world in terms of the consistency of what we will encounter within it. This search for consistency is a feverishly sophisticated game; resplendent with exquisitely tortuous devices for ensuring our continued distraction. It is also a surreptitious process. It runs at twenty-four frames per second, like a movie – fast enough that the individual pictures cannot be clearly seen, encouraging the illusion that it is natural and unfabricated. This process even includes a way of viewing the uncomfortable anarchy of 'the unknown'. It is labelled simply as 'mystery' – a convenient compartment that makes sense of itself by not making sense. Once something has been labelled a 'mystery' it can be safely held within the horizon of conventional comprehension. We could burst out laughing and the whole structure would collapse – but that kind of laughter is not often heard. We would rather reassure ourselves that this is a reasonable way to behave: "After all," one might say, "I must make sense of the world. . . mustn't I?"

We could spend a lot of time trying to convince ourselves of this – people almost invariably do – but actually the world makes its own sense, and there is really no need to impose an artificially constructed one upon it.

The kind of sense our world makes is immediate. It is spontaneously apparent. We can embrace it. We can be embraced by it. We can dance – but only if we let go of our obsessional pre-ordained systems of sense-making. Our world is not static. There are no rules that can always be applied. Each situation is fresh and new. So why imagine that we can pigeon-hole our experience? Why is it that we want to reconstitute life according to some stale set of conceptual constructs inherited from the past? Why are we so convinced that life has to be made comprehensible in terms of pre-constructed regulations? Why do we need to squeeze phenomena through numerous filters of our own devising?

Asking these questions could become quite interesting. It could even become outrageously fascinating – if you applied them to your own emotional history. You might find that the more you question, the more you discover about the nature of distracted-being. It is actually rather bizarre to be talking about discovering the nature of distracted-being. If we are talking about our obvious condition – the way we are – there should be nothing much to discover. But there are many things we do not understand about ourselves. For example, the way we walk. One could ask: "How do you walk?" and, maybe, the answer might be: "I just do it – I put one foot in front of another and it happens". One could say: "I learned to walk as a child". One could say: "I was helped by my parents". One could say: "I experimented with balance, and now it comes naturally; as do all the other skills I have". One could say: "I did it the same way that I learned to swim, cycle or ski".

But if we think about it a little more, we find that we actually have a vast range of skills that cannot really be explained in terms of ordinary trial-and-error learning.

We all have the skill of enjoying certain tastes. We have the skill of listening to music. We have the skill of looking at paintings and films. Maybe you have never considered these aptitudes to be skills that have been learned. Think about walking – it seems so simple. But if you look at the work that has been done in the field of robotics, you might be surprised at just how intricate a process it actually is. The act of walking has been analysed – mapped out by computer – and the resulting information has been used by scientists in experiments to imitate walking mechanically. But the engineering difficulties involved in this 'simple act' are in fact so complex, so sophisticated, that success in this endeavour is considered beyond the reach of current technology.

For example, it was found that a point on the hip, when mapped through the passage of a few steps, traced a rolling distended coil – something that is practically impossible to duplicate mechanically. The joints move both vertically and laterally. For mechanical joints to perform this function as smoothly as the human apparatus, fantastically elaborate technology would be required. There are thousands of delicately balanced movements coordinated through muscles, tendons and ligaments. Attempts to reproduce these movements show us just how surprisingly complex the process of walking actually is. But we just do it. It is as simple as that. It is also as complex as that.

We just perceive. It is as simple as that, and as complex as that. It is quite likely that some people would disagree with the idea that the broad range of our sensory perceptions is learned behaviour.

But if you disagree with this idea, you need only consider the range of foods and drinks that are described as being acquired tastes to suspect that there must be some kind of sensory learning process taking place. At the very least we must recognise that this holds true for those tastes we have acquired. There are all manner of things one might end up eating or drinking. The world is a strange place.

We have looked at an apparently simple physical skill. But what happens when we look at the 'skills' of our sense perceptions? The patterns become infinitely more elaborate. The structure of thought, the convoluted geography of our personalities, the world of ideas is far more complex and subtle than the articulation of limbs. If we put ourselves in the position of thinking about the way we think, we have a tricky situation on our hands, to say the least. We are obviously limited in our thinking, by our style or manner of thinking. So; something apart from thinking needs to look at thinking. But what could this be? Buddhism describes this 'something' as the open dimension of our being. It is the discovery of space.

The discovery of space begins with shi-nè.[5] Shi-nè is the practice of letting go of our addiction to the thought process. We will need to look at the practice of shi-nè in order to gain some sense of what is meant by 'the discovery of space'. But before we explore the idea of shi-nè, we will need to make some further exploration of the evolution of our perceptual 'skills'. We will need to ask some questions about the familiar yet somehow unfamiliar landscape of distracted–being.

[5] *Shi-nè* is practised in all vehicles and schools of Buddhism. There are many types of shi-nè, but the method referred to here is linked with the practice of the Four Naljors. The Four Naljors are the *ngöndro*, or preparatory practices, of Dzogchen Sem-dé – the Great Completion Nature-of-Mind Series. The Four Naljors consist of *shi-nè, lha-tong, nyi-mèd* and *lhun-drüp*. The method of shi-nè is outlined in Chapter 4.

In a relative sense you could say that our being is distracted from
be-ing. Our sense of what and how we are wanders interminably
in a miasma of cross-referencing fictions. This faculty of cross-
referencing includes every function of the intellect. It builds itself
out of the compartmentalising, labelling and judging department
of our conceptual bureaucracy. This conceptual bureaucracy sets
itself up in order to maintain the illusion of duality, and it does this
through continually seeking assurances from the world – assurances
that we really exist. Somehow we seem to be in doubt about
our existence – we have a sense of unease about it. This sense
of unease would be very disturbing – unless we simply remained
unconscious of it. The fact that this doubt exists is actually
evidenced by most of the philosophies that have arisen in the
world. It would seem that no sooner have Maslow's 'hierarchy of
needs'[6] started to be met, then people start to question their own
existence.

Many people would say that they have no doubt of their existence
at all. They would say that they felt as real as the next person,
or perhaps even more real. Some people would state quite
categorically that they are certain of their existence. They know
they exist; and what is more, they are annoyed and insulted by the
apparent stupidity of this kind of question. But from the Buddhist
perspective, this is not a completely honest response – it is a response
based on fear. If people are so convinced of their existence, why
do they continually seek assurances and proofs of it? Philosophers
have been doing this for a long time. Various pronouncements
have been made, such as: 'I think therefore I am'. People may of
course wish to disassociate themselves from the ruminations of
philosophers.

[6] Abraham Maslow (1908-1970), American psychologist, listed a hierarchy of basic
human needs: hunger/thirst, shelter, sleep, sex, safety/security, love and belonging,
self-esteem, and finally, self-actualisation.

They may deny that they seek reassurances of their existence. This is not really surprising – no one in this society is brought up to recognise their fundamental perspectives described in this way. It is not so easy to see the manner in which we live our lives as a process of doubt – as a context of unease. We are geared into the machinery of our distraction. We imagine our acts and motivations to be 'natural'. But this doubt of existence is chameleoid – it takes on the hue and tone of every aspect of our mutable emotional colouring.

But from where does this doubt stem? Is it an aspect of our realisation, or an aspect of our confusion? The answer to this question may be a trifle bewildering: the doubt of our existence is both an echo of our enlightenment and an echo of our fear of the space of our own being, which could also be called our unenlightenment. We continually seek assurances from life that confirm the unconfirmable. We seek security, and that is a problem. It is not that security does not exist, but that the security that is available is not the kind of security that we want.

For example: we can be secure in the knowledge that we are going to die. We can be secure in the knowledge that we are going to get older hour by hour, day by day, month by month, year by year. We can be secure in the knowledge that we are going to get ill from time to time; and that one day the illness will be our final illness. We can be secure in the knowledge that we are going to lose our entire material context at the moment of death.

It could be said that insecurity is the only real security. This might seem a singularly unappealing concept until we consider that pain and misery also cannot be established as unchanging. The phenomenal world is unreliable, if reliability requires stasis.

We cannot rely on the phenomenal world to provide either continuous pleasure or continuous pain. We can be surprised: good friends can turn against us, and generous support can be forthcoming from unlikely quarters. The 'security of insecurity' and the 'insecurity of security', is a theme that will run through this book; and, any other book that deals with Buddhist psychology. This is a crucial idea to understand if you seek to experience a happy life, let alone to seek liberation from duality. It is not even that the existence of certain seeming securities is being brought into question – it is more that the process of seeking security itself needs to be viewed as inherently problematic. Whether we seek security or not, what we get is a combination of 'security' and 'insecurity' – and from the perspective of personal history it can, hopefully, become difficult to distinguish which is which.

There is something suspect about our inability to enjoy anything unless we can define it as lasting forever. In actuality *nothing* lasts forever, and yet we act as if *some things* do – in order that we can enjoy them. The fact that *nothing* lasts forever is very interesting – it is true in two entirely different senses. We can say that 'nothing' lasts forever, and that no 'thing' lasts forever. Nothing is emptiness, which has no beginning or end. Things or phenomena are form, and therefore have beginnings and ends. Interesting paradoxes are wrapped up in this: we own emptiness because it cannot be owned; we cannot establish ownership of that which is already ours, without distorting it into something that we cannot own. We can only own forms on a temporary basis, and as long as we relate to these forms through ownership – we cannot own them. If we understand that ownership of form only exists in the moment of appreciation, then we automatically own the entire universe of form. But we cannot own anything as long as we try to own ourselves.

Paradox is the heart of Tantric understanding, and once we begin to get a taste for what it means at an experiential level – the amazing world of *what we actually are* starts to open up to us. When we begin to accept our emotions *as* the path, we can also begin to understand something fundamental: that as long as we continually attempt to establish ground – we can never really experience ground. Our dualistic method of establishing ground, is to validate ourselves as being *solid, permanent, separate, continuous* and *defined*. These form-criteria for evaluating ourselves arise out of the nature of the dualistic elements:

> *Solidity* is the *form quality* of the earth element.
> *Permanence* is the *form quality* of the water element.
> *Separateness* is the *form quality* of the fire element.
> *Continuity* is the *form quality* of the air element.
> *Definition* is the *form quality* of the space element.

And all form is inherently impermanent. Paradoxically, we reject the criteria that actually validate our existence – because they are exactly the emptiness-criteria which we fear as undermining our existence:

> *Insubstantiality* is the *emptiness quality* of the earth element.
> *Impermanence* is the *emptiness quality* of the water element.
> *Inseparability* is the *emptiness quality* of the fire element.
> *Discontinuity* is the *emptiness quality* of the air element.
> *Undefinability* is the *emptiness quality* of the space element.

Nothing that comes into existence, has form qualities as permanently reliable characteristics. Because our experience does not conform permanently to these form-criteria, we cannot succeed in establishing our existence through attaching to them. Our attempts to define ourselves in this way are bound to be self-defeating.

When we engage in this strategy, we subvert the brilliant immediacy of our experience with our endless attempts to establish reference points. This is the major problem we face as human beings. In struggling to maintain the illusion of duality, we are fighting a losing battle. Nothing will serve us as a permanently reliable reference point, because everything within the world of form is inherently impermanent. Phenomena will only ever afford us temporary proofs of existence according to their qualities of: solidity, permanence, separateness, continuity and definition. These are the *form qualities of emptiness* and their major characteristic is that they are ephemeral. Phenomena are solid, permanent, separate, continuous, and defined on a strictly temporary basis. So, these existential criteria cannot possibly afford us proof that we could be any different. Everything we encounter in our lives is impermanent by nature, and will have limited duration over the course of time. Even if we encounter phenomena that outlive us, we lose them when we die. At the time of our deaths we lose everything anyway; and we in turn are lost to our companions, family, friends and lovers.

Impermanence is not only a quality of phenomena in terms of duration – there is also the question of ownership and proximity. Our possessions may have many more years in them, but maybe not in our keeping. Whatever we have may be stolen, or sold because of a sudden shortage of money. More subtly, there is the extent of our own interest. Our prized possessions may remain with us as long as we live, but they may not always be prized so highly. Fashions come and go. Jumble sales are full of the clothes that people once wore with delight. Fashion is a great teacher of impermanence.

I remember, when I was in my early adolescence, I badly wanted a ten-gear racing bike. Every other young lad seemed to have one.

But when I finally got mine, no one was noticeably impressed. This was due to the fact that I bought it at the 'wrong time'. Not long after I saved up enough to buy the bicycle, the first motorbike appeared on the scene. This resulted in my peers deriding me for the fact that I could have hung on to the money a bit longer and put it toward a motorbike. So the object that had afforded me pride very soon was transformed into 'just a push-bike'.

Making ourselves feel solid, permanent, separate, continuous and defined – by constantly scanning the phenomenal horizon for reference points which substantiate these criteria – is a convoluted process. The phenomena of our perception will only serve us temporarily in this capacity. So if we take this course, we sentence ourselves to the continuous activity of establishing and replacing reference points. When we engage in this process, we convert our perceptual circumstances into a prison. In fact, our perceptual circumstances not only become an incarceration, but a very subtle personal torture chamber. We need to be continually on the look-out for new reference points. We need to reassess old reference points. We need to imbue ourselves with a certain pervasive nervousness. We need to foster a sense of unease about the whole process of experiencing existence. It could become unrelenting hard work in our own personal forced labour camp.

In our attempts to establish reference points we react to the phenomena of our perception in three ways. We are either attracted, we are averse or we are indifferent. *Attraction, aversion* and *indifference* are usually referred to, in the translations of Buddhist texts, as *lust* (desire or attachment); *hatred* (anger or aggression); and *ignorance*. Although these words have a distinct application to the three distorted tendencies (usually referred to as 'the Three Poisons'), they have connotations in English that lend them the tone of 'the Seven Deadly Sins'.

44

Buddhism does not really deal with the concept of 'sin' – it simply deals with the mechanisms of confusion, and the means of liberation. There is no guilt attached to being confused, and no sense of deliberate 'wickedness'. The terms 'attraction', 'aversion' and 'indifference' have been chosen because they are mechanistic rather than emotive – they describe the machinery of dualistic perception.

If we encounter anything that seems to substantiate our fictions of solidity, permanence, separateness, continuity, and definition – we are attracted, we reach out for it. If we encounter anything that threatens these fictions – we are averse, we push it away. If we encounter anything that neither substantiates nor threatens these fictions – we are indifferent. What we cannot manipulate, we ignore. But what is left of our responses if these three fictions dissolve? The question of what our experience would be like without attraction, aversion, and indifference poses an interesting challenge to our rationale. In fact, we cannot approach this question at all, if we approach it through conventional reasoning. Fundamentally this question deals with the nature of experience itself. If attraction, aversion, and indifference dissolve, what remains is not any 'kind of experience'; it is simply experience – *experience as such*. In terms of experience as such; we are completely present, open, and free in the experience of whatever arises as a perception.

In this totally spacious condition there is neither attachment, manipulation nor insensitivity. We are discussing straight experience here, in more or less the same way that we might discuss a straight drink. We are describing an undiluted shot of single malt, rather than some fancy cocktail, overloaded with tinned fruit, and decorated with a paper parasol. We are concerning ourselves with the essence – the undiluted experience of our own intrinsic condition.

We rarely have a straight experience. This is because we are almost invariably bound up in the convolutions of compartmentalisation. We have a vested interest in establishing reference points – attempting to prove that we are solid, permanent, separate, continuous and defined. We are either nervous about our situation, or we throw caution to the wind. Both are methods of attempting to manipulate the world referentially. Caution is calculated manipulation. Throwing caution to the wind is desperate manipulation. It may seem difficult to imagine recklessness as a form of manipulation, but we are only ever reckless as a last-ditch stand – the 'make-or-break' method of securing reference points. We stipulate the exact ingredients of our joys and sorrows and react in accordance with how closely circumstances conform to our pre-determined specifications.

I remember playing mime games as a young child. One game was to pretend to scale the garden as if it were a mountain. I would have to find imaginary foot-holds and crevices for my hands. Sometimes I would really have to stretch for a ledge that was almost beyond my grasp – it was difficult, but I would always finally do it. Games can be enjoyable, if we know that we are actually playing them. But when we are unaware we are playing a game, and it suddenly becomes clear that something painfully real is taking place; we have trouble on our hands. Life starts to get very serious. The problem with these perceptual games, that constitute our life experience, seems to be that we are not really enjoying them. Our games are not really working out well according to our desire to establish reference points. People never seem to want to play with us without changing the rules to their advantage. When we forget that we are playing a game of distancing ourselves from what is actually happening, something ludicrous occurs. We begin to think that 'this' is reality.

It would appear that we would rather climb imaginary mountains than stroll in the garden. We spend so much time setting up 'base camp' among the runner beans that we never have time to pick them for the table. How could we ever consider approaching real mountains when our own garden is such an ordeal?

We cling to pain as desperately as we cling to pleasure. We seek security in intensity, as well as in safety. We turn pain into a reference point and use it to prove that we exist: 'I hurt therefore I am'. If 'I' am in emotional pain at least it pin-points me as 'someone in a state of trauma'. We tend our pain meticulously, and cultivate it through the process of thinking about it. The more we think around our emotional pain, the more we cripple ourselves with the artificial intensity of it. We create conceptual scaffolding to ensure that our pain will not collapse. We experience our pain as security, because it seems to prove that we exist. In fact we often actually cling to pain in order that it will serve as a reference point. We could allow it to dissolve into the sky-like openness of direct experience; but somehow we feel more secure with our pain as a definition of being. It seems to substantiate something about us, to make us feel more solid, more permanent, separate, continuous, and defined. The experience of pain appears to be comfortingly familiar – it is something that we know quite a bit about. We are actually terrified at the possibility of liberation. We feel more at home with restrictions – with our miasma of constricted energy.

Question and answer commentary

Q   Could you say something more about our enlightenment
being beginningless?   I always find that a hard concept to grasp.

Khandro Déchen   I think that's the point, really.

Ngak'chang Rinpoche   It's not really a concept to be
'grasped'. Trying to grasp this intellectually is actually an obstacle
to understanding. I think that the word 'grasp' is probably the
clue to the problem.

Q   Oh... so there's no point – [interrupted]

NR   No [laughs]. Or maybe I should put it another way.
There's nothing either to understand or not understand about
such a statement. The only thing you can 'grasp' at the intellectual
level, is that nothing is logically tenable apart from beginninglessness
and endlessness... If Mind were not beginningless, then it would
have to have had some beginning – and, if Mind had a beginning,
then there would have had to have been a cause. Then you'd have
to ask where the cause came from...

Q   Ah... so that's where the idea of God comes in?

NR   Yes. The theists get round this problem of an original
cause with the idea of God – the uncreated creator. But that
creates a duality between 'God' and 'not God'. So the *tirthikas*,[7]
or monists, say that everything is God or an aspect of God.

---

[7] *Tirthika*: philosophical extremist, i.e. people whose spiritual view was distorted by
adherence to one, or any combination, of the Four Denials: monism, dualism, nihilism,
and eternalism. Monism is a form of non–duality in which the God/not-God
dichotomy is evaded by saying that 'everything is one', i.e. that multiplicity is an illusion.
Dualism is the ongoing attempt to split emptiness and form. Nihilism is the denial of
pattern or meaning (form). Eternalism is the denial of chaos or randomness (emptiness).

But that creates further problems about why all these fragments of God don't realise that they're God. It's actually far more complicated to devise a theory around our enlightenment *not* being beginningless. If it had a beginning, that beginning would have to have occurred with reference to something else, and that would mean that Mind was distinct in relation to something else. But the primal quality of Mind is that it has no characteristics – it is simply the source of all characteristics.

Q   What about the idea that we are all the dream of Brahma?

KD   It's a charming idea but not particularly useful, because it creates a fatalistic approach to life, and to one's spiritual practice. If you simply have to wait for Brahma to wake up, then there's nothing that's worth doing. He'll just wake up in his own good time. If there were something you could do to help him wake up, then somehow you'd be on par with him.

Q   Could you explain how abandonment to the heights and depths of feelings could be 'constrictive'?

NR   Well, it's constrictive because more often than not, it's manipulative. It's a *strategy* of intensity rather than simple self-existent intensity. There's no real abandonment. Manipulating life in order to create or sustain intensity cannot be defined as abandonment. It's not real because there's a vested interest in those heights and depths providing some form of validation of our existence. There's no sense of expansiveness in terms of the ground in which heights and depths exist as ornaments.

Q   What do you mean by 'ornaments' in this context?

NR   That's not so simple to explain. . . I guess there's an easy finger-painting type of answer, and there's a more detailed answer. I'll try the finger-painting first.

Emotional heights and depths exist as ornaments, in the sense that ornaments don't alter the basic nature of the person who wears them. You can *wear* joy, and you can *wear* sorrow. When you have the experience of joy or sorrow, you can have the sense that you are not actually totally defined by either. That is to say: who is it who wears this sorrow or this joy? Now, to make it a bit more detailed, you could say that an ornament is that which adorns something. Ornaments belong to a person, but they're not to be confused *with* the person. That's the basis of how the word is used. But in terms of inner Tantra,[8] ornaments are actually no different from the person who wears them – even though they don't define the person who wears them. Ornaments are as real as the person who wears them; when they *taste the same* as that which they adorn.

KD   Ornaments are as real as the person wearing them; when their *taste* is the same as their wearer's – unless, of course, they're viewed as being real in themselves – and if they're viewed as quite distinct from ornaments that adorn others.

NR   Exactly! It's always a matter of perception, and the need to cling to form. You see, if the ornaments are real and distinct from the ground in which they exist, and if there are other ornaments which appear to be different – in that case you'll have entered into judgements about the relative dimension of the ornaments. You'll have come to see them as independent and separate from the space of their origination.

KD   In order to understand what this means, you need to have some experience of *nyi-mèd* or *lha-tong*[9] practices, in which stillness and change are experienced as ornaments of mind.

---

[8]   The inner Tantras comprise of maha yoga, anu yoga and ati yoga (Dzogchen).

[9]   These practices are explained in detail in *Roaring Silence* by Ngakpa Chögyam, to be published by Aro Books in 1998.

Q   That's the Dzogchen view isn't it – that the state of no-thought and the movement of thoughts, are both ornaments of the state of rigpa?

NR   Yes. It applies to the experiences of *mi-tog-pa* – identification with the condition of mind in which thought is absent; and *gyo-wa* – identification with the movement of whatever arises in mind. When those two experiences are recognised as having one taste, they become ornaments of rigpa – or the enlightened state. But that's a vast and difficult discussion.

Q   Can I go back a bit and ask what would constitute real as opposed to artificial abandonment?

KD   Real abandonment would have no investment in hope or fear.

NR   Real abandonment would not objectify focuses of intensity into reference points. You see, with manipulative abandonment, the emotionally neutral middle ground is rejected – it's seen as a reflection of emptiness. As soon as there's a field of experience which is seen as 'low intensity', it has to be fabulously hyped in some way. We've seen that happen with books, haven't we? Someone writes a book, and manages to collect enough famous names to endorse it; and then the publisher hypes it, and you see it everywhere... literally [laughs]. Then everybody buys it as if it were worth reading.

KD   In terms of the three distracted tendencies, this relates to attraction. Either that or... the neutral ground has to be regarded as pain, which relates to aversion. Or else it becomes just a place to zone out – to fall unconscious with the fatigue caused by cycling back and forth between the heights and depths. This relates to indifference.

NR So you buy the hyped book: attraction. Then you start to read it and it turns out to be recycled nonsense: indifference. Then you feel a bit conned by the whole thing and want to throw the 'timeless classic' into the bin: aversion. These three happen all the time – it's called samsara.

Q You said that we have a compulsion to divide perception and field of perception – why is it that we have this compulsion? What do we get out of it?   Why do we do it?

NR In order to control the uncontrollable qualities of experience.

Q So... you mean we don't actually succeed in controlling them?

KD No [laughs], it would be like trying to control an orgasm!

Q [laughs] Then... [interrupted]

NR Then, why do we do it?

Q Yes, what do we get out of doing that?

KD We have the feeling that we might succeed.

NR We feel that if we were able to be ever, ever, ever so tricky – that we might... just... pull it off. We see it as a gamble, but we're gamblers on a very definite losing streak.   If you gamble on duality giving you a good deal, then you're in for a big let-down.   In the end you're going to lose your shirt *and* your underwear – even if the cards you've been dealt look like a sure thing.

KD So, what we get out of this is not much different from what a gambler gets out of playing and continually losing – simply the hope that we might win.

Q And that's enough?

KD It would appear to be.

Q   But the gambler does have occasional wins.

KD   Yes. And so does the duality gambler. But what is a 'win'?
A win is a temporary illusion before losing again.

Q   Or losing is a temporary illusion before winning again?

NR   That's what the gambler hopes [laughs]. Maybe it's what
you're hoping. This is why Rig'dzin Chögyam Trungpa Rinpoche
used to talk about hopelessness. He said hopelessness was the
essential basis for the practice of Tantra. Without a sense of duality
being 'the hopeless hand that we deal ourselves' – the idea of being
a tantrika is actually fatuous. Let's not be under any illusions at all
about this.

Q   You mentioned earlier that we weren't separate: in what
way is this true? I guess it's just an idea to me, and I don't really
understand it.

NR   No. It's not a conventional rational statement. And, it's
not as simple as saying that we are not separate... actually, simply
to say "we're not separate" would be a statement of monism – an
'everything-is-one' philosophy. From the Buddhist perspective,
we're both separate and non-separate. This applies to the emptiness
and form aspects of the elements. According to the form aspects
of the elements, we are solid, permanent, separate, continuous, and
defined. According to the emptiness aspects, we are insubstantial,
impermanent, non-separate, discontinuous, and undefined.
Glorious isn't it!

Q   Yes... but also terrifying!

KD   ... and that terror is also form and emptiness.

Q   So how does that work at the relative level of our being
here together?

Does it suggest that at one level we're all here together; and that at another, we're still each in our unique position? Like, we're both here, but you're here and I'm there?

NR   Why not? That's certainly one way of expressing it.

KD   While we experience existence within the field of 'here' and 'there', we experience paradox. Your 'here' is my 'there'. My 'there' is your 'here'. Or in a decentralised mode, as you've just expressed it: 'we're both here; but you're here and I'm there'. But essentially – at the level of emptiness – we're not separate.

NR   There is no distinction between your emptiness and my emptiness. At the level of form we are separate. But form is emptiness and emptiness is form. This is the teaching of the Heart Sutra – it's very, very important, and absolutely crucial to the understanding of Tantra. Without this understanding, Tantra could seem like a variety of pantheism; or demonolatry. When we take the statement 'emptiness is form', and apply it to the issue of separateness, it means that we are essentially non-separate. But this essential non-separateness is not separate from our sense of separation. When we take the statement 'form is emptiness', and apply it to the issue of separateness, it means that we *are* separate. But this separateness is separate within the empty field of non-separateness. You could also say that the empty quality of our non-separateness has the form quality of impermanence; and that the form quality of our separateness has the emptiness quality of permanence [laughs]. You could say all kinds of things.

Q   Is this an example of the way that talking about non-duality, in the language of duality, always results in paradox? Because paradox is the result of holding two dualistic aspects in choicelessness?

NR   Quite so.

Q   You were talking about rationality earlier, and it was weird to hear the process of rationality described as a 'compulsion'. I always thought that rationality was something like the basic structure of the brain!   So does this mean that it's useless to try to understand these things rationally?

KD   Yes and no.   If you try to tackle these questions rationally you experience the 'emptiness' or the inoperability of rationality. If you let go of the rational process, you experience the 'form' of the irrational – or of non-rationality.

Q   So it's not even a matter of rationality being right or wrong – [interrupted]

NR   Or useful or useless.   Rationality is useful within the conceptual field – that does exist, you know, or at least it did a few moments ago [laughs].   But rationality is useless beyond the conceptual field.   But because conceptuality and non-conceptuality are reflections of form and emptiness, in their natural condition, they're not separate from each other.   So in practical terms, you have to have a sense of humour about rationality. . .   You can use your rationale to take you beyond rationality; but, if you hang on to it, it becomes an obstacle.

Q   Can I go back to what you said before – about experiencing the 'form' of the irrational – or of non-rationality?   I don't understand what would be the form of the irrational.

NR   It's more a question of how the non-rational appears from the point of view of rationality.   From the point of view of rationality the non-rational is emptiness – the absence of form. But form is emptiness and emptiness is form.   Once you let go of rationality, you can appreciate the form of the non-rational.   You see, the form of the non-rational cannot be appreciated from the perspective of the rational *as* form.

It doesn't behave according to the self-referencing criteria of rationality. The form of the non-rational is *moving* – the form of the non-rational is not constant – the form of the non-rational has no particular direction – the form of the non-rational is not linear or goal-oriented – the form of the non-rational only exists in the moment. Yes.

Q   Thank you. . . there's a lot to be explored there, isn't there? But in a way that won't become obvious before I'm there in the midst of whatever is becoming.

NR   Sure.

Q   You have spoken of the way that people cultivate their own pain through the process of thinking about it. . . How would you say this relates to counselling or therapy?

KD   Counselling and therapy. . . those can certainly be ways in which people can cultivate pain through the process of thinking about it.

Q   But don't you think therapy can be valuable?

KD   I used to feel that counselling and the various forms of psychotherapy were very useful. I used to be quite enthusiastic [laughs]. Now I'm not so sure. I still feel that these methods can be very useful for certain people, at certain times; but I also feel that they can be a way of remaining at the level of self-obsession, or of cultivated inadequacy. If you end up making a hobby of your pain, as I have seen many people do, then you just build yourself a different kind of prison. Counselling and therapy are valuable for people who get locked into the patterns of their own trauma and can't find their way out. It can be very helpful for people with high levels of distress, or who have been hit by appalling life circumstances.

Q   What do you mean by 'appalling'?   Doesn't everyone who goes into therapy think they've had appalling life circumstances?

KD   Possibly, but some people feel they've had appalling life circumstances if the tooth fairy missed them one time!   Appalling life circumstances involve events that are actually appalling – the kind of things you tell people and they're appalled by them. I think that if we were to look the word up in the dictionary, we'd find it meant 'appalling' [laughs] – that an ordinary everyday person would be shocked by the pain of the circumstances.

NR   Scuffing your shoes is not appalling.   Having parents who didn't do a perfect job of parenthood is not appalling.   Life not turning out the way you hoped it would is not appalling.   To a certain extent, people simply have to get on with it.

KD   I know this might not be a popular view among those connected with therapy; but I've seen too many people who've made hobbies out of their real or imagined pain – aided and abetted by therapists.   There are certainly some therapists who encourage people in the idea that exploring pain is what gives meaning to life.

NR   Many would have you believe that unless you go back into the past and root through the fæces of all your frustrations, there's no way forward in terms of being able to enjoy yourself.   In many ways therapy can simply be another trap.   How does it feel to hear me say that? [laughs]   Stay with that feeling! [laughs]

Q   I guess I feel I had a very positive experience with therapy, and I think it helped me arrive at a position from which I could start to practise Buddhism.

KD   Yes.   We're not saying that therapy can't be useful. Counselling and therapy can be profound avenues of exploration for those who aren't interested in spiritual practice.

And, possibly, spiritual practice could be the outcome of such methods. I would also say that counselling and therapy can be useful for practitioners especially in the early phases of relating with the Lama – especially in terms of separating out the need for a parent figure from the need for a spiritual teacher.

NR I'd also say that psychotherapy could be crucial for anyone entering into the vajra relationship of Tantra – because although Tantra can side-step the need for therapy, if you should slip from the perfect precipice of devotion – you're back in the pit of your neuroses again, and they're all wound full volume. But, having said that, counselling and therapy are very definitely 'long-process'. And Tantra is very definitely 'short-process'. At the end of the day you either take refuge in therapy, or you take refuge in the teachings. That's the difference between being a regular Joe with an interest in Tantra and actually being a tantrika. I'm not saying this in order to make a strong value judgement. Short-process is only useful to a person who is capable of making use of short-process. Some people are simply not equipped for it.

KD For some people, a lot of long-process work may have to be the ngöndro, or preliminary practice, for Tantra. But if you have a Tantric teacher, and you have a close connection, then it might be different. If you are able to work very closely with a teacher then it's possible to bypass long-process methods; but you do need considerable devotion and determination.

Q How would that work? I mean, if there was someone with a problem – say it was a bad self-image – how would that be worked with in terms of short-process as opposed to the long-process of therapy?

KD Well, there are two aspects to this. The first concerns the development of vajra pride.

The second is how the Tantric vajra master would work with the individual at a very personal level. I can't describe the second because it's not possible to talk hypothetically, but I can say something about vajra pride – in which one enters into the sense of actually *being* the yidam.[10]

NR   This is a very important aspect of the practice, because by this means we can let go of the concept that we are 'poor little things'. You say to yourself: "My Root Teacher has told me that essentially I am Yeshé Tsogyel! Isn't that amazing! Isn't that fantastic! I'm not just the product of a dysfunctional family background – I'm Yeshé Tsogyel!" So I can enter into what that feels like through the practice of visualisation. Then I can expand that into my daily life. But it has to be real – [interrupted]

Q   Couldn't that be kind of psychotic? I mean, what's the difference between that, and someone in a mental hospital who thinks he's Jesus?

KD   Having the sense of being Yeshé Tsogyel has to be based on one's devotion to the Lama. It has to be based on the knowledge that Yeshé Tsogyel has limitless compassion for all beings. You have to understand that Yeshé Tsogyel is essentially emptiness. Yeshé Tsogyel is ultimately empty form – the non-dual experience of emptiness and form.

NR   We're not talking about changing your name to Yeshé Tsogyel, or dressing like her – that's what the psychotic might do. You would simply be acknowledging that that is what you are beneath the veneer of neurotic behaviour. It can't merely be an idea I'm trying out because I'm just this wretched little *schlemiel*[11] with halitosis and a twitch...

[10] *Yidam*: awareness-being, wisdom being or meditational deity.

[11] *Schlemiel* (Yiddish): a foolish, rather pathetic person.

It can't simply be a half-hearted try at feeling better about 'me'. You'd also be acknowledging that everyone is essentially a wisdom being. You've got to have the strong devotion of a tantrika to cut through in this way. Otherwise it's back to long-process.

Q　In order to experience yourself as Yeshé Tsogyel wouldn't you need to know a bit about what she was like as a living historical person?

KD　That's one possibility for the Western mind... but actually, no. You don't have to know much at all. All the information you need is there in the visualisation.

Q　Would it be at all helpful then to read about her life and her personality?

NR　Possibly... if such literature existed. But all you'll find is the mystical hagiographies. The best one to look at is *Sky Dancer*. [12] That has a really excellent commentary which says a little more about Yeshé Tsogyel as an historical personage, and about the whole field of Tantra and Tantric history in general. We would heartily recommend it.

Q　I'm wondering why didn't anyone write about her as she was in terms of her personality? Is that just the Tibetan cultural style; that the actual day-to-day manifestation of individuality is not what's considered interesting?

NR　Well, in terms of Sutra, personality is an aspect of delusion – so it wouldn't be interesting. Then, from the perspective of Tantra, personality would be seen as something very secret – so it wouldn't be discussed openly. Most of the *namthars* (mystical hagiographies) available discuss the outer and inner levels only. Secret namthars are very rare.

[12] *Sky Dancer*, by Keith Dowman (Routledge & Kegan Paul, 1984).

There is a secret namthar of Milarépa in the Drukpa Kagyüd lineage of Shakya Shri which mentions Milarépa as having a *sang-yum*,[13] but you won't find mention of this anywhere else as far as I know. In general, the lack of 'intrusion' of personality into a namthar gives more scope for projection; and to a Tibetan audience, that provides a strong basis for devotion. But I don't feel that encouraging projection as the basis of devotion is useful for Western people.

Q Why is it exactly that projection is such a problem for Western people?

NR Projection of any kind is a problem for anyone – because realisation is not a projection. For Tibetans projection often may have served a useful purpose – if individuals had no projective needs based on inadequate parenting, which does not often seem to be the case in the West. Projection could arouse the inspiration necessary to pursue practice; but, fundamentally, projection turns the practitioner into a child. If the Lama is a projection, then the Lama is going to disappoint you. The Lama is even more likely to disappoint you than any other focus of your projections, because the Lama's rôle is to undermine projections.

Q I remember how annoyed some people were when John Lennon sang: "I don't believe in Zimmerman, I don't believe in Beatles".

NR Yes. It can be deeply disturbing to people when their idols don't live up to their projections. Now there'll never be another Beatles album! What have I got to look forward to? How dare you split up and become less than you were! How dare you change your style? How dare you play electric rather than acoustic! Or in the case of a Lama: how dare you give up your robes and marry! How dare you drink sake!

13 *Sang-yum*: spiritual wife or consort. Spiritual husband or consort is *sang-yab*.

How dare you wear a suit! How dare you insult my fantasies of living in a Tibetan dream world! How dare you ridicule my working-class angry young man mentality!

Q Great! [laughs] So, in terms of relating to Yeshé Tsogyel, what about understanding the symbolism associated with her image?

KD This might possibly be useful, but what is most important is entering into the visualisation. The visualisation has self-existent meaning; it explains itself.

Q It explains itself? That's an amazing idea... How can that be?

NR There is not much time to go into that here, but I can say something briefly. What is most important about the practice of visualisation, is that it's a way of using your own visionary capacity to instruct itself. The visualisation of Yeshé Tsogyel, for example, has self-existent meaning; and that meaning explains itself *through* itself. Simply by being Yeshé Tsogyel we find out what it is that she means. It's an understanding that has nothing at all to do with words or concepts. It can be expressed in words and concepts, but that is very much a contraction of the experience. Yeshé Tsogyel explains herself, because she is none other than the visionary code that unlocks your own enlightened state. It's like, the number 108 unlocks my suitcases – I guess anyone can rob me now [laughs]. But if you concentrate too much on intellectual meanings, you lose the opportunity to discover that they are simply *there* as an intrinsic part of what you are. You *are* Yeshé Tsogyel – so Yeshé Tsogyel is a method of introducing you to yourself. Kyabjé Chhi-'mèd Rig'dzin Rinpoche would very rarely give any explanation of the meaning of symbolism for this reason.

But it seems as if my rôle in the West is to approach symbolism in terms of explanation. . . hopefully as a method of overpowering the intellect with the innate glory of meaning.

KD   If it would help you, you could read a description of Yeshé Tsogyel before beginning her practice – but you'd have to let go of the intellectual meaning in the actual practice, or visualisation would merely become some kind of intellectual fantasy. . . Anyhow I can give you some idea of the appearance of Yeshé Tsogyel: she sits in the Dzogchen yogini's posture with a wrathful five-pronged vajra in her hand, subduing the dualistic appearances of all apparent phenomena.   She holds the trident which pierces the heart of attraction, aversion and indifference.   The trident, or khatvangha, is her secret inner method nature through which she can manifest whatever needs to be manifested for the benefit of everything and everyone everywhere.   Her gaze is at once soft and penetrating; compassionate yet playfully wrathful in token of her ability to infuse all circumstances with opportunities for realisation.   Her wide open eyes sparkle with the electricity of existence and non-existence.   Her mouth is open and her strong laughter overpowers all dualistic conceptions.   She is naked in token of utter lack of pretension and complete fearlessness.   She wears the six human-bone cemetery ornaments in token of having accomplished the paths of the six Tantric vehicles.   She wears conch shell earrings in display of her mastery of all siddhis.   She sits on a tiger skin because she embodies in her appearance all the qualities necessary for beings to attain liberation through her practice.   There is much more, naturally, but maybe that's enough to be going on with for the moment.

Q   Thank you.   So, if one really felt that. . . [interrupted]

NR . . . then one couldn't possibly have a bad self-image. One couldn't possibly feel like some miserable *schlemazl*[14] – one would never have to wear a shirt with a button-down collar again!

KD Vajra pride means assuming you are the Buddha that you actually are.

NR It's a vajra-assumption, or maybe vajra-presumption. . . but whatever; if you *are* Yeshé Tsogyel, then you are full of love and kindness for everyone and everything everywhere. That is very important. You have the capacity to free all beings from the stained underwear ambience of samsara!

Q Would you say that our emotions are closer to our enlightened state than something like our physical sensations, for example? Or are emotions just a kind of easy access point?

NR 'Easy access point'. . . Mmmm. . . yes, but so are our physical sensations. That is what is so wonderful about this cycle of teachings – every delusory aspect of what we are is an access point to what we actually are. Every aspect of our unenlightenment is close to our enlightened state.

Q You said that attempting to prove that perception and what we perceive are independent causes monstrous confusion. I guess what I always wonder is what is the purpose of everyone running around being confused on this point.

NR Walking is also possible. . .

Q [laughs] I mean. . . is there something inherent in being born in a human body that causes duality to naturally arise as some reaction to that? Because we have to be able to function in the physical world?

[14] *Schlemazl* (Yiddish): A useless, clumsy, accident-prone, unfortunate individual.

Differentiating between perception and field of perception is
something babies have to learn, isn't it? Some psychotics never
do learn it and stay confused. I can't quite put all this together in
a way that makes sense, though that may be my whole problem –
that I'm trying to. . .

NR Yes [laughs]. I actually talk about this in *Roaring Silence*.
But to say something brief. . . The psychotic state and the infant
state do reflect aspects of the non-dual condition; but it would
be wrong to assume from this that these states are in some way
'closer' to the non-dual condition. Those states are not actually
particularly desirable, and practice isn't designed to produce
them. Perception and field of perception are both separable
and inseparable; and, we can experience these simultaneously.

KD Otherwise we'd end up on the 'enlightenment ward'.

Q You were saying that, in order to allow space for experience
to be precisely what it is, we need to stop grabbing at phenomena.
But how do we get rid of our obsession with relating to everything
as a series of reference points?

Q Could you explain what is meant by 'reference points'?

KD Reference points are aspects of our world that we attempt
to freeze, because they seem to substantiate our existence. The
main thing about reference points is that they're not actually
reference points at all. They're temporary experiential coordinates
– emptiness qualities of form manifesting as form qualities of
emptiness. So we get rid of our obsession with relating to
everything as a series of reference points, through coming to
understand the nature of reference points. Reference points are
the non-existent products of our dualistic relationship with the
phenomenal world.

Q   Has this got anything to do with what you said about the free condition and how you said that patterns are either absent or they're present but existing in a state of unconstrained flux?

KD   Yes.   Unconstrained flux – that's what the perceptual horizon is when we don't attempt to convert it into a series of reference points.

Q   Rinpoche, you said that attempting to establish the separateness of perception and the field of what we perceive creates confusion.   But don't some forms of mental illness involve a *failure* to separate your own perception from what is perceived?

NR   Well. . . I wouldn't actually argue with that - it's perfectly valid.   For anyone with a poorly-developed ego – in the modern psychological sense – this kind of teaching could encourage pathological tendencies.   You see, it's not a problem that descriptions of the enlightened state resemble certain aspects of pathology – in fact, it would be surprising if there were no connections of that kind.   Every aspect of our dualistic condition, no matter how deranged, is connected with our enlightened state.   That is the wonderfully creative aspect of Tantra.

KD   So, from the perspective of someone with a healthy ego, this teaching represents a challenge.   We're quite good at being distinct.   We're quite good at functioning in the world.   We're quite good at boundaries.   There's nothing wrong with this. . . apart from the fact that there's a whole realm of experience that we lose.

NR   We lose it in order to function crisply.   You see, with the divisive logic of our highly functional crispness, we create a kind of analytical distance from direct experience.

Q   Yes!   Now I see why perception and field of perception are what experience actually is: it's their inseparability –

NR . . . that is the point-instant of experience. Inseparability is the unique moment of recognition.

KD It's their indivisibility that is the real nature of our experience.

Q So. . . in all this discussion, I seem to understand you to be saying that it's only dualism that makes dualism possible.

NR Yes [laughs] that's very observant of you.

Q But if we're not actually separate from enlightenment, then in some sense. . .

NR Exactly.

Q Isn't it enlightenment that makes dualism possible?

NR What do you imagine?

Q It seems that way, but I don't understand what I'm trying to ask. . . I thought ego or dualism was supposed to be treated as an illusion. Isn't there a danger of setting up a new duality between enlightenment and unenlightenment, which we're simultaneously trying to break down?

NR Perhaps your difficulty here is based on the fact that, for once, I'm avoiding the use of paradox.

Q So, when you talk about entering into duality are you talking about something we did once a long time ago, or something we do from time to time, or something we keep doing at twenty-four frames per second twenty-four hours a day?

NR Something we keep doing at every point-instant of perception [laughs]. I think, maybe, that the frames per second might vary slightly.

Q When you say that the world has its own sense, and that there's no need to impose sense upon it. . .

This sounds just like what I do. But isn't this drawing of connections, this association with past knowledge, crucial to our survival? To have some way of seeing the whole picture when you only have part of it in front of you; to be able to predict outcomes – all of this takes perceiving the present through the past with its categories of experience. I understand that this distorts the present, but wouldn't we have to recognise that survival was actually possible without it before we could give it up?

NR That's why we sit. That's why we let go of the thought process.

KD But to go back to the earlier part of what you said: drawing of connections and association with past knowledge is important in the relative sense – but we allow that process to dominate everything else, and we impose systems of categorisation onto our experience. You see, there's always a process of abstraction going on, and in some ways it's useful and in others it's not. Abstraction is important while we're engaged in 'mapping' an area – it's not possible to put every tree and stone onto the map, or the map would be as large as the area we were mapping. So we have to abstract. These maps are valuable, but if we believe in them too much – especially maps of 'life' or 'experience' – then we risk disbelieving reality when it conflicts with the map.

NR Even in Buddhist circles people do this. Reality is defined by the texts, and the texts are written in the archaic prose of a foreign culture. Maybe some people can read these maps... Maybe Tibetan Lamas can read these maps... But what if the maps become uncommunicative? What if no one ever visits the places to which the maps refer? What then? This is a difficult issue, isn't it? Even in terms of psychological health, we need to remain open to continually re-drawing our maps of reality according to what is really there. Maybe Mount Meru isn't really there.

KD   To be real practitioners we have to be continually open to comparing the map with the actual landscape of experience we find in our silent sitting practice.   In spiritual terms, map and maplessness, or map and uncharted territory are non-dual. They are simply form and emptiness.

Q   It really hit me when you said that people cling to pain as much as they cling to pleasure.   Why is it that we're so desperately avoiding our own enlightenment?   It seems to me that we're avoiding facing the demons in the shadows, death and pain, but you were saying that it's not pain we avoid but emptiness.

KD   Yes.

Q   But couldn't it be said that we also seek emptiness?

NR   Sure.   We couldn't cling to form as ferociously as we do without also seeking emptiness.   You see. . . if we ever actually got hold of total form – it would simply reflect emptiness.

KD   Total security would be totally static.

Q   Yes I think I see that. . . and 'static' would be empty because it wouldn't move – nothing would go anywhere.   But. . . I was thinking more about emptiness, in terms of a vacation on the beach in Tahiti with nothing to do and only space to dissolve into for a week.   Or an hour or three as a couch potato on a Sunday afternoon. . .   Or are these only moves toward emptiness that stop short at some last-chance gas station – we never quite head out across the empty desert?

NR   Even heading out across the empty desert could be form. You see, all these 'emptinesses' are just ways of backing away from emptiness.   When form gets too solid for comfort, we move toward emptiness as a means of avoiding emptiness.   I'm sorry if this is getting too paradoxical, but samsara is rather complicated.

Q It must be. It seems impossible to work anything out according to any kind of linear system – there's always some kind of circle or closed loop that forms out of any direction I take in thinking about it.

KD That's why it's called samsara – going round in circles.

Q What is it we know about enlightenment that we're so scared of that we'd rather live in torment for æons?

KD It's more: what do we know about samsara that makes it worthwhile to keep pretending that it exists. . .

Q . . . right, so why is it so difficult to stop the existing samsaric pattern for even a few moments and try out emptiness and make an intelligent choice?

NR Because that's what we *want* to do.

KD We might think we're making an intelligent choice – but maybe we need to sit and let go of choices altogether.

3

View, Meditation and Action

Being is not attached to reference points.
Being does not rely for its existence on any style
of perceptual cross-referencing. Trying to pin-point being
is like attempting to suspend time and movement –
it is not possible, so we might as well simply be.

In order to realise ourselves, as we actually are, we need
to gain some understanding of exactly how we have
distanced ourselves *from* ourselves. We need to recognise
the mechanisms by which we have distanced ourselves from our
essential being. To do this, we need to explore the geography of
duality. We need to do this because every aspect of our personal
duality is dynamically linked to our intrinsic enlightenment – our
liberated-being. Exploration of this nature progresses on three
fronts; and in the Tibetan tradition these are known as *view,*
meditation, and *action.*[1]

We can develop our *view*. *View* in this sense has nothing to do
with philosophy. *View* is the uncharacterised way in which we
see ourselves and our surroundings.

[1] In Tibetan, view is *tawa,* meditation is *gompa,* and action is *chodpa.* These also equate
to *chö-ku* (dharmakaya, the sphere of unconditioned potentiality), *long-ku* (sambhogakaya,
the sphere of intangible appearance), and *trül-ku* or *tulku* (nirmanakaya, the sphere of
realised manifestation).

That is to say: it is not a constructed conceptualised way of seeing the world. It is simply *seeing the world*. It is *intrinsically effortless and uncontrived*. *View* involves our ceasing to employ preconceptions as part of the methodology with which we investigate our situation. *View* is the recognition that logical analysis is limited. It is the recognition that intellectual comprehension is no substitute for direct experience.

The development of *view* is encouraged by *meditation*. In the context of starting out on the path, *meditation* is the practice of shi-nè: the discovery of space. From the ultimate perspective,[2] meditation is not a fabricated state that needs to be artificially maintained; it is our *natural state* and as such only needs to be *discovered*. It is actually quite hilarious, that the method of discovery *is* the discovery. This hilarity itself is only possible because our innate realisation sparkles through. The real quality of meditation is sheer effortlessness, and shi-nè is a way of approaching this state. It is a way of encouraging ourselves to dispense with the illusion that we are unenlightened.

View encourages us to gain direct experience through *meditation,* and *meditation* gives us confidence of *view*. *View* and *meditation* are the basis of *action,* which is the dynamic of our relationship with the world. That is to say: how we respond when *view* and *meditation* are present in the moment. *Action is the endless and spontaneous dance ignited by precise sensitivity to whatever happens.* We flow harmoniously with what is, wherever we happen to find ourselves. *Action* is not a 'way of acting' – it is being: unrestricted, uncontrived, unconditioned, and unlimited. In the Tibetan tradition, the development of these three – *tawa, gompa* and *chodpa* – is the principle of the path.

---

[2] The perspective of the realised state itself.

74

In this exploration of emotions we are dealing largely with *view*.
In the development of view we come to recognise the different
patterns that evolve from referentiality. We recognise the different
styles of distraction that are available when we distance ourselves
from experience and drift into indirect experience – duality.
These patterns are pale and painful imitations of our liberated
energies. The pain that we experience arises from our continual
struggle to maintain our illusion of solidity, permanence,
separateness, continuity and definition.

Being is not attached to reference points. Being does not rely for
its existence on any style of perceptual cross-referencing. Trying
to locate being is like attempting to suspend time and movement –
it is not possible. So, we might as well *simply be*. Ironically, in
order just to *be*, we need discipline. This is necessary because
from our bizarre standpoint we apparently do not know how to be.
We seem to have the idea that there is a special method involved
in being; but being is methodless. However, the methodlessness
of being is something that the limitations of our foggy faculties
cannot encompass. Conventional perspectives cannot handle that
principle; in fact most avenues of approach cannot cope with it
at all. So we need to *feel* our way with delicacy, daring and
determination. We have to acclimatise ourselves to the method
of non-method. We discover the effortless spontaneity of being,
through the practice of shi-nè – the introduction to space.

Question and answer commentary

Q   Could you clarify a little more what you meant when you referred to 'non-method'?

Khandro Déchen   'Non-method' is the condition in which you might find yourself at the end of a meditation session. You stand up, and somehow – that's not the end of the meditation. . . but we still need to avoid pretending to live as though we're enlightened.

Ngak'chang Rinpoche   Methodlessness is something of a wild card that doesn't fit in with the game we've chosen to play, so it's very difficult to enter into that through our games of wanting to be enlightened. You see, without the lived experience of space, it doesn't work very well. Trying to be unrestricted, free and spontaneous whilst divorced from the experience of space is doomed to failure. The qualities of freedom and spontaneity can only be discovered within the condition of space. So *trying* to be free and spontaneous is like trying to hang-glide with a feather duster.

Q   When you say that we should avoid pretending to live as though we were enlightened, I don't understand exactly what that means with regard to how a person might behave.

KD   Well, one simple example would be adopting a style in which the range of emotions was very subdued. You'd avoid all display of anything but an ever-present bland smile. This would be to deny any kind of strong feeling both positive and negative – because supposedly it's not 'enlightened behaviour' to feel anything strongly. The problem with this is that it's fundamentally sterile; but it does have an advantage as far as duality is concerned. . . It feels safe.

Q   I guess everyone wants to feel safe. . .

KD   Well. . . yes and no. But both answers need to be
qualified in terms of each other; and, to varying degrees. You see,
when you feel threatened by your everyday existence; when you
sense that there's no real security anywhere – then you want to
feel safe and secure, and you might grab at almost anything that
represents solid ground for you.

NR   When you're feeling a bit lost and intimidated by your life
circumstances, you don't usually sign up for an outward-bound
course or a trekking holiday in Ladakh. But when you begin to
feel too safe and secure, you start to need some sense of risk: some
slight danger, some uncertainty, some excitement. This is really
an example of how the *play of emptiness and form* can function in a
person's life. When you play with risk too much for your own
sense of structure and well-being, you back out. But when you've
created the impression of enough safe ground, you come to a
point where you feel hemmed in by that. We cycle between
these continuously.

Q   Why is that, Rinpoche? Isn't it possible to arrive at a
point of balance?

NR   No [laughs], that's the whole point; that's why it's called
samsara, or *khor-wa* in Tibetan – it means 'going round in circles'.
The point of balance is unattainable because it's a self-undermining
point. When you arrive at this illusory point of balance it then
becomes your ground or your security in some way. As soon as
the point of balance becomes a point of security it starts to feel
claustrophobic. It becomes form. The only real point of balance
is what is there all the time. . . actually there is nothing *but* the
point of balance, whatever is happening. There is nothing but
the point of balance, because there is nothing other than the
play of emptiness and form.

Q   Samsara sounds truly diabolical...

KD   Yes, truly!

NR   It beats any concept of the Devil hands down. But; to return to the question of imitating enlightenment... We were saying that this imitation was concerned with feeling safe, rather than with taking risks. But actually; it's not even a matter of risk or safety, as we've discussed. It's a matter of strategising...

Q   So the problem is the fact that our strategies aren't working, that there's something wrong with them?

NR   Possibly... your guess is as good as mine [laughs]. You see, it's not really a matter of a strategy that doesn't work... it's a matter of strategising – at all!   *That* is the problem.

KD   There's actually nothing at all wrong with imitating enlightenment, if what you're doing is attempting to act with kindness. That is a really useful idea – simply being kind for the sake of kindness, because kindness is its own reward.

NR   But if there's any other motive in mind, the whole thing becomes diabolically complicated. If there's some goal in mind beyond the kindness itself, then there's some kind of tension – hope and fear. But in addition to this, I would say that the most noticeable problem with people attempting to imitate enlightenment is that they falsify themselves: they close down; they refuse to engage with the world; they try to ride the ups and downs of everyday existence with a fabricated calm, that is born out of the fear of being real. Men often have the worst problem with this. Men often like to tidy their emotions away; especially any sense of vulnerability or dependency.

Q   So you're making a distinction between acting as if you're enlightened and the practice of emulating enlightenment through practices such as the Six Paramitas.

NR   Yes... as long as you're actually practising the Six
Paramitas, and not acting 'as if' you were practising them. There's
a way of trying to look 'as if'; or, trying to persuade yourself that
you can force these qualities to manifest. If you try to be a saint,
for example, and you're not a saint, you get experientially tighter
and tighter until there's some kind of implosion.

Q   Implosion? [laughs]

NR   Yes. You'd just get enormously resentful. You'd either
quit or become a Buddhist robot. Or, in terms of Tantra, you'd
become some sort of vajra android. I've met people like this.

Q   Yes – there was this Western Buddhist nun once... I
heard that people had nicknamed her 'Ani Getchergun' [laughs]...

NR   Mmmm... Some people seem to have discovered a
method of disguising a lack of simple regard for other people
through affecting an 'artificial Buddhist personality'. They attempt
to hide their aggression in stylistic Buddhist stances. This is a
subject that makes me rather sad, to be honest. Human suffering
is sad enough without converting the means of its alleviation
into a method for punishing and humiliating people.

Q   But people do seem to catch on to the fact that there's a
pretence being put on... There was another guy who got called
'the K-Mart yogi', I guess because he was so obnoxious about
how enlightened he thought he was...

NR   Yes... It's rather sad when people become parodies of
what they thought they were trying to become. In Tantric terms
that's known as vajra hell; and intellectual academic prowess is one
of the quickest routes to that sorry state that I can think of at the
moment. Fundamentally, you have to be real in your neurosis if
you want to be real in your realisation.

If you defraud yourself by taking on the outer appearance of realisation, you merely become a 'wisdom-cookie Buddha'.

Q   I was thinking of what you said about action being the endless spontaneous dance ignited by sensitivity to whatever happened... Would this be the same as lhun-drüp?

KD   Yes. Lhun-drüp means *spontaneity.*

NR   This is the final practice, if one can employ such a term, of the four methods of remaining in the natural state – the Four Naljors. It is the actual practice of Dzogchen, the practice in which everything is integrated with the non-dual state. This means that you stand up and get on with whatever there is to do next in terms of the life that you happen to be living.

KD   It's also called *gommèd* or non-meditation, according to the four levels of formless Mahamudra in the Kagyüd School.

Q   What did you mean when you said our unenlightenment wasn't real?

NR   Actually, our non-liberation or non-enlightenment is something of a joke – it's as real as having a drink when you're no longer having a drink. Where or what is 'having a drink' when you're no longer having a drink? You can't find it except by having another drink. We can't even compare the 'having a drink' that is happening now, and the 'having a drink' that happened before.

KD   One is an experience and the other is a memory. As soon as you try to make any kind of comparison of present and past experience, present experience turns into a memory. Because it's no longer your present experience anymore.

NR   In the act of comparison, we wrap up our present experience in a bubble-pack of intellectualisation. If we try to define *being* it's the same.

As soon as we attempt to locate or describe being, we distract ourselves from being. But *being* is simply *being*. It cannot be confined to 'this kind of being' or 'that kind of being'. It cannot be defined as 'being this' or 'being that'.

Q   It's frightening to think of life without method. It's not just alien to my conscious experience; it's the very essence of what's so frightening about space. I'm amazed that you define the approach to life without method as requiring delicacy, daring, and determination. That seems like an understatement...

KD   Perhaps – but that's what's required. But life without method is the *goal* – it's not the path, even though methodlessness may be reflected in the path. But you're lucky really... having it be terrifying for you to consider life without method, is something of an advantage. It sounds like quite a real statement. It's better to know the nature of your fear than to romanticise about a Tantric fantasy world in which you are some great non-dual heroine.

Q   It sounds like view is the result of shi-nè – being able to see and be in silence. But I don't understand how view encourages us to gain direct experience *through* meditation. Isn't view itself direct experience?

NR   Actually, yes. In reality view, meditation and action are simultaneous.

Q   So not being able to understand the difference between view and successful shi-nè...

KD   Is just fine and dandy.

Q   So then how does view relate to emptiness?

NR   View *is* emptiness.

KD   Emptiness equates to wisdom, and view is the manifestation of wisdom – so view is emptiness and active-compassion is form.

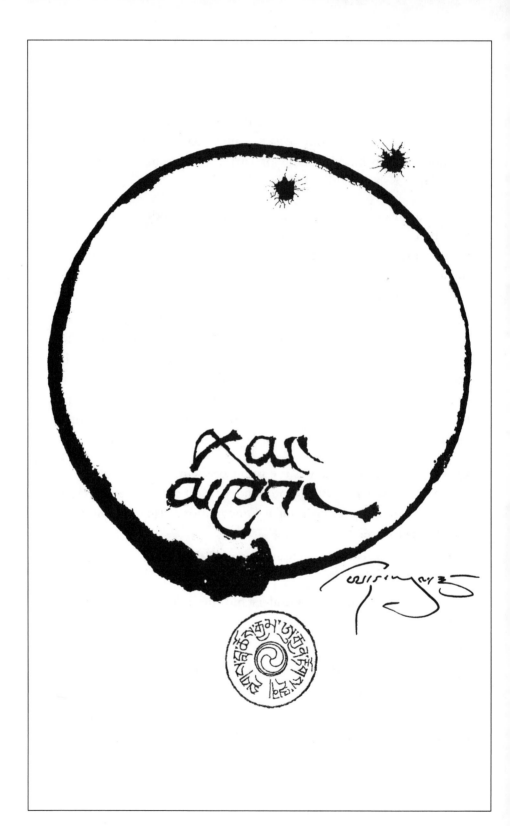

4

Discovering Space

Awareness is the uncontrived, unattached recognition of the
experience of movement – the movement of the arising
and dissolving of thoughts in the continuum of Mind,
the appearance and disappearance of phenomena
in the vastness of intrinsic space. There is only the
sheer exquisiteness of this movement.
This is what we actually are.

To be real is to be able to play with the display of
phenomena without trying to concretise experience in
the vain hope that it might remain forever. To be real
is to relax; to rest with non-referentiality. To be real, we need
to discover ourselves in *actual experience*. To do this, we need to
encourage some practice of non-referentiality. In Tibetan this
practice is called *shi-nè*. Shi-nè means 'remaining uninvolved'.

With the practice of shi-nè; it is not important to sit in 'lotus',
'half-lotus' or even the cross-legged posture. The most significant
aspect of posture is that your back should be vertical and relaxed.
Your back should not be held 'straight', but neither should you
slump forward or lean back. There is a natural, comfortable
position where the spine will balance with ease.

You need to find that position by experimenting. Sitting in a good, solid and fairly upright armchair is fine, and probably best for a lot of people over forty. This is an especially important consideration for people who are not as supple as they might like to be. Some people treat the lotus posture as if it were an attainment in itself; but it is only a way of remaining physically still – alert, stable and undistracted. Tibetans were not brought up to sit in chairs – so they do not find such postures difficult. But Western people are not culturally or physically accustomed to sitting on the floor, and so it is important to recognise that you may have physical limitations that are culturally acquired.

However, if you feel compelled to sit cross-legged, get yourself a piece of dense industrial foam that raises your buttocks high enough off the ground for your knees to hang comfortably below the level of your hips. Sitting in this way will ensure two things: first that you don't get 'pins and needles'; and second that your spine will settle in to its natural position. If you try sitting on a cushion, you may find that your knees are too high off the ground, in which case your legs will 'go to sleep'. Another problem with having your knees too high is that you will be unstable and either slouch forward or attempt to keep your back straight and end up with mid-back pain. If you have to strain to keep your back vertical, you are in the wrong position! The spine is not actually straight but vaguely S-shaped, so attempts to straighten it, for whatever purpose, are not part of the practice of shi-nè. All straining and stiffness should be avoided. Forcing your posture only causes strain and discomfort, that will quickly prove to be very distracting. The less you are distracted by bodily aches and pains the better.

Khandro Déchen and I have met numerous people who have
given up practices of meditation because they could never get past
the pain barrier of trying to sit in a 'spiritual position'. This is a
great shame. It is also rather ironic, because the lotus position
originated as an aid to meditation. The lotus position keeps the
knees lower than the hips and allows the spine to sit easily; but
if the pain of staying in that position, or trying to get into it,
outweighs its advantages, it is best to forget about it. So sit any
way that proves comfortable; but make sure that you keep your
spine vertical and that your general posture keeps you alert.
This is one reason why it is difficult, although not impossible,
to do this practice lying down.

When you are comfortable, allow yourself to breathe naturally
and easily. There is no special breathing technique. Just let your
breath flow as it will. You may like to start with a few good deep
inhalations and exhalations, to make yourself fresh and clear.
At first you should simply *find the presence of your awareness* in the
inward and outward movement of your breath. If thoughts arise
do not try to block them. Just let them be. If thoughts drift
away do not detain them or grasp at them. Just let them go.
Rest your attention in the movement of your breath. If thoughts
come and go, simply allow them to lap like the tide. Allow them
to be a background of 'coming and going'. If you get caught
up in a thought-story and lose the *presence of your awareness* in the
movement of breath – just return to it as soon as you become
aware of having drifted off. There is no need to get angry or
irritated with yourself – these reactions are just opportunities to
indulge in referentiality. Maintain an open, humorous and relaxed
attitude. Expect nothing. Be attached to nothing. Reject
nothing. Just be in the present moment.

The practice of shi-nè is one in which you make the commitment for set periods of time not to become involved with thoughts. You do not examine the content of your thoughts. You just let your thoughts come and go. You simply let them move, without deliberately forcing them out or feeding them in such a way as to prolong them. You allow your thoughts to arise and dissolve without intellectual intervention. You sit in a comfortable way. You keep an alert posture. You simply let go and let be. See what happens.

This practice of stilling the neurotic thought process introduces us to a new dimension of ourselves, in which we can find a sense of spaciousness. We can learn through the practice of shi-nè that, when we relax and loosen up enough, we begin to discover space. When we allow our thoughts to arise and dissolve without commenting on them, or becoming involved in them, we discover that between the thoughts there is space. This is not an empty space. It is not merely an absence of thought, but a *vibrant* emptiness – an emptiness which is in itself pure potentiality. We can discover that all thought and indeed all phenomena arise from and dissolve into emptiness.

In Tibetan this emptiness is called *tong-pa-nyid,* and is recognised as the source or ground of being. It is this recognition of space, within the practice of shi-nè, that enables us to appreciate the nature of direct experience. The artificial division between perception and field of perception evaporates into this emptiness. In this context of no-context our being is characterised by direct contact and immediacy. There is no longer any need to evaluate experience within the framework of referentiality. Awareness is present and flowing with whatever arises in the field of our perception. Phenomena and awareness of phenomena are an instantaneous occurrence.

Awareness is the uncontrived, unattached recognition of the experience of *movement* – the movement of the *arising and dissolving of thoughts in the continuum of Mind,* the appearance and disappearance of phenomena in the vastness of intrinsic space. There is only the sheer exquisiteness of this movement. *This* is what we actually are. It is infinitely and infinitesimally subtle. It is completely ordinary, humorous and somewhat magical.

In terms of embracing emotions as the path, the practice of shi-nè is absolutely necessary. In order to embrace your emotions you need to have sufficient clarity to see what is happening. You need to become transparent to yourself. This means that you have developed sufficient recognition of space to be able to observe yourself in operation. It does not mean that you become involved in looking at yourself in an analytical manner. It does not mean that you become self-conscious in the sense of losing all spontaneity. This is the observation with no observer – it is simply the sense of openness or presence that is made possible through shi-nè.

When you begin to develop a sense of observing yourself in operation, you will cease to be a mystery to yourself. Perhaps you could say that you have simplified yourself. You have simplified the way that you perceive and respond. You experience straight pleasure and straight pain. It is not a complex or elaborate affair. There is no need to embroider your sensations. You do not underpin your image of yourself with quite as much justification. You do not feel so compelled to rummage through the cumbersome baggage of past experience in every new situation. You discover a sense of real spontaneity, and are a little less menaced or lured by anticipation.

The main reason we find our emotions so difficult to understand
is that we are unable to see clearly what is happening to us.
If you are somehow outside the process of yourself, everything
about what you are becomes obscure and opaque – as if you were
experiencing yourself through frosted glass. This obscurity is
caused by the frosting activity of thought – this activity to which
we feel so attached. Kyabjé Chhi-'mèd Rig'dzin Rinpoche once
gave a singularly amusing and earthy example of the process of
thoughts chasing thoughts in circles: "You have a pile of dog dung
outside your door that has hardened in the sun. As long as it
remains undisturbed it won't disturb you. As soon as you start
stirring it round with a stick, the stench of it drifts into your room
and makes you feel ill. So let your thoughts come to rest and
they will not distract you from your awareness".

If we have no sense of the space of our own being we will be
unable to observe our energies directly. We need room to
experience ourselves – to get a look at what is going on in the
context of how our habits function. This space is the ground of
our natural clarity; and the arising of a more spacious sense of
being enables this clarity to operate more precisely. In everyday
terms, this means that you stop talking yourself into unnecessary
suffering. You stop misappropriating your own resources. You
stop selling yourself down the river for a handful of plastic buttons
and coloured glass. You learn to take a break from over-reacting.
You cease adding to your problems, and come to see them a little
more lightly.

There are, relatively speaking, two kinds of problems. There are
the problems that arise out of the random functioning of the
universe – the ones that life seems to hand out gratuitously.
Then there are the problems that we are responsible for ourselves.

The problems for which we are responsible are those that have arisen from our attempts to manipulate our circumstances. The more actively we try to establish reference points, the more problems we create. We create these problems when we refuse to accept our world as it is. We respond to what is happening to us in too extreme a way. Acceptance of what is happening does not constitute some sort of social irresponsibility or political impotence. This is a commonly-held misinterpretation, and one that it is important not to make. We are part of our world and cannot operate in isolation. We are responsible to each other and should discharge that commitment through taking an active part (where necessary and appropriate) in shaping the future for the peace, joy and freedom of all. We need not brutalise ourselves because it is supposed to be 'spiritual' to have a sense of acceptance. Seeking liberation is not a devious authoritarian conspiracy designed to keep people quiet. It is about opening ourselves. It is about losing our limitations. It is about taking action with awareness, freedom and personal responsibility.

Creating conducive circumstances, for ourselves and others, involves planning and making efforts which in many respects is a 'dangerous' game. Plans can be made and plans can fall apart, but that is no reason not to make plans. The failure and success of plans simply gives us an opportunity to experience failure and success as the *ornaments of equanimity.* If we have some sense of space, this is a distinct possibility. Life is 'dangerous' when we make plans, and engage with the swirling patterns that arise from emptiness. But unless we embrace the monastic life, we have to work with the richness of the dualistic condition in all its complexity: monochromatic boredom and technicolour excitement; joy and sorrow; decisions and dilemmas; set-backs and exultations; misfortunes and rewards.

It is a fantastically fertile field of learning but we have to find the *experiential space* in which we can pursue plans very *lightly*; and, with a pronounced sense of humour.

We need to accept the success or failure of whatever we do with a sense of wryness. We need to treat these two impostors just the same – or at least to begin to have a sense of how that could feel. And that is not as far away as it may seem. With the discovery of *experiential space* we can let go of the emotional investment we put into all our plans and efforts. Things actually become easier when we allow ourselves to *play* with our situation, rather than having to take it totally seriously. The lightness of this approach is a manifestation of our developing clarity.

The development of *clarity* arises from our growing awareness of the natural spaciousness of being. With growing clarity, the life problems that occur cease to manifest so painfully. We no longer add to their intensity as an automatic reflex. Ultimately, our lives are our own responsibility. Our problems are for us to work through. There is no use in blaming the state of our lives on anybody else. Taking responsibility for one's life is an attitude worth cultivating. Obviously there are many situations and predicaments in our lives that could accurately be described as having an external impetus. Somebody or something has created or caused a sequence of events that has unfolded to your apparent detriment. The landlord or landlady might be evicting you, because they want to sell the building; and maybe you cannot find another place to live. You may get made redundant because the company for which you work has collapsed. A tree may have crushed your car on a windy night. You cannot take responsibility for the fact that you are being attacked by an unknown assailant intent on besmirching you with strawberry jam.

You cannot take responsibility for government policies that alter
the level of your pension. You cannot take responsibility for being
crippled by an inebriated hit-and-run driver. You cannot take
responsibility for the natural life-span of those around you. We
cannot be responsible for many things. But we are all responsible
for *how we feel* about the things that happen to us.

To embrace our emotions as the path, we must take responsibility
for the style of our responses. If your lover walks out the door
with someone new – you are responsible for how you feel about
that. You can't say, "*You* have broken *my* heart! *You* are responsible
for the misery that *I* am feeling". We are sad because we are sad.
We are sad because we don't want our lives to change. Your
father and mother may not have loved you enough, but you
cannot spend the rest of your life bemoaning that. It has never
really helped anyone to use that as an excuse, for the fact that they
destroy relationships, or fail to keep jobs. Life may not have
turned out quite the way you thought it would; but if you allow
yourself to get caught up in the idea that your pain has been
caused by somebody else, you may feel you have to throw a tantrum.
People get into some terrible difficulties over this, and act in ways
that only make their situation worse. Rejecting responsibility for
feeling as we do spawns jealousy, bitterness, resentment, recrimination
and vengefulness. Rejecting responsibility for how we feel has
never created the causes for pleasure, enjoyment or emotional
fulfilment.

Some people may say that they have every right to feel that
their emotions are caused by others; but it is doubtful whether
anyone would actually find that these emotions do them any
good. I doubt whether anyone would argue that bitterness or
recrimination are a positive experience, in the long run.

In a situation where you are feeling very hurt, it would be helpful to tell yourself that: 'No one has done anything to me – someone has merely done what they wanted to do; because *they* wanted to be happy'. The fact that the thing that makes another happy makes you miserable, is a theme that runs throughout the history of human beings on this planet.

Accepting sole ownership of our emotions can make an enormous difference to our lives. Unless we accept the responsibility of owning whatever we feel, we will not be able to embrace our emotions as the path. As soon as we accept that we cannot actually justify our feelings, we can start to approach our feelings openly. To let go of justification requires that we let go of our experientially claustrophobic habit of referentiality. With some sense of space, we can begin to experience our emotions as they are; rather than as if we had rehearsed them.

This fresh contact with the field of our emotional energies opens a portal through which we can glimpse the possibility of our natural unconditioned responses. When we start to find some event in life painful or when we have experienced a series of calamities, it is helpful to avoid involvement in the 'unfairness game'. If you say: "This is unfair! I don't deserve this!" you only succeed in increasing your pain. It would be better to side-step this frustration and confusion, simply by saying: "This is what is happening". There is no consumer-protection society in the sky to whom you can appeal. There is no life-dissatisfaction appeals tribunal where you can demand: "Life isn't what I expected, I want my money back!" This is it. This is what we have. Fair or unfair, our situation is what it is, right here and now: in your front room; in the dentist's chair; in the terminal ward; in your lover's arms; in rush hour traffic; on Death Row; in front of the television cameras; in the gratification of desire; in the car wreck;

in the shrine room; in the airport waiting lounge; in the four-star restaurant; in the context of luxurious possibilities; in the dance of seduction; in the pouring rain; in any context you can imagine. . . It is the texture of your experience, and you cannot disown it. You can only *try* to disown it, by creating a more complex level of confusion around it.

The car you are driving is breaking down. You are late for an important assignation. You feel highly irritated; but your reaction to that situation is completely your own responsibility. You become angry because it seems unfair: "This shouldn't have happened today! Today of all days!" The more you indulge the feeling with justifications for feeling the way you feel – the worse it gets. It gets worse because you have complicated and intensified your initial feelings.

You might inflame yourself even further by shouting at your vehicle. You could also shout at yourself for having allowed the car to get into such a bad state of repair. You could fill your head with ugly recriminations about how you knew you should have had it serviced. That would be one way of passing the time. You could scan the irregular index of your memory for suitable people to blame. We are highly skilled at making our situations worse. These contrived emotional additions to our situations are the computer software of distracted-being, and we have infinite megabytes on the hard disk. . .

So what do you do next? You sit in your wretched car in complete emotional ferment. Time goes by. You try to telephone for help. The phone is out of order. At this point you could throw another tantrum. Failing the tantrum, you could settle for increasing your blood pressure. Then maybe you find a telephone that actually works.

You get through to the auto association who promise to come out as quickly as they can. You feel a bit better. You give them very exact details as to how to find the car but you cannot seem to remember how to spell the name of the obscure little village you are passing through and it seems very much like the name of some other place that could either be quite nearby or in the next county. You feel worse. Then the person on the other end seems to get the picture. You feel a bit better. You head back to the car. A few steps down the road you check your watch. An idea hits you. You run back to the telephone box; but a local, having appeared from nowhere, is in there chatting leisurely. You despondently observe the neat pile of coins they have set up to feed into the slot for more time.

You walk round in circles for a while, looking at your watch approximately every thirty seconds. You make sure that the person in the telephone box notices that you are checking your watch. The person in the box seems oblivious. You tap on the door and tell the occupant that you need to make a very short and important call. You are advised to try the box down the road; but you know that that one is broken. You try to explain but the door has already closed and the conversation goes on, replete with peals of laughter. You consider violence, but think better of it. You consider tears, or maybe even a bribe...

At last you get into the box. You want to apologise that you are going to be delayed, but it is too late, there is no answer. Your paramour must have already left for the restaurant. Panic sets in! You wind yourself up a bit more. You try to phone the restaurant but the line is engaged. You try again and again but the line remains obdurately engaged. The telephone box is like an oven so you try to wedge the door open with your foot to get some air but the sound of traffic roaring past makes it impossible to hear anything.

Every way you turn there seems to be some new and more
devilish torment. You manage to get through to the operator to
have the line checked, and sure enough there is no fault on the
line. The restaurant is actually engaged. You try again but just
hear that irritating engaged tone. It is probably some imbecile
talking to a friend about something completely trivial.

You cannot hang on any longer because the repair van could be
arriving at any minute. You rush back to the car. It is impossible
to relax as you sit there; you are just too wound up. Even the
book that you found so fascinating this morning is incapable of
holding your attention. So you just sit there and drum your
fingers on the dashboard. You brood on the ruination of your
evening. The repair van is a long time coming. You start to
become really agitated. Should you go back to the telephone box
and ring again? Maybe you could give the restaurant another
try... You start to get out of the car but there is an awful feeling
inhibiting you: if you run to the phone, the van is bound to turn
up as soon as you are out of sight. You realise after a while that
you have smoked all your cigarettes and now you seem to want
one quite desperately. Maybe you could just call a taxi and
leave the car there... You continue to drum your fingers on
the dashboard as idea after idea chase their tails through your
tormented consciousness. Now you are really quite angry.
You could have been back and forth to the telephone box several
times by now.

At long last the van rolls up and the mechanic is very courteous
and friendly, your car is put right in ten minutes and you are off
again. This story could go on and on, and we could all add great
long tracts to it from our own experience. There could be a list
of abortive attempts to impress the dinner guest. There could be
an itemisation of the mistakes, or the failed seduction.

Maybe there could be a happy ending. Maybe you get to the restaurant in the end. Maybe you are able to wind down and have a delightful time. Or maybe, you are just so overwrought that you ruin the whole evening and end up going home with acute indigestion. This story could be as long as anybody's life – a long tale of irritation, anxiety, frustration, nervousness, fear and anger. We need to learn to relax with whatever is happening. We need to develop a sense of humour through discovering a sense of space. Real humour only arises with the development of space. Space enables us to recognise the ridiculousness of our own problems.

When the quality of our experience becomes more spacious, something completely delightful happens. This sense of space enables us to develop the ability to see the pattern of our continual attempts to manipulate the world – according to what we imagine would be our advantage. Once we start to see these frantic manipulative strategies as something artificial, they begin to lose their hold on us. Once we see them as something we have deliberately constructed in order to make us feel real, it is no longer possible to take them entirely seriously. *Seeing* the patterns of distracted-being, and recognising them as such, is the beginning of clarity. And, as we discover greater degrees of clarity, we become increasingly transparent to ourselves. We recognise our capacity to embrace emotions as the path. We are on the threshold of discovering space.

Question and answer commentary

Q   You said that making plans gives us an opportunity to experience failure and success as the ornaments of equanimity. I'm not sure I know what that means.

Khandro Déchen   It's a question of the importance of either failure or success. In terms of dualistic vision, it's what failure might mean, and it's about what success might mean.

Ngak'chang Rinpoche   In terms of non-dual vision, 'failure' is simply the colour and texture of one particular moment in time. In terms of non-dual vision, 'success' is simply the colour and texture of one particular moment in time. When failure and success are simply the colours and textures of particular moments in time, they don't actually have to mean anything. Or rather, from the non-dual perspective, we are not *making* them mean anything.

KD   If a certain event isn't what you hoped for, it's called 'failure'. If it is what you hoped for, it's called 'success'. But what if there's no hope or fear?

Q   What would that look like?

KD   Like nothing you can think of from the context in which you're asking your question... But what if you were simply *playing* with whatever came up? What if you were simply doing whatever you're able to do for the benefit of beings?

NR   What if failure or success carried no definition of you as 'a failure' or as 'a success'? What if whatever happens is merely the outcome of events? What if you throw an apple in the air and you're unable to catch it... what does that mean?

KD   Does it have to make you either happy or sad?   Maybe in a game you can laugh... maybe... But what if you're not a good sport?   What if you're a sore loser?   I guess most of us are sore losers at some level, and when it comes to life we all 'lose'. We lose our youth.   We lose our innocence.   We lose our virginity.   We lose our parents.   We lose our range of choices. We lose our independence.   And then, finally, we die.   We view the loss of life as a very serious loss [laughs].   Do you see that?

Q   Yes... I see that gain and loss arise from attachment. It's the idea of their being 'ornaments' that I find difficult. I thought the idea was that one transcended failure and success; but it sounds like you're saying something slightly different.

KD   No... you're right.   We *are* saying something slightly different.

NR   From the Tantric perspective, it's rather more subtle than saying: "I cut attachment and then failure and success are transcended!   I'm now beyond enjoying or regretting the outcome of events".   That view is a trifle simplistic, if you'll excuse my saying so.   There is always the tendency to look at the enlightened state as removed from all aspects of everyday existence.   But this idea comes from a misinterpretation of the Sutric concept of non-attachment.

KD   Non-attachment doesn't mean that you become disconnected, and enter into a position from which nothing matters.   Non-attachment means non-attachment to reference points – not manipulating reality in order to substantiate your existence.

NR   If your sense of existence doesn't depend upon anything, then failure and success can be *simple failure* and *simple success*. When failure doesn't threaten you, then it's just failure.

You might even be able to laugh about it! When success doesn't substantiate you, then it's just success – you could be delighted; but with the groundedness that comes from recognising the perfection of all the contributing circumstances. You've simply witnessed the success of a situation in which you've also played a part.

Q   When you say that there are problems we're responsible for, and that those are the ones that have come about because we've attempted to manipulate our circumstances, do you mean that we'll *always* fail to be able to manipulate our circumstances perfectly enough?

KD   Yes.

Q   . . . or maybe, that our desires will change so that we won't like the result in any case?

KD   That's also quite possible.

Q   . . . or is it the mere fact of attempted manipulation that establishes a kind of adversarial relationship with reality?

KD   Now you're getting much closer.

Q   It just seems such an amazing idea to be confronted with; could you say more about it?

KD   I think you've answered your own question quite well – maybe you should just sit with the answer.

Q   But. . . [interrupted]

NR   But that's exactly it. 'But' is exactly why samsara comes into being. . . and, as Khandro Déchen advised, you could try simply sitting on your butt. . .

KD   [laughs] You see, our desires, aversions, and indifferences are always changing.

They have to change all the time, because if they didn't change, then we'd get what we wanted. And if we got what we wanted, we'd be frightened that there was nothing else we could project our hopes onto.

NR   Samsara is dependent on our not getting what we want, but being able to hope that the possibility of getting what we want is not out of the question. You see, the important thing about trying to get what we want, is that it defines us as being in process toward some kind of goal. Once we arrive at the goal, the goal seems to make us feel non-existent. We can no longer account for what we're doing with our time. So now I'm the King or Queen – what do I do now? Now I'm a superstar – what do I do now?

KD   That's why some people travel continually – they're always on their way to somewhere else.

NR   It's all a means of manipulating reality to prove that we exist.

Q   Yes. . . so, going back to the manipulation. . .

NR   I can't wait.

Q   [laughs] I can't quite understand how to make the leap from seeing my behaviour as ridiculous attempts at manipulation, to seeing it as something I do in order to feel real. It seems more like something I do in order to be happy. . . by whatever definition I've got going for happiness at the time. Is there a difference? I mean, I'm not aware of feeling unreal – but I'm often aware of some kind of dissatisfaction that I'm making crude attempts to fix. . .

KD   Some kind of dissatisfaction that you're making crude attempts to fix, yes. That's actually a very good way of explaining the process of trying to feel real.

The fear of non-existence is usually very well hidden within the mechanism of samsara. If it were not so well hidden we would address it.

Q   So... in order that we never address it, we have to prevent ourselves from seeing it at all?

NR   Quite. Absolutely. That's exactly how samsara works.

Q   How can I tell the difference between my enlightened energy and my neurosis?

NR   Not being able to tell the difference is a definition of samsara. Being able to tell the difference is a definition of a practitioner. There actually being no difference, is a definition of the enlightened state.

KD   In a sense, as a practitioner, there's no purpose in trying to see a difference – you can only be open to perceiving a difference through the window of meditation. Then the difference manifests as the creative friction of practice.

Q   Wouldn't it be useful to be able to distinguish what was a liberated energy, and what was a distorted energy?

KD   Possibly. But it wouldn't be useful to categorise yourself in that way... It's more useful to be open to seeing the liberated reflections within your neuroses, and to seeing the neurotic qualities of what you feel to be your spiritual dimension.

Q   Right. That's the same as with the idea of pure and impure motivation, isn't it?

NR   Yes, exactly. It's not worth analysing. In fact, I'd say that it is definitely very tricky to come to the conclusion that one's motivation *is* actually pure – or, that some aspect of one's being *is* the liberated energy.

Q   I guess that would be as problematic as seeing all one's motivation and patterns of energy as distorted...

NR   Quite.

KD   Both are problematic. It's much simpler just to accept that every aspect of your being is mixed – unless you're in the non-dual condition.

Q   I'd like to ask about the idea that awareness is present and flowing, that it moves naturally with whatever arises in the field of perception... the idea that phenomena and awareness of phenomena are an instantaneous occurrence. I'd like to get a clearer idea of what that means, but there's probably no way of explaining it in a more concrete way...

KD   Indeed.

NR   Certainly there's not a more concrete way of explaining it. Unless, you want to make the whole thing ferociously intellectual?

Q   No, I'd rather avoid that [laughs].

NR   Then it's better to feel your way into explanations of this sort. Phenomena and awareness of phenomena are an instantaneous occurrence... What does that feel like? Try to touch that assemblage of words, without using words...

KD   Or maybe just rest your gaze on something, and then try to separate that focus from your awareness of it.

Q   Oh... yes... it's not really possible is it...

KD   That's what I've always found...

Q   Rinpoche, you said that you doubted whether anyone would agree that emotions like anger ever got them anywhere. But don't people sometimes throw temper tantrums and then feel that they've discharged the negative energy and everything is fine?

NR   Mmmm... it can certainly appear that way. But the reality is that this 'feeling fine' again is merely the comfort that arises out of self-justification.

KD   But what does it actually mean: 'to discharge negative energy'? What is it that is 'discharged'?

Q   The feeling?

KD   Possibly... but how do you discharge a negative pattern – the cause of the feeling? What happens to the cause of the feeling?

Q   Oh, I see: you can get rid of the feeling for a while, but you're still stuck with the conceptual pattern.

KD   Yes.

NR   Possibly you can discharge energy in some way, but not patterning. You can't get rid of the pattern by acting it out. Acting out *is* the pattern.

Q   So all you accomplish by acting out is that you create further karma?

NR   Yes.

KD   You complete the third phase of the karma. The first phase is wanting to throw a tantrum; the second is throwing the tantrum; then feeling fine about having thrown the tantrum is the third phase. All this achieves is that you condition yourself into throwing another tantrum.

Q   And I guess that's very far from being free...

KD   Yes. That's what's called conditioning.

NR   This type of emotional conditioning is not what Buddhists call freedom. This discharging business isn't Tantra, it's tantrum.

5

Reading the Fields of Energy

The personalities of the khandros, or wisdom sisters, are the
inner energy of everything it is possible for us to feel.
This is what we are, or what we could become.
Our inner elements are the khyil-khor of the khandros –
the iridescent matrix of being.
There is no more profound khyil-khor
than who or what we actually are in our world.

The symbols that radiate as the communicative display from
each band of the five-coloured rainbow are the warp and
weft of our lives. It is important not to misunderstand
this kind of language. One should not get the impression that
these five expressions of our being are internal visions. Our own
eyes are all we need – our own senses are all that are required, but
they have to be *open* to *perceiving* the world.

Most people will have heard the word *mandala*. The Tibetan
word for mandala is *khyil-khor*. You may be familiar with what
a khyil-khor looks like. You may have seen them in books of
Tibetan art, where they appear in their most complex forms.
Everyone at least has some vague notion of concentric circles
and squares.

But here we are going to look at the most fundamental aspects of khyil-khor. Khyil-khor also can be translated as 'circle', and the Sanskrit word 'mandala' means 'grouping' or 'association', which carries the sense that everything gathers around a central point. It is important to underline the fact that complexity does not necessarily imply profundity. The origin is always of greater profundity than the complexity of the display.

The idea of emptiness and form is central to Tantra. In some of the other religions of the world, the idea of God[1] or a creator is central. The central issue of a political party is its political philosophy, which may be embodied in a prime minister or a president. Around him or her radiate the chief ministers, around them the junior ones and so on. There are different departments, committees and subcommittees which make reports on various issues. All these aspects comprise the energy field of the political party. Everything operates in the same way. When you are young, you have your family – unless you are an orphan, in which case some other analogy would apply. The family is your first external experience of khyil-khor. There are your parents, your sisters and your brothers – they radiate around you. Then you have the other relatives, and the close friends of the family who are always dropping in. Then there are the more distant relations, the ones from whom you get birthday cards but seldom see. This closed system of relatives is known sociologically as the extended family. People are probably more used to the nuclear family or even single-parent families. But whatever the arrangement, there are people who radiate around you – baby-sitters, other single parents, crèche facilitators (daycare workers) and so on. As you grow older your own friends become more important.

---

[1] In Buddhism there is no concept of 'God'. Buddhism as a world religion is unique in being non-theistic or atheistic.

In some instances you might move far away from your parents
and relatives. Maybe you have some falling out with your family,
and your friends become your family. At some stage you connect
with a partner – possibly having children of your own. You
develop a small circle of good friends and a larger circle of friends
whom you see less often. Then there are those to whom you
write, because they have moved away. There are acquaintances,
colleagues, work-mates, landladies, bank managers, local shopkeepers,
restaurateurs, gunsmiths, and the many other people who cross
your path briefly in business or social circumstances. Then
there are the people you see but never meet, the people to whom
you never speak. All these people play some part in your life.
There are others still – those with whom there appears to be no
connection; but who share the same town, village or city. Your
activities radiate from your house, flat or apartment to your friends'
homes and other locations you visit for any imaginable purpose:
theatres, restaurants, cinemas, night clubs, Buddhist centres, topless
bars, churches, shooting ranges, swimming pools, gyms, department
stores, supermarkets, sports stadiums, soup kitchens, railway arches,
condemned buildings, art galleries, auctions. . .

Wherever you are is an aspect of khyil-khor. Whatever you are
doing is part of the energy of khyil-khor. You are simultaneously
centre and periphery of this experience known as khyil-khor –
wherever you are. You are the centre of your own and in the
periphery of the khyil-khors of others. It is a totally inter-
penetrating energy. Even if you are in solitary retreat, you are
not truly isolated – there are people who are thinking about how
you are getting along and wondering if you will be different when
you come out. All these thoughts and ideas link you to their
khyil-khors.

Even if you tried to eradicate your personal history in an attempt to become anonymous, it would be impossible to be free of your interconnections. Even when you die your friends and children remember you in their photograph albums as part of their khyil-khors. It is impossible not to leave a trace that ripples through eternity.

Khyil-khor is a wonderful dancing energy. It is not possible to exclude anyone from your khyil-khor or to be excluded from anyone else's. Even if someone dislikes you, you remain within their field of energy. Even if they despise you, it would make no difference. In fact if someone feels very strong negative feelings toward you, you would figure even more potently in their field of energy. Ultimately, every being is part of your khyil-khor. Everyone and everything is linked with your field of energy; and, you are linked with theirs. Therefore it is vital that we recognise this, or that we work toward this recognition. You cannot really ever feel comfortable in your own skin if you are attempting to be exclusive. It is not appropriate, or accurate, to exclude anyone or anything; because that would be attempting to do something that is not possible. If you do not feel comfortable in your own skin, you cannot have any sense of love for what you are. If you have no love for what you are, then it is not possible to love anyone else. True love (that is to say, being 'in love' with another person), in its essence, is *centreless recognition of khyil-khor*; and the practice of shi-nè is what gives us a feel for this view.

The elements are a five-fold symmetry of symbolism that permeates our reality. They permeate the spectrum of our enlightenment, and our artificially structured perception of the universe. The elements enable us to view the entirety of our perceptual experience as khyil-khor.

Khyil-khor manifests as empty centres – centres of unconditioned potentiality. These empty centres appear spontaneously on the luminous fringes of our perception. Khyil-khor is our experience. It is our sensation, or consciousness, of finding ourselves in our world. It is the rich and dynamic experience of finding ourselves in relation to symmetrically radiating sets of phenomena: conditions, locations, atmospheres, times, seasons, landscapes, environments and circumstances.

Each of the five elements is an expression of being. Each element is associated with a colour and a Tantric symbol. They are connected with seasons, times of day and with the cardinal directions. They can be associated with any aspect of the phenomenal world – types of landscape, climate and weather. No aspect of our world can be excluded. This is a significant understanding, if we are to make a personal contact with the awareness-imagery of Tantra. When you understand that it is not some arbitrary set of metaphysical abstractions, but a field of meaning that includes every aspect of your world, you realise that it is completely workable in every moment. If this symbolism applied to something specifically Eastern and mediæval, we would not be able to relate to it in terms of the landscape of our own domestic dramas. These five fields of energy *are* the conditions, circumstances, situations, personalities, predilections, and interacting forces that constitute our relationships with each other and our world.

The physical aspects of the five elements are known as the five *pawos*.[2] The word 'pawo' means hero or warrior.

---

[2] For detailed discussion of pawo and khandro, see articles: 'Cutting Through Spiritual Chauvinism' in *The Middle Way,* Journal of the Buddhist Society, Vol. 62, N° 1, May 1987; *Tantra Magazine* N° 6, 1993; and *Der Biß des Murmeltiers,* Junferman Verlag, Köln, Germany. See also *Entering the Heart of the Sun and Moon* by Khandro Déchen and Ngakpa Chögyam (in press from Aro Books).

This pawo characteristic applies to the dynamic qualities of the elements: the colossal enduring ruggedness of earth; the powerful surging force of water; the bright lascivious incendiary hunger of fire; the all-pervasive relentless turbulence of air; the fundamental fecundity of space. The five internal energy fields of the elements are known as the five *khandros*;[3] the sky-goers. The magical appearance of the khandros reflects the spatial qualities of the elements. The personalities of the khandros, are the inner energy of everything it is possible for us to feel. They are the magical prism of endless inter-connectedness. This is what we are, or what we could become. Our inner elements are the khyil-khor of the khandros – the iridescent matrix of being. There is no more profound khyil-khor than who or what we actually are in our world.

The character and circumstances of our lives are symbolic of our enlightenment. They remain symbolic as long as we do not know we are enlightened. When we recognise that we are enlightened, symbolism disappears – or rather, the symbol and the enlightened state become indivisible. When symbolism and the state of enlightenment dissolve into each other, we recognise the primal purity of our own condition. The purpose of symbolism is to effect that dissolution. Even at the level of initial experiences, symbolism can have a powerful effect in sparking our innate ability to comprehend ourselves beyond our habitual conceptual frameworks.

---

[3] The word *khandro* is a contraction of *khandroma*. *Kha* is a contraction of the word *namkha* which means 'sky'. *Dro* means 'going', and *ma* is the female ending. In Tibetan, the word 'sky' has a much broader meaning than that which we see when we look upward. Sky carries the sense of spaciousness, and is used in the same way as 'sphere', 'field' or 'world' in terms of all-inclusiveness. In Tantric terminology we can speak of the *skies of the elements*. Each element is a sky of meaning and qualities. To be able to 'go', move or dance in the sky, is to be free of referential coordinates – to be unbounded.

It is quite possible for people to relate to the symbolic systems of other cultures if they feel out of tune with the symbols of their own. But the symbolic systems of different cultures cannot be compared and contrasted to any useful purpose. Each system is unique and valuable in its own right; as is every human language. Every language has its own peculiar strengths and emphases. The English language is amazingly flexible, German is very logical, and Tibetan is rich in subtle vocabulary on the subject of Mind and magic. No language is the 'best' language, but different languages suit people of varied climates, histories and geographies in their own special ways. The Chinese and Tibetan acupuncture systems (as well as their calendars) use elemental systems that have wood and iron or metal as elements, and leave out the elements air and space. But no one finds a problem reconciling these systems in Tibet, even when the same elements may have different meanings in the respective symbolic systems.[4]

Tibetan Lamas often disconcert people by their enthusiasm for the scientific view. His Holiness the Dalai Lama in particular, has a profound interest in the discoveries of Western science, and in discussing the nature of reality with physicists, biologists and scientists from all the fields that relate to the experience of being human. Western people often imagine that Lamas would wish to debunk scientific ideas and hold to their own version of cosmology. But Tibetans already have three separate cosmologies: the ancient Indian Mount Meru cosmology; the Bön cosmology; and the cosmology of the Kalachakra Tantra. So a fourth alternative poses no great threat.

[4] In *Magic Dance,* by H.H. Dungsé Thinley Norbu Rinpoche (Jewel Publishing House, 1981), there is an amazingly profound teaching on the nature of the elements. It contains a unique presentation in which the fire and water elements reverse in meaning. From this it can be clearly understood that the symbolic display of the elements is a vehicle for understanding rather than an ultimate statement on the nature of the elements themselves.

Viewed in this light, Darwin and Genesis could co-exist quite comfortably as alternative realities rather than being seen as rigid ideas in opposition to each other. When it is reality that is important, rather than a personally cherished version of reality, one can be open to everything. The alternative realities of the Tibetan cosmologies continue to be valuable because they apply to the sphere of visionary experience, and the fact that they are not aligned with scientific discovery has no particular relevance.

In Tibet in the nineteenth century the Ri-mèd movement flourished and was heralded as a renaissance of spirituality. Ri-mèd[5] is often translated as 'eclectic', but a more literal translation is 'without bias'. This movement consisted of a number of conspicuously great Lamas who mastered the other Tibetan lineages and became masters of all schools and traditions – without bias. The great Jamyang Khyentsé Wangpo was one such Lama and was famous throughout Tibet for the immensity of his wisdom and compassion. When he gave Tantric transmissions[6] he always gave them in the exact style of the school of their origin. If it was a Nyingma transmission he would give it as a Nyingmapa, and if it was a Sakya transmission he would give it as a Sakyapa.

[5] Ri-mèd (pronounced *ree-may*): *Ri* means 'bias', and *mèd* means 'not' – thus: without bias, or non-sectarian.

[6] Tantric transmissions are often referred to as initiations or empowerments. They are a symbolic method of communicating the essential nature of visionary practices. Tantric transmission has three aspects: *wang, lung* and *tri. Wang* means empowerment or transmission through power (in the sense of overpowering the sense fields with the splendour of symbolic display) and pertains to the ritual aspect of transmission. *Lung* means transmission through sound (in the sense of sonic resonance that is linked with the vital force of the *rLung* – spatial winds or *prana*) and pertains to hearing the sound of the awareness-spell (*ngak* or *mantra*) and the *drub-thab* (ritual text or *sadhana*). *Tri* means transmission through explanation, with regard to hearing, and integrating the meaning – especially in terms of putting the method involved into practice. See *Wearing the Body of Visions* by Ngakpa Chögyam (Aro Books, 1995).

It is important to point out that the idea of the Ri-mèd movement was not to mix the schools but to treat them individually. There was no blending of traditions but rather all traditions were taught by these masters in their characteristic style, without bias.

There were some lesser-known Buddhist Lamas who worked in the same way with the Bönpo, and vice versa. Venerable Geshé Damchö Yönten (a Lama of the Gélug School who lives near Raglan in Wales) once told me that monks of every school would come to his monastery of Séra Jé to learn debate, because the monastery was famous for it. This was so much so that Bönpo monks would also come to study there, and leave sometimes having attained the highest degree of Lharampa Geshé. Tibet is like most places: wherever there are people, there are wonderful and inspiring stories to tell. But wherever there are people, there are also appalling stories of mean-mindedness, bigotry and malevolence. There is no political, religious or spiritual system in the world that cannot be or has not been open to corruption. Tibet has had its share of problems with sectarian disputes and even violence, but a spirit of harmony and respect was the most pervasive influence – and this is what has kept its spiritual culture alive. Sectarianism and bigotry betoken the death of any spiritual culture; even if, ironically, these activities are motivated by the wish to preserve these traditions.

Symbols can be as varied as people and their native habitat. Because symbolic systems contradict each other does not mean that there has to be a problem. There is only a problem for those who feel safer entrenched in dogma, or for those whose interest lies in the intellectual study of comparative religion. But for the practitioner who adheres to one system, there are no such problems.

For the practitioner whose breadth of vision can encompass it, there is also no obstacle. Many systems can be accommodated as circumstances require, and utilised within the terms of their individuality. With awareness and kindness there is no limit to the possibilities available in terms of being human.

Question and answer commentary

Q   You were saying that if someone hates or despises you, that you would figure even more potently in their field of energy. I've always thought that hatred negated people. I thought that it would make someone into nothing if you hated them – you'd cut them off...

Ngak'chang Rinpoche   Well, yes, in some ways. But remember that old song lyric: "You're nobody till somebody loathes you!"

Q   When you say that true love is centreless recognition of khyil-khor; do you mean that this is the recognition that two people share the same khyil-khor?

Khandro Déchen   They mirror each other's khyil-khors.

Q   So the relationship wouldn't constitute a khyil-khor of its own with both of you perceiving yourselves at the centre?

NR   No, [laughs] but, also... no! That's the cute little khyil-khor with roses around the door!

Q   [laughs] So is it centreless because it's not owned by either of you, and therefore really has no centre... or is that an impression created by the flickering backwards-and-forwards dance of mutual-centre?

NR   It's an impression created by a flickering dance within a centreless centre.

Q   If love is just the centreless recognition of khyil-khor, I'm wondering why it is that we don't just fall in love with everybody we meet.

KD It's certainly possible to fall in love with everybody we meet, but maybe the definitions of how that is acted out would have to become far broader. The reason we don't fall in love with everybody we meet is that our personalities are like windows – they only allow us to see and be seen within a certain range. This is both an aspect of compassion and an aspect of dualistic limitation. What would you say, Rinpoche?

NR The same. Compassion is intrinsically communicative. It moves from the enlightened state toward any variety of confusion, with the motiveless intention of facilitating wakefulness.

Q You said that the khandros reflect the spatial qualities of the elements, and that the *personalities* of the khandros are the inner energy of everything. . . Why do you use the word 'personality' in this context?

KD Because we are dealing with Tantra, and Tantra is not afraid of personality.

NR Personality is very important in manifesting compassion on an individual basis. You have to relate in terms of individuality in order to be seen and heard by individuals. If you had no personality, you would not be able to touch individuals.

Q You mean that to communicate with all beings equally, one would have to have some kind of cosmic blandness?

NR Damn right.

KD Yes. Infinite non-specific benevolence would have to be rather bland. That is why greater effectiveness is linked with wrathful awareness-beings than with peaceful ones. The more particular the detail, the greater the capacity to communicate in a direct and highly personal way.

Q   This links in for me with what you said about the character
and circumstances of our lives being symbolic of enlightenment
and that if we recognised that we were enlightened, symbolism
would disappear.   So if we recognised that we were enlightened,
if we were no longer symbols of our real selves, but actually
manifested our real enlightened selves all the time, then *we* could
be yidams that other people could use to realise *their* real selves. . .

KD   Absolutely!   That's why we practise Padmasambhava and
Yeshé Tsogyel – that is exactly what they did!

Q   If all my thoughts and ideas link me to their khyil-khors,
is this like an explanation of karma in four dimensions?

KD   That's one way of looking at it, but why stop at four?

Q   Five?

KD   Certainly – the five elements.   They are the dimensions
or skies of our being and our universe.

Q   The system of colour and element symbolism you've
presented here is part of the vision of Tibetan Tantra.   But there
are many other systems of colour, element and directional
correspondences in the world.   Can you comment on how
this system relates to the others?

KD   No.   Not really.   Some of these systems reflect each other,
and some do not.   Although there are similarities between some of
them, they're never completely externally aligned with each other.

Q   They contradict each other?

KD   Yes.

NR   But this is no cause for alarm.

KD   There's no need for anyone to have conflict about this
unless they need conflict.

NR   Each system, if it is an authentic system, realised through direct visionary experience, functions perfectly within its own context.   People often seem quite confused about symbolism.   When they become aware of 'contradictions' between symbolic systems, they're apt to ask: "Which one is true?"   But this question betrays an absence of understanding of the nature of symbolism.   A symbol is an *interface* between ultimate and relative – between the experience of emptiness and the cultural and personal context of the perceiver.

KD   Let's say that you eat a peach, and that you enjoy it very much.   Then someone asks you, as a peach-eater, what that experience was like.   You might say: "Edible ecstasy!"   This reply would then be the symbol of your peach-eating experience.   But there could be many symbols for that experience, and some could even sound contradictory.   However, the actual experiences of peach-eating wouldn't conflict with each other.   We're speaking, of course, about the experiences of people who enjoy peaches!

NR   Tibetan tantrikas say that white is the colour of water and is associated with the East – with anger and clarity.   But I've heard it said, that the Plains Indians of North America regard white as the North; and the buffalo of wisdom.   In that system East is associated with yellow and the eagle of illumination and far-sightedness.   Blue plays no part, whereas black, which does not appear in the Tibetan system, is the West, representing the bear of introspection.   Green is found in the South as the mouse of trust and innocence.   This Native American khyil-khor is known as the Medicine Wheel, but unlike the Tibetan Tantric system, there's no central pervasive quality of origination which is described in terms of colour.

Q   Is it valuable then to look at all these different systems and learn what lies behind them?

I mean, they must ultimately all express the same truth, wouldn't you say?

NR   Your guess is as good as mine.

KD   Some people might think it's possible to learn something from looking at the differences between these systems; but I'm afraid this would merely yield information. You can learn very little indeed from this kind of comparative study. Nothing that will be of any value in your life can come of this kind of research, apart from the pleasure of gaining artistic or anthropological information. These systems aren't mutually exclusive, but if you attempt to mix or synthesise them; you merely distort them. They each work within their own context. It's not even a matter of choosing one – you can work with two or even more, if you're that expansive, just not at the same time, in some dreadful stew.

Q   How can you know which is a true system?

KD   It's impossible to know. They're all true in that they all function to help people grow. But they're all untrue because they're not the experience of totality. They only *represent* the experience of totality.

NR   Symbols are not ultimate. Symbols are tied to time and place and rely to some extent on a shared cultural context. This may make some people feel that symbolism is a waste of time, but that would be an unfortunate conclusion to draw. Symbolism is highly valuable if it communicates something that connects you with the totality of your being.

Q   You said that it's possible for people to relate to symbolic systems from other cultures if they don't feel in tune with the symbols of their own. This is actually an issue for me – my friends and family are looking askance at all the imagery of this practice.

They think I'm denying what's 'natural' to me and grasping at an alien 'straw'. But if a symbol is an interface with a culture, how can we relate to the symbols of a foreign culture?

NR Well, if you can relate to it, you relate to it. If you didn't relate then you wouldn't be here – you wouldn't be asking the question. But as to what's 'natural' – that's certainly quite an issue.

KD In Buddhism, the idea of rebirth assumes that a person has had many previous lives; and so, what's natural may not always be the spiritual culture of your family. That's especially likely if the spiritual culture of your family is weak or unfulfilling in some way. It could also be that the spiritual culture of your family is so strong that it jars with society at large – that could also send you looking at other systems. But I'd also say that the world is getting a little bit small now to be talking about 'foreign' cultures, as if they were really so different. We live in a very heterodox society.

NR I learned only last week that the paisley pattern on my very English dressing-gown originally comes from India. And I once had to remind a gentleman, who was rather critical of Westerners practising Eastern religions, that Christianity was once an Eastern religion. And there may well have been Celts who were quite annoyed that an Eastern religion was trying to establish itself in their land.

Q I'm struggling with the explanation of a symbol as an interface between ultimate and relative – between the experience of emptiness and the cultural/personal context of the perceiver. Is that why symbolism exists on the Thunderbolt Bridge? Because it travels between dharmakaya and nirmanakaya? Because it's a bridge that looks two ways, towards the relative and the ultimate.

NR Yes. To be perfectly frank, I would be obliged to say that this is one of the exciting things about Buddhist Tantra.

6

Yellow Khandro-Pawo Display

The liberated field of energy of the earth element
displays the glorious warmth and wealth of earth which is
inexhaustible and free to whomever needs it.
Wealth and generosity go hand in hand because
even if we have very little, we can be wealthy and attract
wealth if we have the spirit of giving,
which always enables us to find something to give.

*Y*ellow *is the colour of the earth element. According to the*
dualistic vision of the earth element, experiences of our spacious
nature are perceived as insubstantiality. From this sensation of
hollowness and illusory lack of substance, we generate the distorted energy
of fixity and dominance. According to non-dual vision of the earth
element, experiences of our spacious nature are discovered in their natural
condition as the energy of equality and equanimity. This is something
that can be learnt non-intellectually through experiencing the nature of
the earth element itself. We need merely observe the world around us.

Earth is massive. Earth exists in magnificent forms that humble us
by their scale and grandeur. The Himalayas, the Alps, the Andes,
and the Rocky Mountains dominated the cultures of the people
who lived amongst them.

Earth can be awesome, overpowering, and gigantically solid.
It is easy to feel dwarfed by the sheer weight and volume of the
earth element. Earthquakes exhibit the *neutral arrogance* of the
earth element – they can crumble the labour of years in seconds,
leaving a trail of ruin. Quakes within the earth element of our
human khyil-khor crumble our assumed or assimilated grandiosities,
leaving a trail of wounded pride. Earth can be a staggeringly
fearful energy, when the ground beneath our feet becomes
unreliable or violent. When the earth moves, in this sense, all
security vanishes.

Earth can be built up into monuments that project an image of
importance. One could construct a huge mansion, an elaborate
edifice, sprawling room after room, hall after hall. One could hire
subordinates to perform endless tasks at one's imperious behest.
The cellars could be stocked with vintage wine which one's
servants could never afford to drink. The kitchens and larders
could be stocked with the very best of everything; possibly some
fine samples of 'endangered-species pâté'. Or; maybe, one could
become a business tycoon. One could build a tall, angular
labyrinth of offices – an impressive and dominant structure of
concrete, steel, and glass. One could occupy the penthouse suite,
which could be lavish and overplayed to the point of ugliness.
There could be too many ornaments of untold cost, and masses of
wonderfully crafted furniture that you hardly notice. Ostentation
could become the norm, and any kind of inconvenience might
have to be removed as quickly as possible.

From the perspective of the earth element neurosis, any kind
of discomfort or environmental irritation cannot be tolerated.
If creating comfort for oneself causes problems and hardship for
others, that is a matter of indifference.

One can shrug off other people's discomfort quite effortlessly. One might philosophise momentarily about struggle and dismiss the misfortunes of others as the result of idleness: "I'm not responsible for the position in which other people find themselves". Maybe one could say: "I obtained my situation through making good business decisions; I bought and sold at the right times". Or, if one had not worked for one's exalted status, one might say: "It's my birthright, my inheritance – why should I give it away to those who would squander it?"

From this position one would continually issue directives, designed to remind people just how very important one actually was. Situations would be engineered to convince the world that a person such as oneself had every right to behave in this way. "After all... I deserve it. It is not a crime to want my world to be luxuriously padded – to want every sharp edge cushioned so that I can lay back in my massive seal-skin recliner, dressed in a sumptuous velvet smoking-jacket with an elegantly quilted satin collar. There I can gently roll some extortionately expensive Armagnac around an inordinately expensive crystal glass and contemplate my next million, and how I might bloat myself still further with magnificence."

Earth signifies the overt qualities of the material world, the ways in which we attempt to manipulate reality in order to solidify ourselves. In some ways one would like to be made out of marble; because one would like to make a naïve bid for immortality and omnipotence. Earth element neurotics often come across as strong, powerful individuals; but ironically this style is actually based on a deep-rooted sense of poverty. Our reaction to being confronted with our intrinsic space has been a feeling of destitution.

125

From the point of view of duality, various complex perceptual inversions have taken place. In order to camouflage our feeling of worthlessness, we attempt to own the phenomenal world.

There are songs and films that reflect this sense of worthlessness, such as those that concern young men rejected in love. There is a particular scenario with which most people will be familiar: the young man rejected in love goes off to becomes a very important person, just so that he can come back and say: "If you want me now, you'll have to beg. . ." The story usually involves a tepid melodrama, in which the young man's object of adulation turns up living on the bread-line. She is supposed to see his name in lights and curse the day she so foolishly rejected him. He then discovers her in some seedy dump with damp fungoid walls and at that point she is supposed to squander the rent money on making herself look splendid in order to go round and say: "But darling, it was a terrible mistake, you know I've always loved you". Our hero then sees himself as being in a very powerful position because he has the option of accepting her or casting her out with some sneering remark about the poor quality of her apparel. He usually does the latter but is supposed to enjoy toying with her a bit first. It is not likely that this ever really happens in the actual world; it is largely a male earth-neurosis fantasy. If the young lady failed to be attracted to him in the first place, she is not likely to find him attractive later; unless she is considerably confused herself.

The earth element's distorted energy busies itself with concretisation of self-image. This has a lot to do with territorialism – and through that, with dominance, power, arrogance, prestige, and status. The earth element neurotic wants recognition and dominion, to establish security beyond any doubt – by accumulating and hoarding anything that is held to be of value.

Relationship with the world is based on exploitation, and on
the expansion of territory. But no matter how large the empire
becomes, the earth element neurotic cannot quite get beyond the
fear of poverty. There is always this nagging doubt. There is
always the fear of poverty; that has its origin in the whisper of a
suspicion at the back of the earth element neurotic's mind that he
or she might not really exist at all. Because of this fear, conflicts
create themselves out of a growing sense of despotism. Despotism
creates reverberations and interactions that intensify the sense of
poverty, and even greater despotism seems necessary. Then, in
reaction to this escalating arrogance, the 'subjects' rebel, sections
of empire collapse, and all sense of what is real is lost.

The distorted energy of the earth element does not manifest
only in this far-flung extravagant style; it manifests throughout
the social structure. The empire-building obsession can be seen in
any aspect of life: acquisition of personal contacts in the art world,
spiritual circles, commerce, and politics. Each of these fields is
riddled with social-climbing manœuvres, and attempts to influence
those in authority or privileged positions. Whether we are
after another shirt, another skirt, another Rolls Royce, another
empowerment, another very secret teaching from a very special
and inaccessible master, another country estate, or another country
makes little difference. These drives are based on an inner feeling
of poverty and bankruptcy in terms of the experience of being.

There are all kinds of materialism: some are quite blatant, and
some are more covert. Arrogance, for example, can be the silent
smugness that refuses to open itself to other people. In this frame
of mind one cannot be seen to allow anyone else their own field
of experience. One has to relate on equal if not superior terms
to whatever it is that is being discussed.

Sometimes people are taken in by this. Sometimes they are bored and frustrated by it. Sometimes, if someone has a little awareness and kindness, it just makes them sorry that there can be no real communication. Inability to admit lack of knowledge, and inappropriately assumed expertise merely puts us in a position where we learn very little. We merely increase our own sense of poverty. We cut ourselves off, and render ourselves unable to tap into the richness of the world. Experience cannot be shared as long as we use materialism to cover an underlying sense of poverty.

But intrinsic space is always teaching us. It sparkles through from time to time in unexpected ways, dissolving the conceptual ground of territorialism. These are golden opportunities. If we cooperate with the sparkling through of our beginningless enlightenment and experience the nature of the energy from which territorialism arises, we can release ourselves from the illusion of poverty. Pride is precarious because it depends on maintenance of the status quo. Territorialism depends on the possibility of success in the unlikely project of flying in the face of change.

There are many examples of ways in which we attempt to build up territory. The wonderful house you build could be such a fulfilling project; but it could develop subsidence problems that you had not calculated into the budget. The intimate dinner party you arrange could leave quite a sour taste if your guests developed food poisoning. At the height of a brilliant athletic career you could be cut down by a debilitating illness for which there is no known cure. You might write a book, and be quite excited about it, but it could be ripped to shreds by the critics and your credibility end up in tatters. Some influential person could have written a foreword to it that they later deny writing because it no longer seems to be in their interest to be associated with you.

Life can be like that. It can also be wonderful. Everything could start working out very well indeed. Your book could be heralded as a major work in its field. But then: maybe you have to write another to follow it in order to maintain the momentum; maybe someone writes the book that replaces your book as the definitive work in its field; maybe there are new findings or new ideas that make what you wrote obsolete. Life is not geared to allow the maintenance of fixed territory. It is sometimes not even geared for maintaining reasonable self-respect. In the world of mass-media popularity, people are often forgiven for a certain amount of arrogance – whilst they are on top. But once popularity is spent, arrogance is seen very differently – it seems hollow and pitiful; the object of derision, ridicule and censure.

There are a few mediæval stories that concern the theme of 'rags to riches and back again', so people have obviously been aware of this pattern for quite some time. There is a German tale along these lines called 'The Adventurous Innocent' set during the Hundred Years War. It concerns a young orphan boy brought up in a forest by an old hermit who took him in and cared for him. When he gets to the age where most young people want to set about discovering who they are and taking their destiny into their own hands, the boy decides to quit the contemplative life. He decides that he cannot renounce a world of which he has no knowledge, so he sets out to meet the world face to face and gets into the whole situation with gusto. He is a good-natured young man with a lot of spirit and people like him. He gets on well in the world, without treading on anyone. He enjoys himself with panache, but no sooner has he climbed the ladder of success than some awful mischance flings him back down again. This happens over and over again. It happens because of the extreme instability of the times, rather than through any significant fault on his part.

He is just an impetuous young man with a love of life and its enjoyments, but eventually it all starts to feel a little hollow and empty. At last, sick at heart and wearied by the ways of the world, he gives up and decides to return to find the old hermit. But by this time the hermit is dead. So he buries him in the forest, puts on the hermit's robes and lives out his life peacefully in the cave where he spent his childhood. In Tibetan terms, the young man chose the way of renunciation, but that is not the only method of working. It is also possible to choose the path of transformation and work with the patterns of life without attachment to failure or success. This is the path of Tibetan Tantra which we are discussing.

Since nothing is permanent or secure, territorialism is an encumbrance that could be usefully jettisoned. The only truly stable ground we can find is emptiness. It is only possible to find security in insecurity – by establishing insecurity *as* security. Although earth seems so very solid and substantial, it can be eroded. In spite of this awareness we concentrate our efforts on attempting to maintain our cherished sense of solidity. This need for solidity does not tolerate its dictates being ignored. Territorialism is outraged by any disagreement or criticism – its brittle arrogance needs to see rebels and dissenters punished and publicly humiliated. Any hint of deviation from the established formulas is seen as unacceptable audacity.

But earth cannot be permanently moulded. It has a tendency to crumble, slip and level out, as well as to thrust itself up as the gigantic mountain ranges of the world. The props that we create from the earth are transient. Change and dissolution continually undercut us whilst we cling to the distorted earth energy neurosis. It is delightful to consider that Tibet is the highest plateau in the world and is still rising – but that it was once the bed of an ocean.

The fossilised conches used as horns in Tantric rites, and in the spiral earrings of the ngak'phang sangha, are a strong reminder that change affects everything.

The liberated field of energy of the earth element *displays* the glorious warmth and wealth of earth. This energy is inexhaustible and free to whomever needs it. Wealth and generosity go hand in hand – if they do not then we have neither. Without generosity, wealth is merely stale territory that has no value. Without wealth, generosity is meaningless. But it is not actually possible to lack wealth, because even if we have very little, we can be wealthy and attract wealth if we have the spirit of generosity, which always enables us to find something to give. Even if we have nothing, we can be generous with our time and effort.

I always remember the hospitality and generosity of many poor Tibetan refugees who gladly invited me to share whatever they had. A smile or a kind word at the right moment could be the most valuable treasure that anyone could offer. Noticing a lonely person in a group and engaging them in conversation rather than feeling that it would be more important to socialise with someone 'famous in the dharma'. Telling someone that you like them. Taking an interest in someone else's ideas and life-style. Being prepared to share an experience. All these things can be acts of generosity that enrich our lives and the lives of others. By cultivating the recognition of *intrinsic space* we are enabled to flow in that way.

Miserliness, on the other hand, is the partner of poverty. When we are constricted by the neurotic energy of miserliness, the feeling arises that we have nothing to give. No matter how much we have, we remain impoverished. The primacy of the 'needy-greedy' mentality creates hypersensitivity to loss of any kind.

Yellow is associated with the richness of gold, the warm glow of amber and the lush treacling sunlight that sparkles on burnished wheat and barley. It can be seen in the opulence of sweet corn and the tousled ears of rye, the sweetness of honey, the sumptuousness of butter and the richness of bananas and sesame. Alternatively, yellow as a distorted field of energy can manifest as decay and death, putrescence, the colour of old paper and ageing skin – the colour of disease.

The formalised Tibetan symbol of this energy field is *rinchen,* the wish-fulfilling gem – the exuberant magnanimous source of all wealth and sustenance. Rinchen is the source of all requirements and spontaneously supplies every need. Rinchen is the multi-faceted jewel that reflects light in all directions equally, showering the universe with a warm radiant glow. The cardinal direction associated with the earth element is the South, which has the image of warmth and hospitality. Even the seemingly wealthiest of people appear to be able to draw sustenance from the earth in very simple terms when they are on holiday – they just lie on the sand and soak up the sun. The sun warms us all equally and apart from the cost of getting to where the sun is actually shining; it is entirely free.

The yellow sky dancers and warriors perform in the autumn. It is harvest time: the trees are heavy with fruit; chestnuts are falling to the ground; and, bushes are bulging with berries. Gleaming crops are being gathered in, and grain is being ground and milled into flour. Outrageous orange pumpkins are hung from ceilings in nets for storage, later to be used in making soups and pies. Preserves are bottled, and jams are cooked. Wine ferments in kitchens bubbling merrily in demijohns and carboys. There is an abundance of delightful food.

A sense of nourishment and fulfilment pervades the air. Even if the fruits and vegetables are not picked, their wholesomeness enriches the earth through the process of rotting. Everything returns to the earth as part of the cycle of enrichment and fertility. The earth is a precious treasure-house and as such supplies all our physical needs. This field of energy is associated with mid-morning when the day is full of promise – pregnant with possibilities. The grass is soft and springy under our feet, still slightly moist with morning dew. The sun is climbing in the sky and the woods are full of tasty surprises – hazelnuts, and mushrooms that spring up magically from nowhere.

The kind of wealth we are discussing is reflected by the environment but it is central to our being. With the discovery of *intrinsic space* we find we really do have all that we need. With this recognition we could realise that we are already totally secure in the primordial nature of our being. We have within us the wisdom of equanimity and primordial freedom from attachment. Mind is sufficient to itself and so is our world. Mind requires nothing but is the ground of everything – the unemptiable source of all phenomena.

7

White Khandro-Pawo Display

Non-dual anger is unconditioned clarity.
It is displayed by the brilliance and calmness of water.
The undisturbed surface of water perfectly mirrors the sky.
The crystal clarity of undisturbed water seems
incapable of bias or distortion.
When water is clear it is barely visible —
it seems to possess only the dimensionless
reflective quality of its surface.

hite is the colour of the water element. According to the dualistic vision of the water element, experiences of our spacious nature are perceived as threatening. From this sensation of fear and illusory lack of security, we fabricate the distorted energy of anger and aggression. According to the non-dual vision of the water element, experiences of our spacious nature are discovered in their natural condition as the energy of clarity and luminosity. This is something that can be learnt non-intellectually through experiencing the nature of the water element itself. We only need to look at the ways in which water performs in our world to begin to understand this aspect of what we are.

Water can be opaque. It can surge with glittering bubbles as it thrashes against projecting rocks; or as it rolls and tumbles at the foot of cliffs.

The tremendous power of 'white water' has to be treated with considerable caution – its current of *aggression* is lethal. The river Bé-as, that runs through Manali in the Himalayas, is one of the most dramatic examples of white water that I have ever encountered. I remember it vividly from the times I stayed in retreat near the *gompa* (meditation-place) of Apo Rinpoche. In the warm weather there was always the temptation to venture into it for a swim – but I knew I would be crushed to death long before I had time to drown. There were some side pools protected from the main current by huge boulders that I used to sit on in order to feel the coolness of the vaporised spray, as I practised integration with sound – trying to allow my awareness to blend with the roaring waters. Many glacial boulders lay in the main current of the Bé-as. The spray of the water from these rocks was so violent that even a shutter speed setting of a two-thousandth of a second was not fast enough to freeze the froth on film. But in its rampant ferocity there was a clear, crisp and immaculate beauty that seemed completely pure – utterly unadulterated.

Water can boil and spit with fury in a cauldron, or in a geo-thermal spring. It can froth and spray with vitriolic disregard, it can display qualities of rage, with no sense of self-control. Water displays the *attributes* of anger in a variety of ways. We need only walk along the seashore to observe fragments of wreckage – the battered remains; the flotsam and jetsam of who-knows-what.

But anger is not always so uninhibited – sometimes it can be icy, the cold bitter rage of calculating destructiveness. We may seem to be outwardly under control, while internally atomic war is in progress. Our every action is accurately and finely tuned to have some very specific hurtful effect. Our motives have the sharpness and lacerating precision of broken glass; or fragmented ice.

When water freezes it can be the instrument of severe surgical mutilation. However anger manifests, it has the quality of 'sharpening' our presence. Anger can produce a state of almost one-pointedness. When we get angry about something in particular, all those aspects of life that we usually find irritating, awkward or embarrassing melt away into a blur on the outer margins of immediate emotional awareness. Our usual worries and anxieties no longer seem to provide such a distracting influence: the unpaid milk bill; the broken cistern in the toilet; the fellow next door who plays his saxophone so badly at all hours of the day and night; the disorganised couple on the other side who leave mounds of festering rubbish outside their back door because they never seem to get it past the gate for the dustbin men to collect; the builders who vanish after having charged too much for work that is distinctly questionable; the dog that keeps barking all night because the owners will not let it inside; the person at work who has a distinct attitude problem and insists on inflicting it on others. Somehow these things do not seem quite so horribly irritating any more if one is venting one's spleen about something else.

Anger is a very direct communication. It is an intellectual energy which is only concerned with its relationship to the object of anger. When you are howling abuse at someone because of the pain you think they have caused you, some kind of tunnel vision of the senses takes over. You no longer hear, smell, touch or taste anything else – your sphere of thought is locked into this communication. In a sense this can be a little like living in 'the now', but being so on edge about the brittleness you perceive in yourself that you become increasingly weapon-like; shiny, sharp, and merciless. There is a certain kind of jagged presence in wrath. If we look at the energy of anger in this way, we can see all kinds of positive qualities there.

These are qualities that it could be useful to realise in ourselves in their non-aggressive manifestation. Because anger is a distorted form of clarity, it will obviously still display certain qualities of clarity. These are not two entirely different energies, because anger and clarity are dynamically linked. We are not talking about polarities or opposites – that is a different way of looking at the world. We are talking about an energy that has apparently become distorted. The innate primordial wisdom of clarity is the energy of anger manifesting in the artificial condition of duality.

Anger arises when our reaction to the experience of space is one of fear. We feel the need to make instant reprisals, the moment we sense that someone could be taking advantage of us. Deep feelings of vulnerability, brittleness and insecurity make it difficult to allow any softness of response. It is like being caught on a thin sheet of ice that is ready to crack at the slightest pressure. This gives rise to feelings of aggression and intolerance, as powerful forces that erupt with little warning. We hope that displays of hostility will deter abuse or humiliation – eventually anger becomes our system of communicating with the world. It is a style of communication that sets out to establish unchanging personal identity as real. We feel fragile and exposed, as if balanced on a knife edge. So, any threat has to be dealt with by means of instant reprisals. An old Norse saying runs: 'For a hand, take an arm! For an arm, take a head!' That seems to epitomise the water element neurosis. It is all rather barbaric – but, whether it is the barbarism of a Viking, a Mongol warlord, the sophisticated barbarism of a boardroom power-play, or the aggression of 'spiritual' intrigue makes little difference. When the energy of anger is functioning in its characteristic way, even the most dull and witless person will suddenly find they are equipped with unfamiliar skills.

Incredible memory develops and can dredge up, instantly, all manner of pertinent past events which are guaranteed to cut the object of anger to the quick. The right words are chosen with unprecedented sarcastic precision. Remarks are parried with impeccable speed. Every comment is a rapier thrust that penetrates some vital organ. The more our intellectual faculties are developed, the more possible it is to hone the cutting edge of rage. But inevitably words run out; and when words fail, the energy carries through into physical violence.

Anger and aggression are symptomatic of feelings of weakness and fear. When people resort to anger they are saying that they are afraid – they are saying that they are too timid to express honestly how they feel. Anger only arises when another person is perceived to be stronger and capable of menace. This may be a little hard to understand, especially for battered wives, but strength is perceived in many different ways. Merely because a man might be capable of physically assaulting a woman, does not automatically imply that he feels stronger. There is emotional strength, intellectual strength, moral strength, the strength that radiates from security, and the strength of conviction or faith. Physical strength and verbal aggression tend to be overt and generally non-enduring.

Anger arises as a reaction to confrontation with externally perceived threats. This is especially the case, when the external threat appears to be possessed of a power which one feels to be personally lacking. One might be afraid that 'they' will have all the answers. It could be seen as useless to discuss the matter calmly – 'they' might get the upper hand. To discuss issues calmly would be to expose feelings of insecurity. We could not possibly admit our fearful feelings; because, actually, we could be quite embarrassed about them.

These feelings might not quite match up to our cherished self-image of intellectual prowess or the dogged stamina of bloody-mindedness. We might feel that we would be ridiculed and humiliated if we expressed any weakness. So rather than risk the possibility of suffering disrespect, it could seem preferable to take the line that 'attack is the best form of defence'.

If our aggressive intellectual assaults are adroitly dismantled, then a punch in the mouth seems to be the last resort of the water element neurotic. After all, we would not like to be shown up as being unreasonable, misguided, self-seeking or generally reprehensible in some way... Sadly, though, the punch in the mouth is the first step along the road to atomic warfare. We should take care not to labour under the misapprehension that wars are created by evil power-mongers who are so very different from ourselves. From the perspective of viewing all forms of aggression as having the same root, we need to acknowledge that irritation and genocide simply occur at different points on the same sliding scale. Seen in this way; either the war-mongers do not seem to be so absolutely evil, or we do not seem to be so absolutely good.

It seems very difficult for us to recognise that one of our most immediate strengths lies in acknowledging weakness. Weakness only exists as such because it is kept locked in an emotional high-security vault, designed to preserve self-image and a sense of personal security. A realisation such as this could give us a new perspective on anger, and on the anger projected by others. The idea that angry people feel weak and fearful may seem to be a total contradiction to some – especially to those who fear anger. We feel this way because of what is reflected at the surface level. It could seem quite bizarre to consider that we were having to endure the projection of anger because someone feared our strength.

If we were to realise that anger is often projected at us, simply because strength is imputed to us – we might be able to be gentle with people who act in angry ways. If instead of protecting ourselves from anger, we were able to recognise our own strength as the ability to expose feelings of vulnerability, we might find that people who are angry at us become unable to maintain it. If in the midst of anger, the notion of personal fear could be understood, an important discovery could be made. We could realise that we have sufficient courage to make that admission of vulnerability to another person. Having done this, we may well find ourselves reassured by the other person. We may find that our feelings of insecurity and inadequacy are groundless. Usually we are so afraid of self-disclosure that the 'anger/attack' and 'assault/defence' habits repeat themselves throughout our lives.

As a transmuted energy, anger is mirror-wisdom – undistracted, undistorted clarity. But in order for us to find this clarity, to polish this mirror, we need to cut through the insidious process of justification. Justification is the authority we invoke to license our anger. Because of this it is important not to allow space for the distorted indulgence of justification. This can be very difficult because the process of justification is a strong part of our education and a salient feature of the world's cultural heritage. The nuclear balance of terror was part of that process. Totalitarian political movements (either extreme left or extreme right) are a manifestation of that process; and, unfortunately, it has also become part of the very ideologies that have arisen to benefit humanity. How often have we heard people saying: "Of course I'm angry! Wouldn't anyone be angry?" And, of course, this is a purely rhetorical question. The concept that we have every right to feel anything that we feel needs to be called seriously into question. At best we can say that we simply feel what we feel.

There are no rights about it. You might say that these negative emotions are only 'natural'. But what does 'natural' actually mean in that sense? What is natural? We can feel hot in the summer; that is natural. We can feel cold in the winter; that is natural as well. We can feel hunger, thirst or physical pain; these things are also natural. But our emotions are not so easily defined. Because emotional responses differ from person to person, there have to be variable factors at work. In Buddhist terms these variable factors include conceptuality. Emotional feelings fall into an entirely different category than feelings of hot or cold. Feeling cold is devoid of concept; apart, that is, from how you may feel *about* feeling cold – that could be highly conceptual. Concepts may arise from your feeling of being cold; but were the concepts to disappear, the coldness would remain.

But what of the emotions? What remains of emotions when the concepts disappear? This is the frontier of experience we explore when we practise shi-nè. This is what we are investigating when we attempt to rediscover our authentic nature – our actual state of naturalness. What is it natural for a human being to feel?

We are not issued the official handbook at birth. We could say that loneliness was 'natural' if we are deprived of company. But in all cultures there are hermits who do not fit in with that idea. There are also misanthropes and 'loners' – people who actively like to go off on their own; people who feel crowded in by others. There are people who will soon remind you that they need their space if they perceive you as having impinged too much. Such people are not just exceptions to the rule that to need company is natural. If we look at the broad range of people in our lives, we can always find some who do not appear to share our needs. We can also become aware that some people seem to have needs that we do not share.

Most of us are aware of people in our lives who seem excessively 'needy' and yet have little or nothing to give to anyone else.

This discussion of what is 'natural' is not an argument in favour of imposing a régime of mortification on ourselves. The Tantric path does not require that we ignore every emotional need. We can respect our own unique pattern of energy and learn to work with it in a creative open-ended manner. We can develop a recognition of how we can be tied by emotional needs, and how emotional needs can create life crises when they conflict with *what is actually taking place.*

It is a delicate balance: to acknowledge emotional needs, on the one hand, and to have a sense of these needs being conceptually generated on the other. This balancing act requires the experience of emptiness, because without it, we either indulge ourselves or brutalise ourselves. The experience of emptiness, in this sense, helps us to view our emotions with a degree of humour – with more sanity and true perspective. With this sense of space we can find ourselves adopting a very powerful stance – the stance of a practitioner. Then it is no longer possible to say: "*You* have made *me* angry!" All we can say is: "*I* have made *myself* angry in reaction to what *I* have perceived you to have done to me". In this way we make ourselves completely responsible for what we feel. That is really wonderful, because from this perspective we stop laying this responsibility on other people. Taking responsibility for whatever we may happen to be feeling is what enables us to *kill* justification.

In addition to the sky-dancers and warriors, the Tantric traditions contain many other anthropomorphic symbols of our enlightened consciousness; and some of these appear as terrifying beings.

Ekajati, the Single-plait Mother,[1] grasps a ripped-out heart in her hand, symbolic of how justification should be uncompassionately murdered. Spilling the heart-blood of justification allows us to be gentle people. We become more relaxed, and more able to discover ourselves. Discovering the intrinsic space of our beginningless enlightenment is the source of kindness for others – for everyone and everything everywhere.[2]

This does not mean letting people walk all over us. It simply means taking responsibility for how we feel, so that we can be clear about how we respond. We do not need anger to help us right the wrongs of the world. We can work for peace, equality and harmony just as determinedly without anger. If there is injustice in the world, or in our personal situation – *anger does not help*. Anger merely occludes our ability to see clearly. With the discovery of space we find ourselves able to respond openly about how we feel. Tantra does not inhibit us from taking action based on heart intelligence. If we allow people to destroy us, or our shared environment, we are certainly not doing anyone a favour. So, in the practice of embracing the sensation of anger, there is the need to rely more on our own intrinsic space,[3] than on the neurotic thought processes and habitual responses that usually infest conceptual consciousness.

---

[1] Ekajati ('Single-braid Mother' in the U.S.) or Mug-nak-rGyakmo (the maroon queen) is the main Protector of the Nyingma School, and specifically of the innermost Tantra – Dzogchen. She is often depicted as the pre-eminent Protector of a group of three, known as the *Ma-za-dor-sum*. Ekajati is *Ma*; *Za* is Rahula (Lord of Lightning); and *Dor* is Dorje Legpa (Vajra Sadhu or the Benign Thunderbolt). *Sum* means 'these three'. There is also a special form of Yeshé Tsogyel manifesting as Ekajati that is particular to the Aro gTér, in which she is practised as a yidam rather than as a Protector.

[2] This is usually expressed as generating bodhicitta (Tib. *chang chub sem*) – compassion for all sentient beings.

[3] Space is experienced through the practice of shi-nè.

Painful emotions are maintained through the process of thinking about them. We continually regenerate our painful emotions by intellectualising about them – rather than experiencing them at the non-conceptual level. The only way out is to let awareness find itself in the dimension of whatever emotion has arisen; and to experience it purely. When we are able to let go of justification we are no longer as involved in maintaining the integrity of our self-image. When this neurotic involvement is reduced, the energy of anger is no longer coloured by the need to prove our existence through the manifestation of aggression.

When the 'subject-object dichotomy' dissolves into space, anger can no longer exist as anger but transforms into total clarity. This clarity dispassionately reflects all that it sees. Nothing is left out. Nothing is added. We see the whole picture in all its vibrant detail. Non-dual anger is unconditioned clarity. It is displayed by the brilliance and calmness of water. The undisturbed surface of water perfectly mirrors the sky. The crystal clarity of undisturbed water is incapable of bias or distortion. Clear water is barely visible – it seems only to possess the dimensionless reflective quality of its surface. We can see the pebbles, shingles, stones, rocks, weeds and fish as if there were no water present. This pure and undistorting reflective quality is symbolised by the *mé-long* – *plane* or *mirror of Mind*. The mé-long is a very special symbol in Tibetan Tantra because it displays the intrinsic quality of Mind in terms of its innate reflective capacity.

In the teaching of Dzogchen[4] there are three methods of transmitting teachings: *oral, symbolic* and *direct*.

---

[4] Dzogchen means 'great completeness' or 'utter totality', although it is often translated as 'great perfection'. It is the innermost vehicle of the nine vehicles of the Nyingma School.

Oral transmission consists of the verbal or 'whispered' instruction that a Lama gives to a disciple. *Symbolic transmission* consists of the Lama showing a symbol such as the mé-long or a crystal in order to convey meaning at a less conceptual level. *Direct transmission* consists of Mind to Mind communication which is entirely free of concept. The mé-long is a circular mirror, usually made of silver or silver-bronze. It is used frequently in *symbolic transmission* and conveys a very important teaching on the nature of Mind. This is something of the explanation that accompanies the mé-long:

Although the mirror has reflections, they are not the mirror itself; neither do they define the mirror. The reflections only exist because the mirror has the capacity to reflect. But although the reflections are not the mirror, they cannot be divided from the mirror. We only see the mirror by virtue of the presence of the reflections. If there were no reflections, there would simply be empty space. We define the mirror as being the reflections we see in it, and rarely glimpse the empty mirror. The empty mirror is the fundamental creative capacity which allows reflections to arise. We see the mirror because of the reflections in it. Whether the reflections are beautiful or ugly, the mirror itself is unperturbed – it reflects everything equally, accurately, and without judgement.

This explanation of Mind grows in meaning as the practice of shi-nè develops and becomes profound. In the awareness-imagery of Tibet, the mé-long is sometimes worn as an ornament hanging on the chests of Lamas of the Dzogchen tradition. Some examples of this are Adzom Drugpa, Khandro A-rig Shé-zér, and Drupchen Namkha'i Mélong Dorje.[5]

---

[5] Adzom Drugpa Drodrül Pawo Dorje, 1842-1924, was a Nyingma Lama of the nineteenth century; A-rig Shé-zér Khandro, also known as A-shé Khandro, 1912-?, was the elder of the two sang-yums of Aro Yeshé, 1915-1951 (the son of Khyungchen Aro Lingma); Drupchen Namkha'i Mélong Dorje lived from 1243 to 1303.

The mé-long can also be held in the hand in awareness-images such as that of Khyungchen Aro Lingma.[6]

Water can have the crispness and the sharpness of ice, with no blurred edges, no areas of confusion. Nothing is indistinct, hazy, or difficult to discern. The landscape glitters with the patterns of frozen water. The cardinal direction associated with the field of energy of the white sky-dancer and warrior is the East. The East is where the sun rises; streaming with the cool dispassionate light of dawn. The formalised Tibetan symbol for this energy-field is the *dorje,* the thunderbolt, which is said to have qualities of sharpness, total precision and absolute indestructibility. It is immovable, which is to say that it is undistractable and devoid of inherent tendencies. It is the hardest substance and as such it is able to cut through everything without itself being cut. It is completely and directly incisive.

The season associated with this energy-field is winter. The landscape is pristine and clear-cut. The snow has made drift ridges that curve with beautiful precision. The white hills in the distance hold no secrets. The landscape is open and devoid of confusion. Sounds carry in the clear cold air and find no surfaces from which to bounce distorted echoes. There is an enormous sense of tranquillity. There is the purity of silently falling snow, and the sparkling geometry of crystalline structures.

---

[6] Khyungchen Aro Lingma is the origin of the Aro gTér. She is often pictured holding a mé-long. When the mé-long is held by a lineage Lama, it usually has a *chö-phen,* or 'streamer of reality' appended, displaying the five elemental colours.

8

Red Khandro-Pawo Display

*When the essential nature of the fire element is
experienced beyond dualism, we realise that we do not
have to seduce the world. . . Every activity becomes the
consummation of the love affair with emptiness and form.
We are free of reference points as objects of desire.
We burn with the wisdom-fire of centrelessness and realise our
capacity to extend our realisation to everyone.*

R*ed is the colour of the fire element. According to the dualistic
vision of the fire element, experience of our spacious nature is
perceived as isolation. When the texture of our experience is
felt in this way, the sense of loneliness (illusory lack of connection) generates
the distorted energy of obsession; and, random hunger for focuses of
comforting proximity. According to the non-dual vision of the fire
element, experiences of our spacious nature are discovered in their natural
condition as the energy of discriminating awareness – the wisdom of pure
appropriateness.*[1] *This is something that can be learnt non-intellectually
through experiencing the nature of the fire element itself. We need merely
observe the sun, moon, stars, and the fire in the hearth.*

[1] Compassion: the aspect of enlightenment described by Rig'dzin Chögyam Trungpa
Rinpoche as 'the passion beyond passion'; or 'non-dual passion'. In the view of Tantra,
compassion cannot be actualised if passion is negated. Passion, together with all forms of
communicative appreciation, are aspects of compassion.

Fire is a vital passionate force that devours its own world. It is omnivorous: consuming everything with which it makes contact. Fire is a sensuous energy. We speak of ardour being kindled. We tell of burning passion, and of flames of desire. Popular love songs contain references to 'setting the night on fire' – sexual arousal is spoken of in inflammatory terms. Poetry has explored different forms of combustion to describe passion; from sparks and embers, to conflagration. You can say that you have 'the hots' for somebody; but, if the relationship 'fizzles out' and you are left desolate – you feel cold. The perceptual frame of reference in which one is abandoned or heartbroken, projects coldness onto the world.

These inflammatory aspects of language are by no means accidental or coincidental. We are actually always in touch with the empty essence of the elements, because enlightenment is always present – it is simply unmanifested. When the need to possess arises, it can become ravenous. It can feel choiceless – leaving no room for self-observation or circumspection. Because distance cannot be tolerated between the subject and object of desire, we can have little or no perspective. When there is no room for the discriminatory faculties to function, obsession becomes increasingly rampant. There is no room left to actually appreciate objects of desire, because our perception is fettered by the increasingly intense claustrophobia of grasping.

When the fire element neurosis is in full swing, people throw themselves into life and invariably overdo it: staying up too late; getting too drunk; going to too many parties; indulging in too many highs; and, attempting to squeeze every last drop of pleasure out of everything. Over-indulgence becomes a way of life.

Dissatisfaction with anything gentle, simple or unmixed becomes
a driving force that sucks in further and further phenomena.
Multiple activities suck the space out of every moment: talking
to a friend on the phone; glancing at a picture book; smoking a
cigarette; drinking a cup of coffee. Multi-media entertainment is
required: a stereo system; watching television with the sound off;
'channel-surfing' on the remote to make sure of not missing out
on more tempting images. Every moment-particle of space is
saturated with entertainment or creative stress of some kind. The
'wiring' of the human frame is overloaded and the fuses eventually
burn out.

Sensation has to be escalated, enhanced or boosted. Fantasy is a
prime arena for installing turbo-drive into all permutations of
possible gratification. "Wouldn't it be great to make love to the
most beautiful person in the world!" Various people come to
mind. We picture the scene: wild synthesised music; fine old
Calvados brandy to sip; soft, beautiful lighting... No, even
better: a strobe light, a red one; the ceiling above the bed has a
large mirror on it; there are mirrors all over the walls... No,
perhaps even better: a video camera relaying every moment to
television monitor screens banked up all over the walls! But no!
Something yet more delightful! It only really takes a moment to
switch the whole picture round: wrapped in passionate embrace –
free-falling from an aircraft over the Sahara; landing in a fabulous
oasis; a refrigeration plant with ice-cold coconut rum and freshly
squeezed orange juice; the sound of a frenzied arabesque zither;
heat haze over the shimmering dunes; mirages of everything
imaginable lap-dissolving – lyrically incandescing with the fluttering
wings of the music... It sounds wonderful, perhaps – and
perhaps it is, if it is actually happening.

But unfortunately this infatuation with 'more' tends to be rather sad: a daydream that denigrates your life, and the real person to whom you may be relating. It is denigrating because there is no appreciation of the amazing qualities of what is actually unfolding in the present moment. There is nothing right or wrong, good or bad about daydreams; but if they are not actually connected with our real life, how do we appreciate our real life? If we make these daydreams more important than our real life, we simply generate a sense in which nothing real can be good enough. If we prefer our dream to what is actually going on, our relationships and our situation are insulted and degraded.

Fire simultaneously exhibits both the qualities of desire, and the textures of objects of desire. Fire is provocative, seductive, and flirtatious. The lascivious quality of fire is illustrated when logs in the hearth are described as being 'licked by flames'. Fire displays glamour. Fire displays both the tinsel qualities of surface attraction, and the fireworks of life's magnificent pyrotechnic performance. Fire can warm – it serves human needs as a centre, or focal point, of comfort and sustenance. It maintains bodily temperature. Without the fire of the sun our world would be a dense mass of ice like the far planets beyond Jupiter. The startling bright forks of fire's flames keep away predatory beasts of the night and provide protection. We use it to cook food; its heat brings out the subtle flavours of ingredients that blend together harmoniously to furnish us with gastronomic delights. It is used to fashion metal implements and vitrify clay into ceramic vessels. Its incandescence illuminates the darkness of winter. It enables people to read, or carry on other activities, when the light of the sun has gone. Its visual excitement and cheering crackle are stimulating. It puts people at their ease. It is a source of comfort and well-being, that enables us to be merry.

One could sit and gaze into a fire for hours, hypnotised by transmogrifying forms – intrigued, delighted and fascinated. Fire is a shamanic art. Lighting a fire in the open air with flint and tinder can take the fire-maker closer to the fire element: a relationship is developed.

We discover that we are surrounded by fire: the fire of the sun and stars; the cold fire of angler fish and glow-worms; fireflies; fox-fire; the northern lights; the fire of our interaction with our world; and, our fire of enthusiasm – the 'good heart' that extends itself to others. But fire needs to be respected because control can easily be lost. Desire needs to be experienced with a certain sense of spaciousness or the flames of desire can escalate into emotional napalm. It is worth cultivating the art of 'dream-like window shopping'. It is worth learning to admire and enjoy the passing display of phenomena; without feeling a need to grab at them, and turn them into reference points.

It is a dangerous business playing with fire, or desire, unless we have some experience of spaciousness. This is not to say that we should avert our gaze from all objects of desire; or that everything that is attractive should be ignored. Refusing to acknowledge the beauty or value of anything that does not belong to us, is simply a method of 'playing it safe' – and it pauperises the field of our experience. This is a rather mildewed caution that is not prepared to taste anything that appears to be beyond our grasp. Nothing can be ours forever; even if we are able to obtain it. Total renunciation of the world is not required in terms of Tantra – merely in terms of referentiality: 'I enjoy, therefore I enjoy' – rather than 'I enjoy, therefore I am'.[2]

---

[2] *Sambhogakaya* or *long-ku* (the sphere of energy, the visionary sphere) is often translated as 'the sphere of enjoyment'.

With the development of view, which is discovered through the practice of shi-nè, the experience of emptiness allows humour to develop. With humour as a function of the fabric of perception, it becomes possible to be childlike. We need to be able to *play* with the phenomenal world; through touching, hearing, seeing, smelling, and tasting. We need to be able to appreciate phenomena in the fullest sense – but then; we need to be able to allow them their freedom. We need to be able to let go.

There is a story of two monks who dealt with this issue in different ways. They came upon a very dignified lady on the bank of a wide but shallow river. The monks were quite used to wading across the river but the lady was quite nervous about the prospect of crossing the stream in all her finery. She was dressed for a very special occasion: the wedding of her friend in the next village. Like the monks, she was used to wading across the river; but on this particular day she was worried about the possibility of losing her footing. It would have been a shame to have arrived at the wedding dishevelled and drenched.

One of the monks saw her predicament and offered to carry her across. She thanked him and accepted. He picked her up in his arms and waded across to the other side. The monks accompanied the lady a mile or two along the path until she turned off into the village where her friend's wedding was to take place. The monks continued on their way. After a while of walking in silence, the monk who carried the lady appeared to be in good spirits, but the other was very obviously pondering serious issues, and had to make his thoughts known. Suddenly he asked his friend: "Do you think it prudent for monks to have such close contact with ladies?" The other monk let out a great laugh and said: "I put the lady down back at the river but it looks as if you're still carrying her!"

154

The distorted energy of the fire element might seem very similar in some ways to the materialism of the earth element. But whereas the distorted earth element acquires and hoards without any real joy in possession, the distorted fire element energy consumes and discards with a certain fevered glee. It is more important for the earth element to solidify ourselves with immense quantity; but we are not necessarily able to appreciate the quality of what we have. The earth element neurosis applies to status rather than to sensual enjoyment and appreciation. The social status value of the 'quality items' we might possess is more important than the pleasure that might exist in terms of any individual object, situation or person. The earth element neurotic simply needs to feel strong and impervious to threats of impoverishment. But with fire, security is found in the moment of consumption. Once the desired person, situation or object is obtained, it is swiftly relegated to the repository of forgetfulness.

With the fire element, confrontation with *intrinsic space* is feared, because it exposes the sense of isolation. Fire element neurotics feel very alone in the world, so they need to possess and be possessed in order to cover this feeling of isolation. The act of anticipating impending ownership, of planning the acquisition of focuses of desire, are crucial aspects of the fire element neurosis. Human relationships are often approached in the same crude way. Fire element neurotics live for the moment. They live for the orgiastic instant when they pass the money over the counter. They live for the point at which they can exultantly caress the new lover; play the new CD; drive the new car; shoot the new gun; put on the new coat; open the pages of the new book; slide into the new elk hide trousers; slip into the luxurious suede shirt; gaze into the lustrous surface of the period viola da gamba; get their fingers on the keyboard of the new computer...

The new whatever, it does not matter, but it has to be: more, faster, bigger, better, smaller, lighter, heavier, more sensuous, more virile, more muscular, more voluptuous, more... just continuous new 'more'.

These are all approximations of exterminating isolation. We have the belief that it is actually possible to abolish our sense of isolation through achieving ecstatic union with any focus of our desire. But no matter how often desire is consummated, the sense of isolation cannot be assuaged. The 'threat' of intrinsic space cannot be appeased in this way. The entire phenomenal world could be poured into this sense of isolation; and, it would simply vanish. There is no answer to this void we feel – this sense of being isolated and incomplete. There is no cure for this emptiness in terms of filling it. There is no cure apart from *staring* into desire with non-conceptual attention. This liberates the boundless energy of desire into the desireless-desire of compassion.

The distorted energy of fire depersonalises our relationship with everything. Fire element neurotics are unable to relate properly to anyone else, because they are always using others to obliterate their terrible loneliness and isolation. They want everybody to love them or at least like them – but if they can't be liked they would rather be loathed. They want their partners to love them more than their own lives. If they make a new friend they tend to call round too often. They crowd people's lives with their presence. Sometimes they can seem very generous; but it is not real generosity – it is usually only an urge to swamp others with the field of their own desire. Anything rather than being alone!

The liberated field of energy of the fire element displays the discriminative quality of fire. This can be seen in terms of how fire helps us in specific ways.

The oxyacetylene torches of those who work with precious metals enable them to direct fine needles of flame to the exact point required. In medicine, laser beams are used in micro-surgery to achieve unprecedented precision in the art of healing. Once we have some recognition of intrinsic space, a great discovery can be made – loneliness is actually aloneness or uniqueness. There is a positive sense in which aloneness is an uninhibited, unattached frame of non-reference. We no longer feel the burning need to grasp or possess according to ourselves as the sole focus. We no longer feel irredeemably impelled to fill our own sense of unfulfilment by seducing phenomena. We can simply experience the coital quality of *intrinsic seduction* as the fabric of reality. We can liberate desire to accommodate the desires of everyone and everything everywhere.

Our entire experience becomes more spacious. It becomes possible to centre on the isolation, vulnerability and insecurity of others. The fire of passion moves beyond personalised or isolated/isolating passion. This can be called active-compassion or pure appropriateness. Indiscriminate grasping is liberated into the pure energy field of discriminating awareness. Discriminating awareness means being in tune. It means being able to listen without the interference of interminable internal gossip. Ceasing to operate from the centralised desire-fulfilment machine of duality, makes it feasible to extend infinitely to all beings. We have immediate awareness of exactly what is needed, and where. When people approach with their problems, we do not feel the need to manipulate the situation to satisfy our need to feel wanted. We have no need to make people feel dependent; but rather, we can facilitate their growth or healing in a skilful way that is not 'sticky' with our thirst for gratitude or accomplishment.

We neither give too little, nor do we give too much; because we are not governed by our fears and anxieties. There is a distinct difference between the real compassion of *pure appropriateness* and the 'idiot compassion' that helps people to vegetate in long-term self-indulgence. It is 'idiot compassion' to assist others in remaining incapable – purely because that is what they wish to do.

When the essential nature of the fire element is experienced beyond the constrictions of dualism, there is no longer a sense in which the world has to be seduced. It is already seducing itself through us, through itself, and through the endless beings who manifest. We no longer have to consummate our relationship with each focus of comforting proximity in order to establish our existence. We are already in coital union with every nuance of phenomenal reality that touches the spheres of our senses. We realise that we already possess everything simply through being sentient.

Every activity is experienced as the consummation of the love affair between emptiness and form. We are free of reference points as objects of desire. Space becomes the open dimension of experience and we can enjoy the spontaneity of its play without feeling isolated. We burn with the wisdom-fire of centrelessness. We realise our capacity to extend our realisation to everyone.

The formalised Tibetan symbol for this field of energy is *pema*,[3] the lotus. The lotus is an important symbol in Tibetan Tantra, and all awareness-beings used in the practice of envisionment or visualisation are described as sitting on lotus-thrones. Padmasambhava, whose name means 'lotus-born', crystallises the essence of this symbol in his being.

---

[3] Padma in Sanskrit.

The life of Padmasambhava, which continues through his deathlessness in the energy of his accomplished lineage, is the epitome of everything that can be understood through this symbol. The symbolism of the lotus is that it grows up out of the murky mud and slime of polluted water into dazzling sunlight. When it opens, its petals are pristine and unaffected by the stagnant sludge. Its petals have been pure from beginninglessness. The lotus remains pure through the illusion of renunciation, of apparent obfuscation, and the transmutation of apparent obscuration into clear light.

The colour red is vivid. It reminds us of youthful rosy cheeks and many of the vibrant, vigorous aspects of life. It can be 'painting the town red' – either in glorious abandon, or as a desperate attempt to mask isolation. The cardinal direction of fire is West. West is where the sun sets. The sun dipping on the edge of the sea has tremendous scenic grandeur – its polychromatic festival of light is an entrancing spectacle. We are lost in appreciation of a sunset in some tranquil place of natural beauty. Soft green cliff tops provide a comfortable place to sit. We take our ease; back against a rock, warmed by the day's sunshine. The sea laps at miles of fine golden sand. The coast line is filigreed with coves and large free-standing columns of granite that have the simple perfection of a Japanese rock garden. The cry of seagulls descants the rippling ocean. There is a soothing breeze fresh from the sea that eases the heat of the day. We feel alive, invigorated, scintillated and relaxed. There is a feeling that everything is just as it should be. What are these many little flowers that scent the breeze? There is densely packed chamomile cushioning the place where we sit. The sun becomes a brilliant deep red. It is a translucent disc of light that scatters reflections on the numberless waves, that sparkle and glitter for our pleasure. The colours of the scene are soft and velvety.

We luxuriate in the accommodating simplicity of it all. We feel young. We feel healthy and expansive. The vastness of the multi-coloured sky is open to us.

The wish to share the delightful efflorescence of this scene with others is spontaneous and unfabricated. The thought of wanting to witness this brilliant display on our own simply does not arise. The performance is far too lyrically generous, to engender the need for ownership. It is too expansive to own – it is something we naturally wish to share. It is appropriate that there should be a full house for this performance. It is appropriate, not only for the sake of the actresses' and the actors' efforts; but for each member of the audience to celebrate their shared appreciation. Even if there is no one there to share this fabulous spectacle – feelings of warmth and good heart toward others extend as a natural reflex.

This field of energy is associated with spring. It is associated with freshness and vitality – the charming play of young creatures, and the joy of being able to leap with excitement at any age. There is the wonder of growth: buds succulent with life decorate the bare branches of the trees, bursting into leaf or blooming into flower. There are catkins and bluebells in the woods – delicate green shoots sprouting into the light. The atmosphere is one of joyous frivolity and lightness. Cultivating real frivolity means abandoning the habit of taking one's 'self' so seriously. Cutting through seriousness enables us to feel the sunshine. It enables us to climb out of the vast vat of porridge built of self-righteousness and sanctimonious attachment to a constipated sobriety. It enables us to feel the fine nourishing rain that refreshes the world and fills the sky with magical rainbows.

9

Green Khandro-Pawo Display

The wisdom of self-fulfilling activity is free of all hindrances.
We can pacify what needs to be pacified.   We can
enrich what needs to be enriched.
We can magnetise what needs to be magnetised.
We can destroy what needs to be destroyed.   Our activities
are self-accomplished; their completion is implicit
in their inception.

G reen is the colour of the air element.   According to the dualistic vision of the air element, experience of our spacious nature is perceived as groundless anxiety.   When the texture of our experience is felt in this way, a sense of panic – the illusory sense of pervasive yet infinitely evasive sources of menace – generates the distorted energy of paranoia.   According to the non-dual vision of the air element, experiences of our spacious nature are discovered in their natural condition as the energy of self-accomplishing activity.   This is something that can be learnt non-intellectually through experiencing the nature of the air element itself.   We need merely observe the sky and the wind in the trees.

The colour green is connected to the element of air, to the distorted energy of paranoia and to the liberated energy of self-fulfilling activity.

Air flurries in all directions: touching everything; exploring
each surface; examining all angles; investigating every crevice.
It is always seeking but never finding. The wind has to press
on; constantly searching, unable to rest.

Air can be a breeze or a strong wind. It can be a forceful,
destructive hurricane – demolishing any obstacle in its path.
The circling energy of a whirlwind energetically mirrors the vicious
cyclical qualities of paranoia. A whirlwind continually chases its
tail; it leaves havoc in its wake in the same way in which people
lash out – dragging others into their paranoid experience of the
world. The circularity of this energy impels itself to go over
the same ground over, and over, and over again. One might be
departing for a holiday and realise that the vital passport is not
where it was supposed to be. So one looks through the same
drawer three or four times, before finding the passport in the
very same drawer through which one had initially searched.

The distorted energy of the air element is fundamentally concerned
with losing ground. Existence is validated in terms of protecting
territory. We have the feeling that our territory is under attack.
This generates the need to engage in constant hot and cold warfare
in order to defend it. Our reaction to confronting *intrinsic space*
manifests as fear of obliteration – we have the feeling that space has
a deadly finality about it. We envisage space as having the power
to undermine through its capacity to conceal devious means.

We fear space as a militant nihilistic conspiracy. Hyperactive
cowardice develops from this, in which any hint of possible sensory
deprivation becomes the focus of paranoid projections. In the
world of ideation there are paranoid projections of what stable
shi-nè may call into form. In the visual world there are paranoid
projections of what darkness may contain.

In the auditory world there are paranoid projections of what silence may hide. In the olfactory and taste worlds there are paranoid projections of what blandness may reveal. In the tactile world there are paranoid projections of what numbness or inability to connect may disguise. In all these sensory fields, we fear losing experiential territory and we create paranoid projections to bolster our sense of self-protection.

The air element has certain similarities with the earth element, in terms of insecurity – but there is a significant difference. The earth element neurotic feels a total lack of territory. There is a lack of identification with solidity in terms of having any kind of coherent foot-hold of personal territory. The air element neurotic does not feel a total lack of territory, but feels totally insecure about the territory he or she may appear to have. The air element identifies itself in terms of the utter vulnerability of 'apparent territory'. There is a lack of any trust in solid ground remaining solid unless it is kept under constant surveillance. This paranoia fixates on the idea that, if territory ceases to exist, being also ceases to exist; and, that territory is, by its very nature, intent on vanishing under all sorts of highly complex circumstances. The feeling that generates itself out of this perspective, is that personal identity could easily be channelled into a maze out of which there might possibly be no escape. The 'solid ground' outside the maze is attainable, but the longer one remains in the maze the more vaporous one becomes – until the time limit arrives, and one disappears altogether.

In contradistinction from the earth element, rather than being concerned with conquering and dominating territory, air element neurotics are desperately concerned with maintaining the territory they have – and the territory they feel they are.

Within the illusion of dualism the air element neurotic is always under threat, but unable ever to ascertain the direction from which the threat is likely to arise. Conspiracies are suspected, both inherent in the world and contrived by parties known and unknown. Plots to undermine or obliterate personal territory are continually inferred. The quality of existence becomes a self-protecting mechanism.

The dualistic perspective of the air element relates to a sense of ourselves in terms of innumerable perceived undermining interconnections with our environment. Because we have no feeling of inner security or safety, anything 'other' seems more real and reliable. This means that other people's territory seems highly secure. Other people's territory appears secure because other people *seem* so relaxed. They *seem* unthreatened about giving access to their territory, so the access they give feels unreliable. Other people's territory seems secure because they appear to be so expert at excluding anyone at a moment's notice. Air element neurotics experience themselves as being powerless to do anything about the process by which they are welcomed or excluded from the territory of others. Because of this, their identity is established according to the perceived security of others, and they find it impossible ever to feel safe or included in anything.

For the air element neurotic, any aspect of the world that is perceived to be reliable automatically generates the maximum possibility for vulnerability to increase. Any encroachment on reliable territory becomes intolerable. If our sports team or political party is vilified, we feel it as a personal blow. If other people's taste in music includes styles that we do not understand, we feel a need to make disparaging statements about it and express our conviction that 'this is not music'.

If other people have different ideas about life-style, culture, architecture, interior decoration, kitchen appliances, preferred beverages, literature, clothing, garden furniture, or anything imaginable; we must vociferously express our contrasting views in order to maintain a sense of reality. We feel a need to condemn everything that is different; and this condemnation can be based on any set of criteria that is felt to be personal solid ground. We could become entrenched in a pseudo-class orientation and condemn working-class tastes, or we could align ourselves with working-class values, and criticise everything we see as middle-class. But our criticisms have less to do with the arbitrary designations of class than with our need to defend what we perceive as our territory.

The air element neurotic has a tendency toward paranoia, and in some cases can suffer from serious mental illness. The use of the word 'territory' is both physical and psychological – it refers to the inability to distinguish the abstract from the concrete. In extreme cases someone might be severely threatened if they were told that someone else disliked their favourite colour. That might be a personal disaster; a gigantic humiliation beyond endurance. For the air element neurotic, threats seem to come from all angles. They are always on their toes – ready to run for their lives or to attack without mercy. They seem to feel a need to be on edge – they worry as a means of trying to control their world, but this merely turns the world into an even more frightening place. The vulnerability experienced by air element neurotics makes them feel as if others are 'out of control'. They see freedom of action as insanity, and project their feelings of fear and insecurity onto others in the form of aggression. This need to be 'on guard' creates some sense of security – which is why it is maintained, sometimes against all reason.

But this security is completely insecure, because it merely serves to increase the sense of threat. If one must maintain constant vigilance against suspected adversaries who may be hatching plots against one, energy is drained in that all-consuming effort and one feels progressively more vulnerable.

It can also be much more subtle. Rather than vigilance against suspected adversaries hatching plots, it could take the form of vigilance against impending disintegration. Air element neurotics feel that there is something crucial about the world that they do not quite understand. People have secrets that they will not share. People give each other knowing glances when they think that you are not looking. If you catch them at it they turn and smile, which seems infuriating. Other people seem so confident that they do not even care that you might be aware of their strategies. From the perspective of this dualistic derangement, others seem completely solid and assured; not at all open to attack.

Air element neurotics even suspect people who are close friends. They engage in espionage concerning others: 'Do they know I know or do they guess?'; 'Do they know that I know they know; or do they suspect?' When they talk to people, they somehow know that others are not saying quite what they mean. Others have some kind of information that they are not going to divulge. Questions are asked but no answers are forthcoming; or if they are, the answers seem couched in such a way as to harbour a multiplicity of interpretations. Ambiguities are seen in harmless comments. People who call to say "hello" might have some other intention in mind. Friends are interrogated for answers as to what is being said, and either there is no response, or there is the feeling that the truth is not being told. The belief arises that something sinister is going on. Someone wants to keep you in the dark.

Air element neurotics can become highly sophisticated in their encyclopædic analyses. They dissect every word, nuance and gesture to discover its meaning. These meanings need to be taken into calculation, in terms of 'making sense' of any situation. They become ridiculously nimble – preposterously alert. There is a readiness to repel invaders at any moment. This acute alertness is a state of high tension, a state in which agitation has become the norm. If this state continues to feed into itself, one could eventually become clinically psychotic.

Of course there are air element neurotics who are not such pronounced caricatures, and more sympathetic pictures of the air neurosis could be painted. The air element type does not always have to be a paranoid personality looking for ulterior motives in every facial expression. It could be someone with shaky confidence in their sense of who they are, or what they have. It could be someone who 'just *knows*' that most friendships are a sham, and that they are just about to dissolve into the vagueness of past association. Jealousy of the seeming security of other people breeds a sense of inadequacy at the level of our own interpersonal emotional technology. Envy of what seem to be other people's sophisticated security systems, cripples our ability to interact. Other people seem to have what it takes to enable them to operate with ease and confidence – but they act as if it were natural. Investing energy in attempts to fathom the motivations of others becomes a preoccupation. Suspicion about why people may be trying to befriend you becomes a barrier to allowing yourself to feel accepted anywhere. You cannot quite shake the idea that 'Maybe they're trying to lure me into a false sense of security in order to take advantage of my weakened boundaries. They want to undermine my identity or steal my ideas!' You might wonder: 'Why do these people want to help me?'

'They must have some ulterior motive'. This continual mental scanning uses up our physical and mental resources, and leaves us exhausted. Attempts to understand the endlessly interconnected conspiracies that seem to exist, simply create more evidence of collusion and possibilities of betrayal. We can arrive at no firm conclusions; just further unanswerable questions. It does not occur to us that there is an alternative to this convoluted personal torture and, if it is suggested, it seems to imply some sort of ostrich-like naïveté.

Of course it *is* possible to adopt an ostrich-like stance about our life circumstances. We could become completely unsuspecting and terminally naïve; but that is no answer to paranoia. To deny the intricacies and schemes of the world, is merely to lose contact with reality. If we lose contact with living according to our perception (because it seems less complex to swaddle our senses in candy-floss) the machinations of society are experienced merely as unexpected and meaningless pain. As dualistic reflections of wisdom and compassion, both naïveté and cynicism are actually necessary. Naïveté relates to wisdom, because of its openness and lack of tension. Cynicism relates to compassion (method), because of its ability to zero in on situations and catch signs of dishonesty. Naïveté when integrated with cynicism manifests openness, trust, and confidence. Cynicism when integrated with naïveté manifests capacity, capability, and direct uninhibited action.

The sensation of paranoia cannot simply be countered by retracting from the complex tension of the distorted air element. The paranoia in this frame of reference needs to be wordlessly observed in the moment of its arising. We need to look at the manner in which our attention functions. Attention is our capacity to concentrate on any designated object or area.

If people are low on the scale of psychological health they often have difficulty with concentration, because of their need to fantasise. Failure to concentrate is a coping strategy, which allows people to be evasive, and to avoid issues that they would rather not confront. So, there is an advantage to the paranoid personality in having their attention scattered. It means there can be little capacity for the fulfilment of natural creativity. And unless natural creativity is allowed some space to function, we become unable to enhance our life or the lives of others. Without this natural creativity, we expend energy merely in maintenance of territory and image. We wear ourselves out with relentless thinking; which, ironically, only heightens our sense of nervousness. Paranoia is a self-fulfilling prophecy.

The character of the dualistic air element covers the spectrum from worry to paranoid schizophrenia. This energy can manifest in a great variety of ways according to the evolving history of habitual tendencies. In the 'spiritual world' we flit from one teacher to another, comparing and contrasting but never actually practising. Air element neurotics have to find what they imagine is going to be totally right for them. The teachings have to meet with their strict and highly intricate intellectual approval. They are constantly asking questions and arguing with the answers. The questions have little or nothing to do with real experience, but are based solely on the currents and eddies of the whirlpool of intellect. Intellect generates reverberations of a despotic need for specifically stylised rationalities. In general, this means that when a person says that they are expressing their feelings, what they are actually doing is describing the process of how they are churning up their emotional being with the cyclic processes of intellect. They may become very confused and unable to settle anywhere.

They may become unable to trust anyone, so it is very difficult for them to trust themselves enough to develop any real commitment to a spiritual path.

The liberated field of energy of the air element is the strong steady wind that enables ships to make good headway. It is not the tornado that wrecks them. It is the fresh clean wind in our hair that enables us to shake off lethargy. This fresh clean wind stimulates the feeling that we could accomplish anything. The discovery of *intrinsic space* enables us to let go of anxieties. In fact, within the experience of *intrinsic space,* anxieties dissolve into emptiness. From this experience we realise that the origin of suspicion and worry is simply nonexistent. This realisation is the dawn of the clear knowledge that paranoia, and the vicious cycle of intellect, are just ways of trying to prevent ourselves from vanishing. When we gain some degree of *clarity* through the practice of shi-nè, we start to view vanishing as an occupational hazard of being. We continually vanish and continually reappear. We are continually *leaping out of sheer emptiness into the present instant.*

Learning to trust intrinsic space – the space between known areas of experience – is the basis of growth. Without trusting this space we stagnate. When we go to sleep there has to be some kind of trust in waking up. Trust in the spaciousness of what we are is imperative in the process of allowing paranoia to dissolve into the emptiness from which *self-accomplishing activity* can arise. As soon as paranoia dissolves into *intrinsic space,* energy is released, and is able to flow freely. Being able to *act directly* without inhibition is a quality that arises out of our recognition of intrinsic space. This enables movement that is completely committed – and it can travel in any direction.

There is no requirement for concern with the dubious benefits of military tactics. There is no need to trouble ourselves with the intricacies of rearguard action, because there are no supply lines to protect. This is the innate recognition that there is no hostile territory; so troops have no need of rations and ammunition. The 'troops' of the sense perceptions are all quite merrily enjoying the countryside anyway. We no longer have any concern with launching offensives. There is no longer any need to consolidate defences, because no one is pitting themselves against us. What we thought were enemy troops are just other people; not so very different from ourselves. Maybe these other people have different ideas. Maybe they sing different songs and eat different food. Maybe they speak differently and wear different ornaments. This discovery makes itself, and in that experience the world is a kinder place than we had previously imagined, and the conflicts that exist, are simply aspects of the way that people relate to each other's pain.

The dissolution of paranoia is a colossal relief. There are no more strategies to be worked out, there is no more suspicion of mutiny in the ranks, there is no war to wage. Once paranoia begins to dissolve there is less and less to keep under surveillance. The need to protect our experiential territory from annihilation simply evaporates into itself and the power of dynamic potential is unleashed. There is nothing to guard and no solid, permanent, separate, continuous, or defined 'I' to guard it anyway.

The wisdom of self-fulfilling activity is free of all hindrances. We can *pacify* what needs to be pacified. We can *enrich* what needs to be enriched. We can *magnetise* what needs to be magnetised. We can *destroy* what needs to be destroyed. These are the four principles known as *wisdom activities.*[1] They are the energetic aspect of enlightenment.

[1] *Lé-shi*, or the four Buddha-karmas: enriching, pacifying, magnetising, destroying.

Our actions fulfil themselves, because we do not embark on projects founded on the viewpoint of duality. Our activities are self-accomplishing; their completion is inherent in their inception – begun in their beginning. These activities are not always easily understood from the conditioned, or conventional perspective. In terms of enlightened activity, a Lama could destroy cherished beliefs which ostensibly gave us inspiration. The Lama could enrich a quality in us that we felt was irrelevant to our spiritual growth. But this is not an ordinary perspective. It can only be comprehended from the view based on the realisation of intrinsic space. All activity that springs from this view is present, direct and self-fulfilling.

Drukpa Kunlegs, the famous Tibetan crazy-wisdom master, was a wandering ngakpa[2] renowned both for the profundity of his realisation and for the extraordinary outrageousness of his behaviour. In one story told of him, he came running into a village where a certain geshé[3] was giving a discourse on logic. Accompanied as ever by his dog, he was in hot pursuit of a deer. He happened, 'coincidentally', to slay the deer with an arrow from his hunting bow right in front of the teaching area – a great canopy of cloth rigged up like an open-sided tent in front of the monastery. Drukpa Kunlegs swiftly skinned the deer, spit-roasted it and feasted on the flesh, leaving the rest for his dog. He washed it down with a flask of chang[4] and leaned back to rest in the sunshine.

[2] Ngakpa / ngakma (Skt. mantrin / mantrini): a yogi who has the power of awareness-spell (mantra).

[3] The title *geshé* is awarded to monks who have spent many years in academic study of morality, philosophy and psychology. Only once they have been rigorously examined over days of long, gruelling debate are they given this recognition, and so naturally they are highly respected in the monastic traditions of Tibet.

[4] *Chang* is Tibetan beer made from fermented barley. It is milky in consistency and rather refreshing, though those who do not care for it describe it as tasting like a mixture of kerosene and low-fat yogurt.

When the geshé had finished his teaching, Drukpa Kunlegs let out a resonant belch. He smiled at the angry monks who approached him, intent on rebuking him for his 'unseemly' behaviour. The assembly of monks were horrified and demanded in aggressive voices what right he had to disturb their important study with this cruel display. Drukpa Kunlegs did not seem very concerned about their righteous indignation and said with a grin: "I have simply come to show you the fruition of what you are trying to learn!" At this, he threw the skin of the deer back over its neatly arranged bones; and, at a snap of his fingers the deer sprang up as if nothing had happened. It vanished into the woods to the amazement of the assembly. Drukpa Kunlegs eyed them all with amusement and said: "Scholarship is one thing, but knowing the nature of Mind is another!"

The monks were fairly dumbfounded by this statement. But their surprise was marked not only by what they had seen and heard; but by the fact that the great geshé was laughing as heartily as Drukpa Kunlegs himself. They were actually good friends. The geshé expected his friend the mad ngakpa to turn up every once in a while and perform some such trick. Drukpa Kunlegs spent most of his life shocking the establishment, but everywhere he went to rock the boat a little he is remembered with reverence. Crazy-wisdom such as this, is associated with the awareness-being Dorje Tröllö – thunderbolt wrath. He rides either a pregnant tigress, or a tigress who has just given birth. This is said to be the most dangerous kind of tiger. The tiger symbolises the *passionate space* of Dorje Tröllö's inner khandro, as a manifestation of Tashi Chhi-'dren or Yeshé Tsogyel.[5]

[5] This is according to the Dzogchen dag-ngang gTér of Khyungchen Aro Lingma. From the uncommon perspective of the lineage of Chögyal Namkha'i Norbu Rinpoche, the tiger is the Bönpo sky tiger A-ti-mü-è, rather than a manifestation of Tashi Chhi-dren or Yeshé Tsogyel.

Dorje Tröllö embodies the Three Terrible Oaths:

> Whatever happens – *may* it happen!
> Whichever way it goes – *may* it go that way!
> There is no purpose!

These 'oaths' constitute a stance in which one *positively wills every situation to be exactly as it is*. This is a tremendously direct and powerful expression of living the view, which is, of course, a very advanced stance to assume. It is an attitude toward life to which most people cannot relate, especially in terms of the experience of pain; but, it is an inspirational direction. As an inspirational direction, it affords us the possibility of shedding the cumbersome baggage of 'victim mentality' – even if we are actually being victimised.

The crazy-wisdom activity of any Lama usually carries a powerful message, if we are open to perceiving it. Kunzang Dorje Rinpoche[6] is a master of this kind and there are many stories about his style of teaching that are truly extraordinary; not necessarily for their outrageousness, but for their oblique and subtly unpredictable divergence from anything one might expect.

Kunzang Dorje Rinpoche was invited to Sikkim to be the resident teacher of the royal court of the King. He surprised everyone by accepting the invitation – everyone knew that he had no taste for ceremony and prestige. While he was there, his habit was to use an old whiskey bottle instead of a bumpa[7] when he gave the empowerments that were requested. The King found this style of using a bottle for empowerment somewhat unorthodox.

---

[6] Kunzang Dorje Rinpoche is a Nyingma ngakpa who is one of Ngak'chang Rinpoche's Root Teachers. He is also the teacher of his vajra sister, Jétsunma Khandro Ten'dzin Drölkar.

[7] A *bumpa* is an empowerment jug or vase. It is the first of four ritual objects used to give transmission in a Tantric empowerment.

He presented Kunzang Dorje Rinpoche with a beautiful golden bumpa and requested that he use that instead. Kunzang Dorje Rinpoche used it once, then left the palace and went back to his wandering life, never to return.

There is a story of Milarépa that also illustrates this idea quite well. Milarépa was a naljorpa[8] who lived most of his life in the mountains of southern Tibet. He was the pupil of the great Lama *lotsawa*,[9] Marpa. Marpa was a farmer who lived as a householder with his *sang-yum* Dagmèdma.[10] Marpa gave Milarépa the heart-instructions which he himself had received from the great Indian yogi Naropa, and sent him off to practise in mountain solitudes. Milarépa practised these teachings with incredible diligence, and gained complete realisation. Many people came to him for teachings, and many of his disciples also gained realisation, including the illustrious Réchungpa; and Gampopa, whose incarnation was the founder of the Karma Kagyüd lineage.

One day whilst Milarépa was sitting outside his meditation cave, he was visited by his sister. She had come from a long way off to bring him some food and other gifts. But when she arrived she was shocked at what she saw: her brother was naked. She felt quite ashamed, and told him off soundly for not looking after himself properly, and losing all sense of decency. She then departed to buy a length of cloth with which he could cover himself.

---

[8] Naljorpa means yogi – literally: one who resides in the natural state.

[9] *Lotsawa* means realised translator, i.e. someone who can translate the meaning, rather than someone who merely translates words.

[10] *Sang-yum* literally means 'secret mother', and is often translated as 'consort'. The male equivalent is *sang-yab* or 'secret father'. These are not the ordinary Tibetan words for mother and father; but rather, they apply to the human reflections of the ultimate meanings of emptiness and form. *Dag* means the sense of solid, permanent, separate, continuous, and defined *self*. *Mèd* means 'not', and *ma* means 'woman'. Dagmèdma is therefore an epithet for an enlightened woman.

It took her a few days to return with her purchase because Milarépa lived in a rather remote area. It is often the way with répas, that they live in very inaccessible places. They seclude themselves in order to practise without the constant interruption of people arriving to request blessings, predictions, and other such 'Lama services'.

When she returned she gave the cloth to her brother, who was quite amused to receive such a thing. However, he agreed to cover up his 'offending parts'. Having accomplished the end she had in mind, Milarépa's sister was pleased that her saintly brother would now be suitably dressed when other patrons called to bring offerings. She then went to make a short pilgrimage in the locality before bidding her brother a final goodbye. But after her pilgrimage, she returned to find a sight that astonished her. She may have been outraged by his nakedness, but she was completely flabbergasted by the extraordinarily strange thing that Milarépa had done with the cloth she had given him. Literally every protuberance of his body, including his nose, had been covered with neatly sewn pouches! And there he was; sitting on his usual rock looking utterly bizarre. Confused and enraged by his waste of good cloth, she asked him to explain himself; but his answer was as strange as his appearance. He said: "Well, I thought that as you objected to this," indicating his genitals, "that you might also object to the sight of anything similar". He had covered it all: penis, fingers, toes and nose. At this point his sister broke down and wept, begging his forgiveness. Milarépa had given her *symbolic transmission of the nature of Mind* through his eccentric display! Until that moment, she had not understood that her brother was a realised being and that he was completely beyond involvement with the nonsense criteria of everyday life!

She had also not really understood the true nature of practice, conceiving of it as most people do: as a system of religious observances that was part of the Tibetan culture. At that point Milarépa gave her teaching on the practice of *tu-mo* after which she went into retreat and became an accomplished ré-ma.[11]

The formalised Tibetan symbol for this field of energy is the thunderbolt sword. It displays unconstrained power, direct action, and unhindered effectiveness – the free unobstructed movement of lightning. Lightning does not waver. Lightning does not weigh the pros and cons of the situation, or get caught up in doubts about when it might be best to strike. It does not hesitate before it reaches the ground but moves with complete purpose, charging the air with electricity.

The colour green is associated with jealousy, envy and suspicion, but also with proliferation and growth. The cardinal direction associated with air is the North; where the elements interact in an extreme fashion. The north wind is the strongest wind and the weather conditions in the North are erratic and changeable. Air is associated with the summer, when life is teeming. Wherever you look, insect activity is frenetic: fields and meadows crawl with millions of minuscule creatures, all engaged in prolific activity. Nothing is static. Nothing is at rest. The air seems to buzz and shimmer with a haze of heat. Bees hum from flower to flower. Tadpoles become frogs and leap in search of flies to catch on the cusp of an accurate tongue. Sudden dramatic thunderstorms end as abruptly as they commence. Air is associated with early night: the time when the sun has set and the dusk is vibrating with grasshoppers and crickets.

[11] *Tu-mo*: psychic heat yoga, one of the Six Yogas of Naropa. Accomplished practitioners of tu-mo are called *ré-mas* or *ré-pas* (cotton-wearer) due to the thin cotton garments they wear no matter what the weather.

Cawing rooks roosting in the trees jostle each other for perching positions. Late-comers try to find space on the branches, dislodging others and getting dislodged themselves in turn. There is a constant squabble going on that never seems to draw to an end. This imagery displays a small fraction of the incredible dynamism of this field of energy which in its non-dual nature is the essence of power.

10

The Blue Khandro-Pawo Display

*The process of artificially maintaining and intensifying
emotional pain with thought is gyroscopic.
If we keep a cycle of thought constantly spinning,
we generate a charge that actively prevents the dissipation
of pain.   But without conceptualisation,
emotional pain becomes pure sensation and is
released to dance in the vastness of the open dimension of
experience.   Without the strait-jacket of concept, pain ceases to
be pain and becomes a free and ecstatic energy.*

B lue is the colour of space.   *According to the dualistic vision
of the space element, the experience of spaciousness is sensed as
bewilderment.   Bewilderment is the feeling of being overwhelmed
which arises out of the illusory lack of intrinsic expansiveness.   From this
contracted perspective, the distorted energy of depression and oblivious torpor
is fabricated as a means of survival.   According to the non-dual vision of
the space element, experiences of spaciousness are discovered in their natural
condition, as the energy of unlimited intelligence in unbounded space.
This is something that cannot be learnt intellectually;   it can only be learnt
directly, through experiencing the nature of space itself.   We only need to
stare into the nature of our own Mind, or into the vast expanse of the sky.*

Space, because of its infinite immensity, reminds us of death. Space is a dimension in which we could become permanently lost. Space can be misconceived as vacuity or blankness: there is nothing there; nothing happening; and, no one even to perceive that nothing is happening. We could experience sheer terror at the idea of complete and utter absence of everything. We could recoil into a cocoon of our own mental fabrication, in order to protect ourselves from such a threat.

And this is exactly what we do. Without an understanding gained from a creative source, such as the inner Tantras, it is not really surprising that we fear the emptiness of space. But fear of space is a distortion, because most people have only encountered the idea of space as a vacuum. Unending empty space seems to be an arena in which physical existence is absolutely dwarfed. If we only relate to space in terms of our relative dimension, our understanding will merely be a product of *dualistic experiential agoraphobia*. But in comparison to the vast ocean of the space of Mind, the spatial vacuity of the materialist universe is a rain puddle.

From the dualistic perspective, we find it so hard to endure the spatial quality of our own being; that we comfort ourselves by conceptualising the free open dimension of space into the graveless grave of nihilism. Having named space as something we do not want to consider, we lose touch with the open dimension of our own being. Then we conveniently lose ourselves in a contracting cubicle of 'virtual insentience'. This mediocre illusion of self-protection prevents us from relating to any absence of tangibility – no matter how transient or transitory.

Intrinsic space does not conform to any conventional logic, so we need some method of feeling comfortable with it.

It is invaluable then, that Tantra provides a 'logic' in terms of the experience of space – but it is not a logic that provides comfort. The logic of Tantra is simply one which allows us access to a spectrum of ecstasy.

We relate to space in terms of nothingness. According to the prevalent nihilistic outlook, death is commonly apprehended as the end of everything, as the opposite of life. But death is *not* the opposite of life. It is not even the opposite of birth. Birth and death are simply aspects of life that relate with each other in an inextricable process. In Buddhism the words 'life' and 'death' are never used in tandem or contrasted as polarities. Everything, *just as it is,* has emptiness as its fundamental nature. The concept of 'nothing' cannot be separated from the concept of 'something'. The concept of 'death' cannot be separated from the concept of 'birth'. 'The end' cannot be separated from 'the beginning'. Even the idea of vacuum implies substance to which it is contrasted. But the vastness of space encompasses every polarity.

Space occupies an ambiguous position. It is both an element, and the empty potential from which the other elements arise. It is within the space of empty potential, that the elements perform as the *primal play of reality* – the *dance* of the khandros and pawos. Space continually creates and reabsorbs these fields of energy without effort. The four distorted elemental fields of energy operate as defence mechanisms for the primary space-neurosis – the oblivious torpor which arises as a result of conceptualising space into a dull fog of nothingness. Conversely, the four liberated energies arise naturally as the dynamic functions of *ubiquitous intelligence* and *complete openness.*

The dualistic frame of reference of the space element numbs everything into a deadly semi-conscious cosiness.

One plays blind, deaf, and insensate to experience. One feels that life is too much – reality is too painful. At worst one feels hollow and worthless and one's living space becomes a health hazard. One lies in bed most of the day, occasionally getting up to make a cup of tea. Perhaps occasionally a slice of bread is toasted and smeared haphazardly with whatever happens to be lying around in the kitchen – probably some piece of ancient grease that has been languishing in the refrigerator in a mildewed wrapper. The knife is wiped on one's dressing-gown because it is the nearest thing that comes to hand. Crumbs drop all over the floor and one wipes one's mouth on a convenient sleeve. The rubbish bin is stinking and full to capacity. The dishes in the sink pile up until there is nothing left to use before the effort is made to wash up a few things – by simply running the hot tap over them. The bedroom is festooned with mouldering clothes – but nothing is done about it until the combined sock and underwear stench has become so untenably ghastly that one starts to gag. Only basic, minimum, acts are performed; and gradually the quality of life is eroded until a further sense of depression and pointlessness sets in.

In less severe cases we do not become quite so socially incapacitated but we might feel that inebriation would serve best in order to blot out reality. Failing that, we might sit staring vacantly at the television and round it all off with 'feelgood pills'. The last thing we would wish to hear is that there are methods by which we could experience the pure undiluted energy of being. Instead, space-neurotics contrive 'palatable' ways of dealing with their inner gnawing sensations and pain of desolation.

There are five dualistic strategies for manipulating the pain of desolation, so that it provides the illusion of solid ground. These are related to the five distorted fields of energy.

The first strategy is *freezing*. Freezing is connected to the distorted energy field of water. The second is *consolidating*, which connects to earth. The third is *fantasising*, which relates to fire. The fourth is *anticipating*, which relates to air. The fifth is *obliterating*, which is the fundamental strategy for attempting to convert pain into 'reliability' – and this connects with space. Of these five the three most fundamental are *fantasising, freezing* and *obliterating*. This is because these three are linked directly to the three distracted tendencies: *attraction, aversion,* and *indifference.*

Fantasising, as a strategy for dealing with the pain of desolation, is one in which we cling to pain because of the conviction that it is all that remains as territory. We become masochistic vampires feeding on the energy of our own pain. We nurture it with skill and devious dexterity. Intensity often leads to obsession, and obsession has a certain quality of single-mindedness – neurosis is always dynamically connected with enlightened nature.

The space-neurotic sees the pain of desolation as his or her identity and maintains it by grasping for it. The full range of imagination is employed to increase pain, thereby increasing the plausibility of a solid, permanent, separate, continuous, and defined identity. If your partner has left you for another person, you torment yourself by imagining everything they could be doing. You imagine that they are going to all the places you used to visit together. You consider the possibility that they are enjoying themselves just as you used to. You imagine increasingly painful scenarios as a means of feeding your anguish – in order to burst into tears over and over again. Some gift you once gave is being thrown away. They are making some cruel joke about you. Your most guarded confidences are being revealed for their shared amusement. There are some excruciating lines in *Othello* which describe this state of mind perfectly.

You might even roll around on the floor clutching at yourself, actually revelling in the picture of the pitiable spectacle you must appear. The imaginary scene could continue to worsen – it could become sexually explicit to the limit of your imagination – and you would both love and loathe what you were doing to yourself. Having imagined things to be as bad as they possibly could be, it might occur to you, that with a beautifully subtle twist the story could be worse still – and so it continues until, totally exhausted by the process, you cry yourself to sleep. There is obviously a highly perverse sense of enjoyment in all this; but it is rather superficial and unreal. It only serves to establish your identity as 'one who is in pain'. What you are saying to yourself is: "I hurt therefore I am".

Freezing as a process of dealing with pain is one in which the space element neurotic becomes as hard and as cold as ice. Feeling vanishes altogether and you 'get on with life'. Why you should just 'get on with life' is really not quite clear – but 'life is there to be lived through – so that is just what I will do!' Resignation is socially acceptable, and that supports this frozen position. Resignation, though a seemingly admirable stance, is a form of anger which imbues a person with a false sense of dignity. It is another way of establishing a concretised existence, through displaying that one can live without emotions. You cannot admit that you have been badly shaken by your partner having left; and so you might comment: "What use are emotional relationships anyway? They have never done anyone any good". You can hold down a job – you can even make the odd cold but witty rejoinder. You refuse to be touched by the pain of desertion, and retract into a form of rigid stoicism, in which you might indulge in ludicrous types of efficiency.

You get on with the matter in hand; knowing that no one will ever know or understand the pain you have endured. Neither will anyone ever appreciate your strength – well, not until it is too late. You bustle about your home making sure everything is immaculate. Time is spent engaged in organisational procedures, which are carried out alone in order that it is not necessary to smile at anyone. Your face locks into a frost-bitten mask of expressionlessness; or, develops an eerie fixed smile that betokens merely the pretence of gaiety. You may appear to have regained your characteristic emotional state, but all exhibited signs of normality are a charade. You might even form another relationship; but if it is unable to melt the permafrost of your defences, the other person will be emotionally frozen out. Space neurotics in freezing mode are merely actors, and their chilly shallowness provides no communication which would enable a relationship to survive. They cannot allow their new relationship to work, because they cannot allow the other person near enough. They cannot admit pain.

Obliteration as a process of dealing with the pain of desolation is one in which distraction becomes soporific and the pretence that the lover has never really left can establish itself. One can have conversations with an 'invisible partner' – or write letters to a partner who has simply gone away on a long trip. In lesser degrees of denial an attempt is made to take an artificial holiday from pain. Having oscillated between freezing and fantasising, which is the usual pattern, the intensity of it eventually becomes too fatiguing. Distraction requires manifold entertainments. You want to engage in conversation, or involvement in some kind of project. There has to be an activity that will swamp your pain. You might go to evening classes and learn a language. You might do a mechanics course and try to get your car back on the road.

You might take up painting water-colours. You keep your diary well-scheduled with events that distract you. Most people imagine that you are coping quite well; until you fall into heavy alcohol abuse, and end up keeping someone up all night weeping on their shoulder. When you cannot distract yourself you take shelter in oblivion: you get drunk; go to sleep; commit suicide; join a pottery class – anything as a means of escaping what you see as the brutal reality of your situation. It is a constant process of masking painful feelings.

Consolidation as a process of dealing with the pain of desolation is one in which a sense of success becomes apparent – emotion has frozen to such a degree that it becomes an inert insensate crust. One feels one has subdued feeling altogether; endured terrible disaster; withstood hideous emotional injuries. It seems like a great accomplishment, and this encourages a tendency to stiffen into morbid stolidness. This is a method of anæsthetising pain. Freezing enables you to avoid breaking down; but with the strategy of consolidation, the possibility of breaking down is no longer even available. Now all that is left is a self-created emotionally frozen world, in which self-reassurance maintains itself in the conviction that pain will never happen again. This creates an emotional suit of armour which provides the illusion of invulnerability at the expense of sensitivity. No one is allowed close enough to cause hurt or unhappiness – but at the expense of any real pleasure and real happiness. Arrogance gradually builds itself into a fortress. It becomes possible to enjoy despising others who break down, because they appear not to have such an advanced degree of emotional atrophication.

Anticipation as a process of dealing with the pain of desolation is one in which the space neurotic fears the worst in advance, living in dread of what might happen.

This process continually looks ahead, projecting fears further afield. If your partner has deserted you; you are stunned by the collapse of your territory, in terms of what it means for the future. You feel you cannot rely on the future any more, because your projected territory has crumbled. You no longer know how to be in the present; because the future has become void of meaning. Plans cannot be made because the guidelines have disappeared. You feel that you have nothing to base anything on in terms of who you thought you were. You are not even sure who you are anymore without your partner. Your partner was part of your territory and you needed them to validate your existence.

Territory, as the term is being employed here, does not have the possessive quality of the earth element. For the space neurotic in the anticipatory mode, territory is not regarded as a possession; but as an indispensable sign of being. For the space neurotic, the idea of extended territory does not have the consuming quality of the fire element – here, it is more the idea of annexing experientially safe areas. These areas are then seen as secure stepping-stones in the raging river of space. This is obviously not possession of territory in terms of the consummation of desire; but a terrified, white-knuckled grip onto any kind of security. In this frame of mind you cannot easily distinguish between 'I' and 'other'. Your partner had become part of you. When the 'other' in question happens to leave you, it feels like an amputation: legs and arms suddenly end at the knees and elbows.

The discovery of space reveals another way of relating to pain. We realise that if we do not tie our sensation of pain to the criteria of establishing our own existence,[1] emotional pain dissolves.

---

[1] The dualistic criteria by which we attempt to establish our existence are that we are: solid, permanent, separate, continuous, and defined. These are also known as the *form qualities of emptiness.* (The *emptiness qualities of form* are: insubstantiality, impermanence, undividedness, discontinuity, and lack of definition.)

It evaporates into its own free dimension. If we allow our conceptual scaffolding to collapse, the sensation of emotional pain also collapses. The process of artificially maintaining and intensifying emotional pain with thought is a gyroscopic perceptual mechanism. If we keep a cycle of thought constantly spinning, we generate a 'charge', that actively prevents it from dissolving into its own free dimension. But without conceptualisation, emotional pain becomes *pure sensation*. When it is experienced as *pure sensation* it is released to *dance in the vastness of the open dimension of experience*. If we do nothing to, or with, the sensation of pain – if we just leave it as it is; it becomes an immanent possibility of enlightenment. Without the strait-jacket of concept, pain ceases to be pain and becomes a free and ecstatic energy.

Needless to say, it is not easy to allow the conceptual framework to dismantle itself, and to *stare into the face of arising emotions*. But we are all intrinsically qualified to do this – this capacity is an aspect of our *natural condition*. In order to liberate emotional pain, we need to develop the practice of shi-nè. We need to discover emptiness and be able to rest comfortably in that state. Without this recognition of emptiness – which needs to be integrated with all experience – we cannot hope to completely liberate our emotions and realise them as the wisdom dance of khandros and pawos.

The symbol of the space element field of energy is the *khorlo,* the circle which transcends location, direction, form, time and space. Blue is the colour of the sky; it is the depth of the sky, stretching into infinity. It is rich, radiant and empty; unaffected by clouds of any colour. It can also be dull, opaque, dense and flat, or like smoke – impenetrable to the gaze. This field of energy is unconditioned and referenceless. There is no cardinal direction because it is all directions and no direction.

Space allows the possibility of 'direction' and 'location' to manifest. It is not associated with any season or time of day because the phenomenon of time passing arises from the continuity of *now* – the perpetual experience of space. Space is vast, infinite, unlimited, unoriginated and unconditioned. The wisdom of ubiquitous intelligence in all-encompassing space is there as soon as we give up the artificial process of distracted-being. It is immediately present when we stop struggling and let go of indulging in the artifice of contrived relaxation. When we just simply and effortlessly let go and let be, we realise ourselves as completely open and awake.

The practice of shi-nè is where we start. We continue through using our life circumstances as part of our path, and integrating emptiness with sensation and perception. Even the initial glimmerings of emptiness will enhance our ability to work with our emotions. The further we pursue the practice of shi-nè, the greater clarity we will discover. However, even as a psychological construct, these ideas can help us relate to the experience of emotional pain in a more real way. If we can connect with this view it is because we already have the experience of emptiness, since all of phenomenal reality is none other than the indivisibility of emptiness and form. Just as we experience form-clinging within the realm of duality, we also cannot help but experience reflections of emptiness. Our intrinsic enlightenment cannot help but sparkle through – we simply need to cooperate with it.

11

Five-fold Display

Question and Answer Commentary

*The elements are always equal in their essential
pure state.   It is not possible to divide the elements,
because they are completely interdependent;
they are indivisible.   We only talk about them as if
they were separate, in order to understand something about
enlightenment and unenlightenment.   As if enlightenment and
unenlightenment were two different things.*

Q   If our enlightened nature can 'sparkle through', I'm
wondering why wouldn't this balance all the distortions?

Khandro Déchen   It's not a question of balance.   There is no
issue of balance in what we're discussing here.   Neither Tantra
nor Dzogchen concern themselves with balance.   Unenlightenment
isn't spoken of as a state that's 'out of balance'.   Balance, actually, is
a tricky concept because it involves a sense of attachment to form.
'Balanced' and 'unbalanced' are simply reflections of form and
emptiness.

Ngak'chang Rinpoche   You must also remember that the
distortions and the *sparkling through* are both the enlightened state.

The *sparkling through* is simply the sporadic and unpredictable series of open-ended opportunities that occur for a tantrika.

KD   So when this *sparkling through* is happening; there is no distortion, because the distortion has become the sparkling through – if only for an instant.

NR   The point is, that you have to remain with the *sparkling through* rather than taking refuge in the distortions – merely because they are known, and therefore feel safe.

Q   Are we kidding ourselves when we say we'd love to remain with the sparkling through?

KD   Of course. But then again... no. It's not as simple as that.

NR   It's a binary issue – yes/no/yes/no/yes/no – but unlike a computer, we can go beyond that.

Q   To 'yes'?

NR   No.

KD   Beyond yes and no. Yes and no are just polarised concepts. It is not 'yes' or 'no'. It is not 'both yes and no'. Nor is it 'neither yes nor no'...

Q   So is it just because we think of dualistic distortion as *known* that we think of it as safe?

KD   Yes.

Q   So then is it just a question of establishing realised experience as the known, to create a different centre of gravity in our lives?

KD   Yes... if you know what that means.

Q   I'll have to work on that [laughs]. Then would that be the gradual aspect of the path?

NR   Yes, but the gradual aspect is also non-gradual. Gradual doesn't really exist. Gradual is just a long run-up to non-gradual.

Q   You're either enlightened or you're not?

KD   Exactly. Either you're enlightened or not.

Q   When you were talking about the earth element, you said something about how we use pride as a means of covering up poverty. . . Is shyness an aspect of the earth element?

KD   Shyness is a secondary colour of the spectrum; like guilt. Guilt is an aspect of the interaction of the earth and air elements. So yes, shyness is an aspect of the earth element neurosis. But it's like guilt – an interaction of earth and air.

Q   Like a sort of backwards pride? You don't want anyone to know who you really are?

KD   Very well put.

Q   How does that work? The interaction of earth and air?

KD   The earth element neurosis is concerned with territory and lack of territory. Pride is obviously a pattern that comes up in relation to establishing existing territory as unassailable. Shyness is a pattern in which personal territory can't be put to the test in any way, for fear that it will be proved insubstantial. So shyness is a form of unmanifested pride.

NR   Then the air element comes in with a bunch of complexities in relation to the nuances of outer circumstances. The air neurotic sees endless threats to personal territory in the outside world, and their method of dealing with it is to shrink back and hide.

KD   You see; hidden territory, or unexposed territory, can be experienced as secure.

Q   So if you perceive some aspect of the world to be reliable and that perception generates maximum vulnerability, would this be like fixating on a relationship as your territory, and then being hypersensitive to its ups and downs?

KD   Certainly.

NR   Hypersensitivity is very much related to the earth element, but it's very different from being shy. Hypersensitives are usually not backward in coming forward about how hurt they are by what someone is supposed to have done to them. They can be very dominant – they can control a whole room full of people just by walking in and looking like everyone has betrayed them.

Q   Would you call equanimity the personality of the earth element khandro?

NR   Yes, or spacious affluence. . . or spacious grandiosity. . . magnanimous mellifluous magnificence.

KD   [laughs] It's important to be able to stretch these definitions right out to the boundaries of language. . .

Q   You said that the idea that we have every right to feel anger should be called into question, and that there are no 'rights' in terms of anything we feel. But it just seems obvious to me that we do have these rights even though I guess that's a neurotic way of looking at it.

KD   Yes. That's the way justification works. Righteous indignation is the best one – not only am I justified, but God's on my side!

NR   And that's very tricky from a Buddhist point of view. . . You see, a right has to be given – there's no entitlement involved with feeling what we feel – we simply feel it. We cannot blame anyone or anything for how we feel. All we can say is that some person, event, or object, has inadvertently provided the finger that pushed our buttons. If there's no button, then no one can push it. Owning what we feel is actually a very useful practice – but that's not to say that we'll always find it easy.

Q   Does a person who has a lot of anger have more water element in them than people who have less or no anger?   I mean, if a person has no anger in them, would the water element be lacking completely?

NR   It's not really useful to think of the elements in a quantifiable way.   It isn't actually possible for any element to be completely lacking.   If an element were lacking, you would simply not exist at all.   The fact that all the elements are there, is what makes a sentient being.

Q   You mean animals and other creatures, like *yidags*[1] for example, are also composed of the five elements?   How would they manifest in a non-human creature?

KD   Yes, all sentient life is composed of the five elements. How they'd manifest in a non-human creature at the level of the emotions is quite another matter!   In order to answer that question, you'd have to be able to enter into the karmic vision of other creatures.

NR   Shamans of many cultures can do that, but it's not particularly a Buddhist practice.   That's not to say that there's anything wrong with doing it – quite the contrary.   Shamans who are capable of entering into the karmic vision of other creatures acquire the 'medicine' of these creatures.   They're then able to heal people of various illnesses, so it can be a compassionate activity.

Q   But isn't karmic vision what we're trying to get away from?

NR   Yes.

Q   Then . . . [interrupted]

NR   Why am I saying there's nothing wrong with it?

---

[1] *Yidag* (*preta* in Sanskrit) means 'hungry ghost'. Yidags are one of the six types of being, within the realms of being through which one can transmigrate. These Six Realms are essentially psychological perspectives or referential frames of karmic vision.

Q   Yes.

NR   Because anything that is done with a compassionate intention is valuable. Also, anything that concerns the experience of a broader frame of human reference has the possibility of providing a spring-board, or an approach to realisation.

Q   But couldn't you just get trapped in that?

NR   Sure. You could get trapped in anything. You could also convert Buddhism into a trap if you wanted to. Some people do, especially scholars and academics [laughs].

KD   I think it's important not to be elitist about one's spiritual path, and kindness is so much more important than some kind of self-centred grasping for the ultimate.

Q   So shamanism deals with the functions of power through accessing the karmic vision of non-human beings?

NR   Yes, that's a good general definition.

Q   And Tantra?

NR   Tantra deals with the functions of power through accessing pure vision manifestations of the dharmadhatu.[2] In some ways the processes are quite similar, but I'm afraid there is not enough time to explore this at the moment. So. . . as I was saying, the elements. The elements are always equally present, in terms of the *pure elements*.[3] It's also not possible to divide them, because they are completely interdependent. They are indivisible. We only talk about them separately in order to understand something about enlightenment and unenlightenment. As if enlightenment and unenlightenment were two different things.

[2] *Dharmadhatu* (Tib. *chö-ying*) is the dimension of space, the fundamental creative space of reality.

[3] The *pure elements* exist in their self-perfected state within the space of the central channel, but this book does not set out to explore this very difficult area of knowledge.

KD   That's why, when you explore the elements enough, you'll make a strange discovery. You'll find that the further you go in understanding the functioning of any particular element, the more it will start to seem like the others. So although it's useful to divide the elements, we should also understand that dividing them is only possible from the perspective of relative truth.

Q   A lot of people, especially women, seem to cry tears of rage or frustration. Why is this? It doesn't seem particularly clear, in the sense of clarity, but it does seem to be one-pointed... Can you say something about how this relates to anger and clarity?

KD   Well, it may not seem particularly clear, but it is very immediate. That state of being in tears of rage or frustration is something that blocks out other fields of sensation – it's a way of being singular about an issue. You see, you have to be quite broad in your understanding of clarity – especially in the distorted sense of how it manifests through anger.

NR   Clarity could have a lot of other words associated with it, such as: simplicity, directness, immediacy, sharpness, rawness, focus, crispness, visibility, brightness, resolution, distinctness, glare, engrossment, concentration, monotony, explicitness, totality, nakedness...

KD   There are very many words... To cry tears of rage is very dramatic, especially when there's an audience. It impresses people that whatever is going on has to be taken very seriously. That's really quite a 'clear' response – it's very direct, it's very sharp and certainly poignant. There's a sense with all this in which you have to feel your way into the meaning through a growing understanding of how the elements function within yourself.

Q   When you say that 'justification should be uncompassionately murdered' and that 'spilling the heart-blood of justification allows us to be gentle people', that sounds like quite a remarkable stance to take; or like a really powerful atmosphere to live in. But how would I approach that on a practical level?

NR   Just approach it on a practical level. More? [questioner nods] Just find yourself in your life situation and let that interplay be what is real. This, as far as I'm concerned, is the very heart of Tantric practice. The approach is to *hold it in your heart*. This is called *living the view*. You have to allow yourself to take in the transmission that is etched into those words.

KD   There is a feeling there: 'justification should be uncompassionately murdered'.

NR   Stay with that feeling.

Q   That seems difficult to get hold of, like, it's a bit vast. . . Is there something easier or simpler I could do?

NR   There's nothing easy you can 'do', I'm afraid. However, there's nothing particularly complicated about *living the view.*

KD   Easy options are for New Age workshops and I'm not particularly convinced of the use of those [laughs]. Living the view is, actually, a matter of inspired application. On a practical level you would simply attempt to remain in the awareness of the view. You'd make a practice of attempting to remember the view whenever you recognised the pattern of justification colouring your perception.

NR   That's not particularly easy – but it *is* simple. You couldn't get much more simple than that. Also. . . you have to make a practice of forgiving yourself for continually failing. That's a valuable part of the process. It's a practice simply to be a practitioner and, to keep that sense of recognition *present.*

Q I have a question about anger. You said that anger wasn't useful for establishing peace and justice in the world... So my question is: when is it useful?

NR It's *not*! [shouts in an angry tone] Sorry about that, but you see – it's never very useful.

Q But... [interrupted]

KD No [laughs]. It's really not useful.

NR *Whatever* the therapists may say.

KD It's not useful.

Q But what about Lamas who get angry with their students? Kyabjé Rinpoche[4] is known as a wrathful Lama, isn't he?

NR Yes... You see, we're looking at 'anger' as the word is commonly understood. But then there's 'the appearance of anger' as manifested by a realised being. It's not the same thing.

KD An actor can act the part of someone who is angry, but the actor doesn't actually have to *be* angry – he or she simply has to manifest the recognisable outer signs of anger. That kind of anger could be useful in certain circumstances. But feeling anger is only ever a distortion of the natural state of clarity.

NR Also, 'wrathfulness' doesn't even have to be expressed through the appearance of anger. Wrathfulness could simply be: the Lama turning up the volume, in terms of the energy of circumstances. For example, the Lama could suggest a cold plunge, a sauna, a parachute jump, eating a large quantity of garlic, an all-night mantra recitation session – anything.

KD Some of these things could obviously be a lot of fun too.

NR Quite. Wrathfulness shouldn't always be seen as anger.

[4] Kyabjé Khordong gTérchen Tulku Chhi-'mèd Rig'dzin Rinpoche, one of Ngak'chang Rinpoche's teachers.

It isn't some sort of spiritualised irritability, or mystical petulance. Wrathfulness has a far broader meaning – it means activity, energy, movement, directness, velocity, acceleration, change, contrast. . .

KD   Wrathfulness can also be expressed as humour and whimsicality. The wisdom-display aspect of wrathfulness is the vajra-whimsy of Tsogyel Tröllö.[5]

Q   Do you ever manifest wrathfulness, Rinpoche?

NR   Not in the sense of manifesting the appearance of anger [laughs]. I only have sufficient realisation to be a nice guy. Or, rather, to try my very best to be a nice guy. I hope that I succeed as often as not!

Q   Why is it easier to be nice than to manifest wrathful activity?

NR   It's not that it's easier, it's that the consequences of one's actions have to be taken into account. Wrathful activity needs to be absolutely perfect. Wrathful activity requires total precision. If you feel that it's still possible to make a mistake – no matter how small – then it's wiser to aspire to being a nice guy.

Q   Are you saying that there isn't *anything* useful in experiencing any of the distorted energies? Or is anger particularly harmful?

KD   Yes.

Q   Why is that? This is kind of off the subject, but why is it such a problem if you die in a state of anger? Is that worse than dying in a state of fear or lusting after a pair of boots, or some other distorted energy?

KD   Anger is the most extreme manifestation of duality. When you're trying to destroy anything that might threaten you, you're not open to any form of communication.

---

5   Tsogyel Tröllö is the most wrathful manifestation of Yeshé Tsogyel – Yeshé Tsogyel manifesting as Dorje Tröllö.

When you're lusting after a pair of boots, at least you're involved in some sort of communication. Where there is communication of any kind, the situation is not as distorted. Anger allows very little space.

NR Quite. To die lusting after a pair of boots would actually be very interesting... if you knew you were dying. To have appreciation at that point would be quite a statement of openness. You'd have a sense of communication that was quite free.

Q It sounds as if you're saying that there's a link between communication and compassion.

NR Damn right.

KD Yes, certainly, as far as two-way communication is concerned. You see, anger is very much a one-way communication.

Q It seems that when people hang onto fantasy in spite of having an actual offer of relationship, that they're afraid because it's a limited form that threatens to define them within those limits. I know people who won't admit to being in love with someone because it says something about who they are, it admits that they're satisfied with something limited in form. Does the fire element offer us limitlessness of definition, within the illusion of duality?

NR Yes, certainly – and probably a great deal more – as far as the imagination can stretch, and then some!

KD [laughs] Especially 'more'!

Q When you were explaining the energy of the fire element, you said that our language reflected the qualities of the elements in the way we talk about our emotional states. How would this relate to people who use language in this way, but who aren't connected with this view?

KD   Everyone is connected with this view – whether they know it or not. There is no such thing as a person who isn't connected with the fire element or with any of the elements, for that matter. We are all connected with all the elements.

NR   Even if some people are not prone to the wilder excesses of the fire element, they'll still be in tune with the language that comes out of the fire element experience of the world; at least to some small degree.

KD   People can enjoy adventure books without ever wanting to go on an adventure themselves.

NR   Yah. . . Adventures are a nasty uncomfortable business that make you late for your tea. . . or so it says in *The Hobbit*. But we like to hear stories about adventures. Because we all have the desire for adventure in us. So whether we manifest any of the elements overtly or not, we still have the unmanifested seed there and it's always ready to flower into either wisdom or neurosis. There was another part of your question, wasn't there?   Oh yes; how do such conveniently elemental words come about?   They come about because the elements form a continuum – from the physical elements in the world around us, to their essence as the *thig-lés.*[6] This continuum contains our physical form, our intellect, emotions, and inner energy patterns. So it's hardly surprising that there's some connection between them. Language, among other things, is a bridge between the subtle and the overt.

Q   You said, in relation to the fire element, that there was a tendency to burn out. If we burn ourselves out, what element do we then become?

NR   *Fire Element II*?   *Son* or *Daughter of Fire*?

---

[6] *Thig-lé* (*bindu* in Sanskrit) is the essence of the elements; the matrix of primal creativity.

It's not necessarily the case that when an element exhausts itself, that another element arises. There could simply be a repetition of the same element.

Q   Rising like a phoenix from the ashes of the old fire element?

KD   Well, that might be the feeling. . .

NR   Fire element neurotics can certainly be romantic at a grandiose level about their florid ups and downs.

KD   The elements can form sequences of dissolving in and out of each other. Fire *could* be reborn as any of the other elements, or simply re-emerge as more fire. What often happens with fire element burn-out, is that then the space element neurosis manifests. Space, in addition to being an element, is also the fundamental ground of the elements.

Q   And that would be a depressed state?

KD   Yes.

Q   That sounds a bit like manic-depression, if you were to swing from one to the other. Would you say that manic-depression was an extreme form of the alternation between fire and space neuroses?

NR   Quite so. Congratulations.

KD   You see, it *is* possible to understand the elements. Thank you!

Q   Is it any easier to transform the distorted energy of one element more than the others?

NR   No, not really.

KD   However [laughs], you could say that the fire element has considerable scope for transformation. . .

NR   I am very fond of fire element neurotics.

From my point of view, they have a great deal of spiritual potential. That gloriously rampant, over-the-top, audacious, devil-may-care lust for the intensity of life is *wonderful*.

Q   Wonderful?

KD   Yes! Wonderful!

NR   Sure. *Wonderfully* painful! *Wonderfully* pleasurable! *Wonderfully* fire and ice! *Wonderfully there.* You're really wonderfully impelled to have to put yourself on the line almost continually. There's a lot of *wonderfully insane bravery* and compassion in the fire element neurotic. Some would disagree, I'm sure... This *is* purely *our* perspective, you understand...

Q   Talking about the differences between the elements, I wonder if you could comment on whether some elements are more 'sticky' than others in terms of being able to transform them?

NR   'Sticky'... What would you say, Khandro Déchen?

KD   They're all pretty sticky. But I'd also say that space neurosis is probably the most sticky in the sense of being hard to dissolve. It's problematic, because there's so little energy there. The space element is very intelligent and very subtle in its deliberate stupidity. Then... earth, water, and air neuroses are less sticky because they're all connected with types of fear. The least sticky is probably the stickiest of all – the fire neurosis. It may appear very sticky because desire is about sticking to objects of desire, but it's actually the least adhesive – because desire is connected most directly with compassion.

NR   So if you have to pick a neurosis, go for the fire element. I'm only joking...

Q   Could you say a little more about the Three Terrible Oaths? I just find this the most amazing and inspiring idea I've ever heard.

KD The Three Terrible Oaths are: 'Whatever happens – *may* it happen!'; 'Whichever way it goes – *may* it go that way!'; and, 'There is no purpose!' This adds up to positively willing every situation to be exactly as it is.

NR This is a statement of the totality or completeness of our context. It's a statement of the totality or completeness of our relationship with our situation, in which we let go of the urge to manufacture anything. It's the ecstatic appreciation of every moment of experience, in which whatever happens has its own unique texture – and that texture, in itself, is the implicit meaning of the Mind-moment – [interrupted]

Q Excuse me, Rinpoche, I got a bit lost there, could you repeat that?

NR [laughs] I doubt it. It's not guaranteed that I'll remember anything I say. However. . . when I say that whatever happens has its own unique texture, I mean that each moment is fresh. When each moment is fresh, and undiluted by the insipid rationalisations of constipated nervousness, the simple fact of experience is there just as it is. That is both very powerful and very ordinary. That is both terribly claustrophobic and fantastically liberating.

KD Yes. Simply to realise that you cannot help but be 'trapped' by what is, releases your capacity to embrace the energy of your own situation – and that's called freedom.

NR Ecstatic appreciation of every moment of experience is simply what happens when we give up on our attempts to create reality according to the banal dictates of security. When I say that 'the texture of whatever happens is, in itself, the implicit meaning of every Mind-moment', there is the sense in which each Mind-moment is, *in its nakedness,* the state of enlightenment. If you *live* these Three Terrible Oaths it is impossible to doubt that.

And that is somewhat terrible [laughs]. It's also somewhat wonderful. But whatever it is; it's complete. It's undiluted. It's direct. It's unobstructed. It's simply there: with no room for manœuvre; no cubby-hole of cold comfort; no cosy foot-warmer philosophy; no ancient wisdom from Atlantis; no pixie cards; no New Age crystals; no Tarot; no astrology or *I Ching* to which you could refer in moments of doubt. The moments of doubt are also simply there – raw and tingling; both absolutely and relatively real. Relentlessly real, as opposed to anal-retentively unreal.

Q   I'm wondering, how can I let go of the urge to manipulate events? I mean, while still remaining capable of doing everything I have to do in my life. How can I still put one foot in front of the other in a specific direction?

KD   The yogis and yoginis seem to manage. This doesn't contradict making plans – [interrupted]

Q   But it doesn't sound like a recipe for getting anything done. In fact it could sound fairly fatalistic if you misunderstood.

KD   Yes, I think this is often misunderstood. . .

NR   People misunderstand this as a stand-alone attitude or a self-sufficient raison d'être. Actually it's an attitude that flows with whatever direction and purpose may happen to be there.

KD   It is actually being alive and responding to the world in a real and vital way. But 'getting things done' is not a goal for the yogi or yogini – even though they are quite capable of getting things done – they often get a great deal done! What we're really talking about here is the capacity not to attempt to *manufacture* the context in which we get things done.

NR   Yes. We're actually being highly realistic – completely pragmatic. A nut needs tightening or the wheels will fall off. The car needs more gas, more petrol. The oil needs topping up.

I need to send my mother a birthday card. I need to launder my clothes, iron my shirt, and darn my socks. I need to allow the wine to breathe. I need to digest my dinner, or evacuate my bowels...

Q   When you were talking about the space element neurosis, you were talking about suffering and joy as being poles apart. But isn't suffering sometimes very close to ecstasy; like tears of joy or tears of laughter?

NR   That question could only be possible in the West!

KD   Last month a lady in California told me that she was writing a book called *The Joy of Suffering* [laughs].

NR   The human dualistic situation is always mixed. It's not that agony and ecstasy are so close to each other – it's that every emotion is close to the enlightened state. Maybe it's the fact that any emotion could flip into the enlightened state that reflects similarity. Emotional release manifests in many ways, but tears of laughter are very different from tears of misery. However, that's my experience – maybe we should do some consumer research...

Q   When you were talking about the earth element, you gave the example of a male earth neurotic's fantasy and in the example the woman was attracted to him when she hadn't been before... I was wondering what is it then that attracts people to each other?

NR   Enlightenment and unenlightenment.

Q   Does that have anything to do with the different elements?

KD   Yes. But it has a lot to do with all of them! Particularly with the fire element! You could say that in terms of attraction, or romantic attraction, that all the elements function through the fire element. Fire certainly has to be there, at least initially.

Q   Does this mean fire element people will be attracted to each other?

KD   Yes. . . I could imagine that happening quite often.   But that's only part of the picture.

Q   What other elements would be attracted to each other; or is it only like elements that attract each other?

KD   No, it's not really like that at all.   It's important not to over-simplify or to make generalisations about the elements. . . The Tantric elemental systems do not really operate in the same way that Western astrology works.   I've heard people talk about astrology, and about types that are attracted to each other – but it's not so useful to look at the elements in that way.   You see, we are *all* made up of *all* the elements.   And all the elements function within each other.   In terms of what attracts people to each other, that's not so simple as certain elements attracting certain elements. Every element attracts and repels every other element in particular circumstances.   Rinpoche and I discuss this in the book we're working on – *Entering the Heart of the Sun and Moon*.

Q   You were saying that because nothing is permanent or secure, that the only stable ground we can find is emptiness.   I found that very exciting but also very threatening; especially when you said that we can only find security in insecurity, by establishing insecurity as our security.   Could you say more about that?

NR   Security is insecure in its very nature.   The desire for security is based on insecurity, and once you gain security from that position – you can never feel secure about it.   In fact, the more secure you are, the more insecure you feel – because you've got more to lose.   But the recognition of fundamental insecurity is totally secure.

KD Once you accept that everything moves – that nothing stays as it is. . . that has to be the most secure position, doesn't it?

Q Yes, but wouldn't that mean being a renunciate – a monk or a nun?

KD No, certainly not – one always participates in temporary ownership of impermanent objects. You don't have to be a monk or nun to do that. . . you don't have to shave your head *or* your legs!

NR Anyone can participate in transient situations, whatever arrangement they may have with a barber.

KD You can always share and enjoy transient impermanent relationships with people. Even in the same relationship there can be many relationships.

Q Really?!

KD [laughs] I'm not talking about having affairs! I mean that there can be many different phases of relationship within the *same* relationship between the *same* people. You don't need a third person to have a torrid affair!

Q When you talked about the water element, you said that anger arises when our reaction to the experience of emptiness is fear. You said that we need to make instant reprisals as soon as we get the sense that someone could be taking advantage of us. How is this idea an experience of emptiness?

KD Vulnerability!

Q Of course. . . Yes. . . So when you say that anger becomes the system of communicating with the world, and that it's a style of communication that establishes your reality. . . You said that this creates a situation in which you feel fragile and exposed – like being on a knife edge.

But how does this translate into feeling that you're not real?

NR   Here it's more a question of feeling that, very suddenly, you could become non-existent – that is to say, *terminally* unreal.

KD   The knife-edge is quite real.

NR   But on either side of it – there's the non-reality of instant death.

KD   And that produces the sense of not being real.

NR   You see this knife edge is so narrow, this reality is so at risk... that it's not really there. The sense of impending disaster is massive... but of course that can be flipped in the opposite direction too – there's nothing more real than the possibility of impending death! That's why people take risks. That's why people live dangerously.

KD   That's why people play Russian Roulette.

NR   That's the interface between the water element and the fire element. Once you look at any element in sufficient depth, you find the other elements beginning to manifest.

Q   You said that if we were to realise that anger is often projected at us simply because people think we're strong – that we might be able to be gentle with people who act aggressively. So if instead of protecting myself from anger, I was able to recognise my own strength as the ability to expose feelings of vulnerability... you're saying that *that* is strength?

NR   Yes.

KD   What else could it be?

Q   Being a victim?

KD   It depends on whether you're interpreting your situation that way. What if you choose not to categorise yourself as a victim?

[Questioner appears confused] We're talking about how life is lived as a practitioner. These practices, although they are useful for anyone, at one level are not geared to help you live your life in the same way that therapy helps people. There is obviously some overlap with these teachings and the field of therapy – but it only goes so far. If you tend to see yourself as a victim, then you need to look at that first. You see... Tantra is highly unusual. It is not actually aimed at people who find certain aspects of life problematic. Tantra is actually aimed at people who can really *do* life – people who live life to the fullest.

NR   In Tibet there were often really extraordinary practitioners who had previously been bandits. A tantrika requires a certain degree of *chutzpah*.[7] But that's not to say that Tantra can't help you short-circuit insecurity, fear, loneliness, anxiety, and depression. This may sound like a complete contradiction – but there is an escape clause: devotion. You can short-circuit all your neurotic sensitivities if you have complete confidence in the practice. But you can never let that slip.

Q   Or you're straight back in the slimy pit of all your neuroses, and they're going at full volume.

NR   To say the least...

Q   I was very interested in what you said about the recognition of emptiness – that loneliness could actually be experienced as *aloneness* or *uniqueness*.

KD   Yes...

Q   Then there was the idea that aloneness is an uninhibited, unattached *frame of non-reference* in which there's no longer the need to grasp.

7 *Chutzpah* (Yiddish): Guts, uninhibited style, 'get up and go'.

KD   Yes.

Q   Good so far [laughs].   Then we no longer feel compelled
to seduce phenomena.   I follow that, but: 'experiencing the coital
quality of *intrinsic seduction* as the fabric of reality'?   What does that
mean exactly?   I seem to resonate with that statement completely
but at the same time, I don't understand it.

KD   Yes.   Understanding the idea of *intrinsic seduction* is not
really a matter of intellect.   We could talk about it, but I feel that
you'd be better off *resonating*.

NR   [laughs] Yes.   The best way to understand this would be
to remember that it is possible to recognise this as it is happening.

KD   One day, you might just notice the coital quality of *intrinsic
seduction* as the fabric of reality.   Or maybe just try looking at
something that you like.   Look at the colour of something.   Look
at something you find enjoyable, and allow yourself to experience
the enjoyment.   What is the nature of that enjoyment?   What is
your connection with that object?   What is it like to look at a
mountain, or a cherry?   What is it like to hear bird-song?   What
is it like to feel velvet?   Is this a one-way process — or is this, in
some inexpressible way, a communication?   You see, the intellect is
a sense field.   You don't have to understand everything through
that one sense field.   The fundamental genius of Tantra is that the
sense fields are interconnected.   You can feel with your mind and
think with your nose.   There are not such strict boundaries
between them.

Q   Rinpoche, I'd like to know more about Padmasambhava.
You said that his being 'continues through his deathlessness in the
energy of his accomplished lineage'. . . .   That was quite a mind-
stopping statement.   Maybe you could say more about that?

NR It's just a way of describing the inspiration that Padmasambhava provided, and continues to provide. The quality of 'deathlessness' gives Padmasambhava one of his many names – Chhi-'mèd Rig'dzin: the deathless holder of awareness. What is meant by deathlessness, is that every Lama of the lineage can become Padmasambhava. We could say the same about Yeshé Tsogyel. Every Lama can become identical to Yeshé Tsogyel. In that way the accomplished lineage is deathless. Padmasambhava and Yeshé Tsogyel are always with us, because realised Lamas are always with us. Padmasambhava means 'lotus-born' and the idea of being 'lotus-born' applies to us all, because we can all become lotus-born. We can all realise our beginningless enlightenment.

Q Rinpoche, when you were talking about the air element, you said that there was a sensory fear of emptiness involved. . . fear of silence, fear of blandness, fear of numbness. To what extent is this similar to the fire element's trying to have music, food, sights, etc., all at once?

NR It's quite different in one respect, because fire is not particularly complicated. The fire element may complicate things by continually turning up the volume, but it doesn't seek out complication for its own sake. On the other hand, there are similarities, because all the elements carry reflections of each other. So, in terms of the sensory fear of emptiness, such as fear of silence, the fear is not based on isolation but on what may be lurking in the silence. There's nowhere to hide. There's no shelter in the uniform environment of blandness. Anything might lurch out from nothingness. Remember that the root misconception of the air element is groundless anxiety.

Q So the distorted energy of the air element is concerned with losing ground and it validates its existence by protecting territory.

Now it starts to sound like the earth element. I guess that's really clear, isn't it – that they're all aspects of each other as well as what they are on their own?

KD   Quite.

Q   So would this be an example of the way that at the fringes, all the elements come to resemble each other? And is that because space is at the periphery as well as the centre?

KD   Quite. You're getting good at this.

Q   When the air element paranoia gets the idea that if territory ceases to exist, existence also ceases to exist, and if territory is by nature prone to vanishing, and if the feeling that comes from this view is that you could be crushed into nothing. . . Well, isn't this actually true?

NR   Yes and no. Yes; if you're trying to validate your existence by proving that you're solid, permanent, separate, continuous, and defined. But no; if you're happy to be intangible, impermanent, interconnected, discontinuous, and undefined.

Q   You said that intellect generates the need for specific styles of rationality. Does that mean that intellect creates artificial feelings, or magnifies the ones we have? Or does that mean we're just intellectualising about the whole thing and not really feeling anything at all?

NR   The whole range – it depends whether you're psychologically 'mid-range', whether you have a low level of psychological health, whether you're merely neurotic or completely psychotic.

Q   Right. So when a person says that they're expressing their feelings, they're describing the result of intellectually distorting them?

NR   Exactly.

KD   You see, there's actually nothing wrong with having emotions – they can be free energies.

Q   You were saying that if you start to gain *clarity* through the practice of shi-nè, you'd begin to view vanishing as an occupational hazard of being. How do you ever make peace with that?

NR   That *is* making peace with that.

Q   Continually leaping out of emptiness, into the moment?

KD   Yes.

Q   How can you actually experience that?

KD   By practising shi-nè.

NR   If you practise shi-nè, *that* is what you find yourself doing. And at the same time, there is the knowledge of how it is that you stop yourself from doing that. The two are co-emergent.

Q   One thing I don't understand very well is what the energy of the elements has to do with khandro and pawo. I can see them as human neuroses, but I don't know which part is khandro, which part is pawo, or how the enlightened aspect is both, if it is.

NR   The answer to this question would actually make a book in itself. But to be brief... Pawo means the actual physical elements – their dynamism. Khandro means the glow, lustre, or ambience of the elements – their innate vividness. In terms of emotions, khandro is the feeling-tone, and pawo is the activity that is manifested out of the feeling-tone. Khandro is the atmosphere, and pawo is the way that atmosphere plays in creating its own specific direction in time. However... they are always aspects of each other.

So whatever can be seen as pawo, can also be seen as khandro. The beauty of entering this view, is that it can never be frozen – there is never one fixed understanding which can be turned into a reference point without losing the view of khandro and pawo. Or, at least, that's how it's expressed in the *Khandro-pawo-nyi-da-mé-long-gyüd*.[8]

Q   This idea of dance... You were saying that the elements perform within space as the primal play of reality, and that this was known as the dance of the khandros and pawos. What does 'dance' mean in this context?

NR   Dance describes the nature of reality, in terms of the oscillation of unitary reality with multiplistic reality. It also describes the way in which non–duality can be experienced as having two aspects that are not separate. If you look at two people dancing together – you have the spectacle of two people; but they are moving together. So is this singular or plural? Or is it both? Or is it both reflecting both? This is the meaning of dance.

Q   If the four distorted elemental fields of energy operate as defence mechanisms of the primary space-neurosis... do you mean that one is angry or paranoid in order not to face the fear of oblivion? Is that the defence mechanism at work?

KD   Precisely – you just have to catch yourself in the process of creating that mechanism – that is the purpose of staring into the arising emotion.

Q   When you refer to each kind of neurotic, such as water neurotic, it gives me the image of a type, as if we each were one type and should be recognising ourselves as a particular type.

8   The *Khandro-pawo-nyi-da-mé-long-gyüd* comprises the Aro gTér teachings on khandro / pawo reflection, and relationship as spiritual practice.

But we're each all of these types, aren't we, depending on what's going on in our lives?

NR   Yes. We are all the flux and play of all the elements. We speak in terms of neurotic elemental types in order to get an idea of what the elemental characteristics are. We also look at extreme examples because they're more easily recognisable in their extreme forms.

Q   The extreme forms tend to make people laugh a lot – maybe we recognise ourselves in them.

NR   Well, yes. We do recognise these extreme aspects, and we laugh because samsara is comical. We laugh because any extreme is ridiculous. That's why we laugh when people mimic Hitler, or any extreme personality. We laugh because we can see that potentiality in ourselves, and from our current less extreme vantage point – we see the ridiculousness.

Q   I've noticed that you like to make people laugh.

NR   Sure. When people laugh, they open up. When people laugh, they remember the teachings. It's actually very important. But to get back to your question. . . Although we are all the flux and play of all the elements, we can also be dominant in one element. We can be dominant in one of the elements throughout our lives, or we can migrate through them during our lives. It's obviously far more subtle to look at the elements in terms of how they influence each other – but we have to start with the basic picture. Once we're really familiar with the elements as neurotic types, we can explore them in terms of how they evolve in and out of each other.

Q   You said that we should be suspicious of our negative emotions, and the seriousness we invest in them.

Could you say more about this 'being suspicious'? For example, what questions should I be asking myself when I feel defensive?

NR It's not so much that you should be asking yourself questions. It's more a matter of allowing space for the mechanisms of your neuroses to reveal themselves. This attitude of suspicion is more one of not taking the negative emotion as reality. Suspicion, for a practitioner, manifests as the willingness to allow space – to simply sit.

KD If you simply sit, then neurotic patterns can't remain hidden. As soon as they become visible, they begin to dismantle themselves.

NR That's the central point. We have to hide from the operational methods of our neuroses in order that they can continue to function. Samsara only operates behind closed doors.

Q You said, in relation to the earth element, that our experience can't be shared as long as we use materialism – physical, intellectual, spiritual or otherwise – to cover up our underlying sense of poverty. Could you say anything further about that? It would be useful to have an example.

NR An example... yes. When I was a young man at art college, I met a person like this in someone's flat. There was a very interesting conversation going on, to which all but one person had been contributing. I noticed this person sitting there quietly smiling and I wondered what he had up his sleeve. The discussion got into some interesting areas; I was fascinated by the subject matter and the knowledge and wit of the people who were the main contributors. Suddenly the person with the fixed smile said: "I think this is all just intellectual masturbation". There may have been some degree of truth in this – intellectual masturbation is also part of the earth element neurosis.

But it seemed to me that the statement was made on the basis of personal poverty in terms of intellectual territory. It's usually just a way of establishing prestige at the expense of others. Unsolicited remarks which are out of context with the creative atmosphere generated by other people seldom have much value – especially when others may have been taking personal risks by having put their views and ideas on the line. Arrogance-based statements often carry weight if the audience is sensitive and self-questioning. But they are still arrogant and motivated by a need to dominate. Even if the speaker puts forward some 'ultimate' view of how 'it's all beyond words'; this is simply one-upmanship. These ultimate statements may sometimes sound very simple, but they need to be based on experience, to be made with any credibility. In 'spiritual' terms, this neurosis expresses itself in the form of bigotry, self-righteousness and moral snobbery.

KD   The earth element neurotic operates with the pious, and somewhat puerile, violence of one who believes they have a franchise on the truth. Tibetan Buddhism presents ample opportunity for the expression of the earth element neurosis. Having an understanding of the technical vocabulary or learning the Tibetan language can enable earth element neurotics to hide their impoverishment. It can enable a person to wield power over those who are impressed by such things. Many people have a degree of credulity which can mistake comprehension of a foreign language or terminology for wisdom. But having linguistic ability while missing the opportunity to be generous is really a sad waste of talent and creates a distorted relationship with the teachings. In the same way, having a private income gives some people frequent access to Lamas. This could be very fortunate. But if they just use this to marginalise others, then the time spent with the Lama is just a self-inflating sham.

It's not much different than following rock stars around. However the earth element neurosis manifests in the spiritual sphere, it creates obstacles and insulates itself from any kind of real spiritual understanding. The pride and self-satisfaction that arise out of this kind of 'spiritual acquisitiveness' are based on very shaky ground. The sense of accomplishment that comes from trying to buy into the Lama's presence is usually short-lived.

NR Yes. . . territorialism is built on the concept of permanent phenomena, and the Lama's teaching is based on the impermanence of all phenomena. Although I'm not an athlete by any stretch of the imagination, I have experienced what it's like to be cut down in full flight. I was in Germany at one time, teaching *sKu-mNyé* [9] to a group of sixty people. There was one particular exercise called 'dancing garuda' which requires a lot of space, so I had to divide the group into three in order to teach them. I usually practise the exercises that I teach along with my students, so I attempted to complete three sets of one hundred and eleven repetitions of dancing garuda. I was doing quite well through the first and second sets, but toward the end of the third set, my Achilles tendon suddenly ruptured, and that was the end of my capacity to teach dancing garuda for nine months. This was something of a lesson to me. I had never experienced being so fit in my life before, so I had no concept that there was a limit to what I could do. In order to teach sKu-mNyé exercises I had to practise them intensely; and during the course of five years, I had changed my body quite considerably. I had become fit enough to give myself a sports injury! (My childhood friends would be very amused by such a concept!) I must have developed the illusion of some level of physical invulnerability. Finding out that I had a physical limit was quite an important lesson.

[9] *sKu-mNyé* is a system of psycho-physical exercises from Dzogchen Long-dé (the Series of Space) of the Aro gTér.

I had worked quite hard to overcome the physical laziness that I had as a child, but had not learnt to be gentle with myself. It was very interesting to be reminded that I had to accept the limits that my body demanded – to accept my vulnerability and to become comfortable with it. This is simply an example from my own experience of how the earth element neurosis manifests. In my case I had become involved in the 'territory' of physical capacity.

Q   You said that the fire of desire needed to be experienced with spaciousness or the fire could escalate into emotional napalm. What do you mean by 'emotional napalm'? I guess I don't understand how desire can be spacious...

NR   I remember once when I had just returned from my first trip to the Himalayas. I was visiting a friend and we were sitting in the garden sipping orange juice and exchanging stories, when he said how nice it would be to get out into the country for the day. We were in the garden of a house owned by the university where my friend's wife was a student, and we were overheard by a friend who wasn't using his car that day, so he tossed the keys over to us saying: "Pour in some juice and take a ride". The car was a flashy little number – a red two-seater with walnut facia, wire wheels, leather seats, and an impressive in-flight stereo. Off we went! Down the country lanes of Devon, changing gears in time with the rhythms of John Lee Hooker. It was a splendid day and we had made up a very pleasant hamper: a flask of freshly ground coffee; and a bottle of chilled Chablis in a thermo-bag; crisp salad and French garlic bread; and some wonderful Italian cheeses. We got back in the early evening at the end of an excellent outing. We relinquished the car, and sat down comfortably in the living room. Then I noticed that my friend was very quiet. I asked him what was bothering him.

He shrugged my question off a few times, but finally said: "I can't ever see me getting enough money together to buy a car like that". Not having a car like the one we had enjoyed that day, had really upset him; in fact it had made him quite depressed. It wasn't possible for him to involve himself with this desire without getting stuck. The concepts around the car had become like napalm – bits of hot desire that stuck to his vision of himself and his world.

Q   I have been thinking about what you said about how cultivating real frivolity means abandoning the habit of taking ourselves so seriously. How would that relate to spiritual practice?

NR   People on spiritual paths sometimes take themselves so seriously that their spiritual quests become like too much porridge. No one can possibly eat all that awful stuff, so it just hangs around in their mind getting older and harder.

KD   They then offer it to other people who just damage their teeth on it. Some people become so very serious that it seems as if they've been rolling around in porridge. Their homes are full of porridge. They hang porridge on their walls in thick congealed sheets. They fill their vocabulary with porridge and end up vomiting spiritual porridge all over everyone around them.

Q   With regard to the air element, you said that space is feared as a militant nihilistic conspiracy. . .

NR   Yes. It seems possible that space might be some ferocious professional golfing version of the Grim Reaper, surveying his wide selection of horrible bony golf clubs, deliberating with merciless precision as to which club will be the perilously perfect device that will sink you into the 'black hole' of non-existence. From the perspective of dualism, space means death; and death seems to mean 'the big full stop'.

A kind of hyperactive cowardice develops from this, in which any hint of sensory deprivation is regarded with horror.

Q   About air element paranoia, what did you mean about it being a self-fulfilling prophecy?

KD   Well, you think that no one likes you visiting them; and so you question the validity of people's hospitality in such a way that pretty soon, you are actually not very welcome. After a while no one asks you to visit; and that gives you something more real to get paranoid about. The self-fulfilling quality of paranoia adds weight to your belief in the accuracy of your fears.

NR   This process can easily escalate to ridiculous proportions; unless you become so exhausted that space simply happens. Within this frenetic confusion, there's no possibility of harnessing the potential of being. It's not even possible to explore these supposed threats properly. There is always the need to spread our attention over an impossibly wide spectrum of threats; and new threats seem to be arising constantly.

KD   You live in a state of panic about being caught off guard: "It could happen at any moment: the electricity or telephone could be cut off; someone might find out about the night I did whatever it was!" Someone might discover that you are really very frightened. Someone might accuse you of incompetence. Someone might divulge confidences that you revealed in a moment of weakness. Someone might notice that you're getting old. Someone might catch you having to take a nap. Or, on the other hand, it could be that you're getting paranoid about something real. . . because; you're simply not a very nice person at all. Someone might find out you don't actually smile all the time!

NR   Yes [laughs]. Someone might find out that you have a stage act.

You're all sweetness and good humour on stage, but off stage you're bad-tempered, irritable, and petulant. Someone might find out that you're a full-fledged hypocrite. Someone might discover that you have to study furiously the night before you give your erudite teaching. It could all become a nightmare – you may have become famous on the back of a vast hoax, and be wracked by fear about when the bubble is going to burst, or when someone who has become disenchanted is going to leak the story to the press. Whether these fears are real or unreal, you're gripped by anxiety and tension. You can't enjoy the real texture of your life when you're taut as a bow string waiting to release arrows of self-protection. Even if the arrow is released, it invariably misses the mark. Your concentration is split, so often you miss the shot altogether and the arrow slips and rips out your thumb-nail!

Q   Rinpoche, you said that when we gain some degree of clarity through the practice of shi-nè, we start to experience ourselves as continually leaping out of emptiness into the present moment. That's very inspiring, but I don't think I understand what it might mean in everyday life.

NR   I remember a time in my early teens, coping with the push and pull of anxiety. I remember the intense anxiety I felt when I first dived into the sea from a low cliff edge. I'd been watching a woman dive off the cliff for a while and I thought it looked like a lot of fun. I took a walk over to the cliff edge where I had seen her diving, but when I got there I thought: 'No way! I'm not going to dive off here!' I could see the green rocks below the surface of the water and realised that I would have to avoid diving too deeply. Even if that were possible, I might make a mistake. I might snag my foot on some damn thing or other and slide over the edge.

I could almost see the blood and bits of tissue turning the rock pools pink. It was a real problem. It was a problem, because I really wanted to dive. I really wanted to be the sort of person who did that sort of thing. But instead of diving, I spent my time thinking myself into a state of incapacity.

Fortunately this cycle was interrupted by the sight of some lady-birds. They were unusual. There was a yellow one, a few small orange ones, and an enormous red one. I watched the big red one for a while and completely forgot about the dive and the possibility of the gory bits of me that would be left all pink and grisly on the rocks when the lifeguards had hauled me away. The big red one was feasting on green aphids and it was fascinating to watch its movements. Finally it flew away. So I got up. I took a good long run and sailed off the cliff edge. Suddenly I hit the surface of the water – I was in the water plummeting down – then I was turning slowly and rising to the surface. The top of my head tingled, but it felt amazing. Whatever it was that allowed me to make the dive was the space I had experienced while observing the tiny movements of the lady-bird. The decision to dive was the first idea that sprang from that space. If I'd questioned the impulse to dive, I would have been plunged back into emotional turmoil. If the intellect had cut in, it would have been back to the beach for me on foot. But as it was, I swam. This is something that can apply to any area of life.

KD And it doesn't just apply to taking physical risks; it can also apply to emotional risks. There's a saying: 'She who hesitates is lost'.

Q When you spoke of space, you said that it reminded us of death... but in the sense of 'outer space', doesn't it also provide excitement?

And couldn't you say that the prospect of inner space, or the space of mind also provided excitement?

KD Certainly. The night sky, so many stars, planetary systems, meteor showers, attenuated gases... the fantastic whirling shapes of spiral galaxies... Concepts of space have the capacity to fascinate us. Space is awesome. It's an exhilarating open frontier – like Mind.

NR But, like Mind, it's also given birth to a vast quantity of fiction that rivals the spiritual science fictions that are popular [laughs]. Anything that's written about inner or outer space has the capacity to stretch the imagination, to create the sense of excitement, but we have to be careful that we don't forget that we're afraid of death... and space is death as far as duality is concerned.

KD Only from the perspective of non-duality is space *actually exciting* – so let's stay with death until we have *nothing* to get excited about.

Q If I remember rightly, you were saying that the space element neurosis numbs everything into semi-consciousness, in which we play blind, deaf, and numb to experience... I'd like to get more of an understanding of why we do that.

KD Well... it's the thought of 'all that wretched life going on out there' – it's just too much. So you say: "I'm not going to play! I'm going to sit in the corner and sulk!" Experientially, you creep off into some little hidey-hole somewhere to forget about it, and hope that it'll all disappear. You come to the decision that you're not even going to think about the possibility of working with it, or attempting to handle it. Everything has become far too much effort with far too little reward.

But really, in order to fully understand 'why' – you have to observe yourself in process when you decide to sulk. Then you have to discover what you're getting out of it.

Q   So it starts with sulking. . .

KD   Yes. Although we would have to extend the definition of the word 'sulking' to include all forms of retraction from communication with phenomenal reality. In order to become 'the incredible sulk' you actually have to retract from everything – and that is called clinical depression.

NR   It is a way of succeeding through failing. It's really very intelligent – very intellectual; and, very tricky. I have never met an unintelligent depressive.

Q   Could you elaborate a little on the way the space neurotics skilfully nurture their own pain? How do you mean 'skilfully'?

KD   Well, we grasp at the intensity of the pain. We see ourselves as lacking any other form of definition. Pain is what we are – it is all we are, so we have to concretise that; and that is a 'skilful' activity. It's skilful in the sense of having to be subtle enough to avoid seeing anything that is not painful. One would prefer to see oneself as some sort of tragic hero. Maybe, as some character in Shakespeare; or Eugene O'Neill's *Long Day's Journey into Night*. This goes along with the Western concept of the suffering artist. Some people imagine that great things will come out of their agony. Much of our Western artistic heritage has been inspired within the context of human suffering, so it is not really so very surprising.

Q   So it's true that pain can be a catalyst for art? Could you say more about that, and how that fits in with the genius of creativity?

NR   Well, when perception is highly charged with negative
emotion we have the motivation to follow ideas through to a
particular end. With that kind of energy we can be creative in
a way that'll often have the capacity to move people. People are
rarely as ecstatically happy as they're utterly miserable, so it doesn't
require too much effort to understand the mechanism of ordinary
creativity in this sense. Ordinary creativity as a description of
great works of art and music could seem to be an insensitive
misconception; but ordinary creativity is linked to *liberated creativity,*
and so genius flashes through – that can't be avoided. It flashes
through in all manner of circumstances, and in all manner of
confusion. With ordinary creativity, there's not a lot of joyous
art to be seen, heard or read. The possible horizons of *liberated
creativity* are far more vast because it's based on the recognition
of *intrinsic space.*   From the perspective of Tantra, recognition of
intrinsic space as the basis of art, is ultimately preferable to being a
living disaster; even though you might leave a trail of great art
in your wake.

12

Method

*There is no sudden breakthrough that remains forever –
there are only sudden glimpses.   But these glimpses
encourage us to see more.   And so, gradually,
we develop the ability to integrate these experiences
of unconditioned being into our lives.*

We now have a picture of the 'patterns of debility' and the 'patterns of potential'.   These are the patterns that exist in terms of duality and non–duality, according to the experiential vision of Tantra.   It is a picture made up of pictures, a complex kaleidoscopic image of incredible intricacy; and yet, it is piercingly personal.   However; unless we can make use of it in our everyday life experience, it could become little more than a phantasmagoric intellectual pastime.   So unless this picture is to remain just a gossamer of meta-psychological poetry, we must have a way of integrating it at a pragmatic level.

This Tantric vision of being is not an escape from what we actually are; at the kitchen sink; in the office; on the factory floor.   The raw texture of whatever reality it is that we live every day has to be our practice.   This chapter is concerned with what you can do yourself.   It is concerned with making vital and direct use of the material in this book.

It is concerned with *embracing* emotions *as* a spiritual path. To simplify this as much as possible a diagram has been included at the end of the chapter, which gives easy reference to the various interrelated aspects of the five elements. To this end there also follows an essentialisation of the *stages of method* involved in *embracing emotions as the path.*

Where to start? First, it is necessary to be well-grounded in the view. This means that the basic information about the functioning of the elemental patterns needs to be assimilated. The only really effective way of achieving this is through repeated re-reading of the material; and, through actively looking for correspondences with the view in your everyday life situation. If the material makes sense, if it *resonates,* then remembering it will not be a problem. In order to *know* this material we have to *see* it reflected in ourselves. It has to stop being external information and start to become knowledge – knowledge that you discover in yourself. Some sort of synapse has to spark between the point-instant of your perception and the immediate texture of your emotional being – the emotional pattern that characterises you in the moment.

So: first you need to familiarise yourself with the pattern and meaning of the ideas presented so that you can recognise these patterns in yourself as they arise (or as soon after they have arisen as possible).

Second, you need to see what you can recognise of these ideas in yourself. You should perhaps ask yourself these questions: 'Does this pattern of emotional styles correspond with my experience?'; 'Can I understand my own emotions presented in this particular way?'; 'Am I prepared to discover that my emotions function in this way?' If your answers are all 'yes', then you can proceed.

If your answers are all 'no', then you can still proceed, but not according to this methodology. If you cannot see any resonance between how you are, and the patterns that are described here, then you will have to proceed in some other way.[1]

Being able to work with view means opening yourself to seeing the five-fold expressions of duality as being the warp and weft of your life's experience. Working with view means that you have the capacity to see your everyday life as a web of opportunity in/through which you can realise the five-fold expressions of liberated-being.

So: first you familiarise yourself with the view. Then second, you internalise the view through testing it against your own experience.

The third step is to accept the challenge of deliberately naming your feelings of negativity, frustration, dissatisfaction, and emotional pain as doorways to new experiences of being. As soon as you recognise a negative emotion arising, you need to look at it. You need to examine its qualities. When we use the word 'negative' in terms of an emotion, we are talking about something that is painful or frustrating to you or to others who have to experience your having this emotion. Let us take the example of anger. If you are experiencing anger, it is always possible to recognise that this emotional energy is based on fear.

[1] There are many paths to follow in the world. Answering 'no' to these questions simply means that you have found no correspondence with the material as presented here. This is not necessarily a reflection on the essential nature of the material, nor on the Nyingma Tantras; but, rather, on the personal vision and style of explanation which is characteristic of Ngakpa Chögyam and Khandro Déchen. Even within one specific system, such as the Nyingma School of Tibetan Buddhism, the styles of explanation vary according to the *personality* of the Lama. We are merely inconsequential eccentrics, who hope that no one will judge the Nyingma School on the basis of our vernacular explanations.

Something about your personal environment is reflecting the dualistic aspect of the water element in terms of your reaction to emptiness. Our reaction to emptiness can cause us to project hostile qualities upon it. We do this in order to create some kind of security by entering into an attack mode. In terms of everyday perception; anger arises when the world seems as if it is something to be feared. When the world seems to incite fear, we become angry out of insecurity. And when we feel insecure, in terms of the water-neurosis, we need to take violent action to 'save' ourselves. 'The best form of defence is attack' is an archetypal water element stance, from which a pre-emptive first strike seems completely appropriate. Plans for revenge seem quite justifiable because our sense of being at risk is so strong. Perception of the 'strike-potential' of others is magnified by our feelings of fear. It is also magnified by our feelings of inadequacy and insecurity. The water-neurotic has to lash out – to make examples of people. We have to let people know that we have teeth – that our bite is even worse than our bark. Violence, ranging from door slamming and verbal vitriol to physical assault, becomes the arsenal of our response to the world.

Every time you observe yourself conforming to this dualistic pattern, it is possible to distance yourself from the artificial intensity of what you feel. When you are able to observe yourself operating in pre-ordained ways, you can no longer take your moods and temperamental reactions to life quite so seriously. Recognising any negative emotion as a 'perceptual habit' gives you a little breathing space. It is almost as if you have been in some stuffy overheated room, but it has suddenly occurred to you to open the windows wide. As soon as you open the windows, there is an immediate feeling of spaciousness.

We need to respect this spaciousness as being an expression of our innate dignity as human beings. This may have been your first experience of *space sparkling through the knotted web of conditioning.* Learning to be suspicious of our negative emotions, and the seriousness which we invest in them, is a very powerful attitude to adopt. It is an attitude that can enable us to transform our entire array of everyday experiences.

As soon as you realise that your negative emotions are not actually particularly individual or personal, it may be possible to let go of a degree of attachment to them. Surrendering even a fractional degree of attachment is acknowledging that you are prepared to treat your emotions as workable. Once you recognise the habitual patterning of any emotion, the next step is to open yourself to the *intrinsically inviting opportunity* to *stare* at it.

So: first you familiarise yourself with the view. Then second, you internalise the view through experience. Third, you prepare to 'catch yourself out' in the act of conforming to pre-set emotional patterns.

Fourth, you *stare into the face of the arising emotion.* In order to do this it is necessary to relinquish intellectual analysis. You have to abandon intellect as soon as you recognise the emotional pattern. It is enough to recognise the pattern; there is no need to dwell on intellectual analysis once that faculty has performed its useful task. The intellect is valuable within the sphere of intellect. But outside that, it becomes increasingly useless. Intellect *is* a valuable tool; but unless we learn when to use it and when not to use it, the view with which we have familiarised ourselves will just become another unhelpful addition to the giddying whirlpool of our conditioned responses.

To relinquish analysis allows you to *stare directly* into the *face* of an emotion. You can accomplish this by focusing on the physical sensation of the emotion as the subject /object of meditation. Your whole field of attention needs to be immersed in the wordless sensation of the emotion as it manifests in the body. If the emotion you are trying to *embrace* is one of sorrow, you will tend to feel this as a very real and uncomfortable sensation just beneath the rib-cage. This is what is commonly known as 'heartache'. But if you are able to surrender the words – the conceptual scaffolding – then the sensation ceases to manifest as pain. If you can then maintain the *presence* of your *wordless gaze,* the emotion becomes a *free energy.*

At first, thoughts seem to be thrown up by the centrifugal force of the sensation; but, if these thoughts are allowed to fly past and disappear into space you will discover that it is the cyclic nature of thoughts rather than the sensation itself that is the cause of your 'dis-ease'. When you can simply *be with* the sensation of your emotion and experience it fully at the non-conceptual level, you will notice a dynamic reversal taking place. The spinning energy that seemed to be generating rivulets of words and ideas has a *vast still centre*; like the eye of a hurricane. From that experience of stillness it is possible to perceive that the obsessive spinning is not caused by the emotional sensation, but that it is in fact the *cause* of it. When you realise the empty nature of the sensation of emotional pain, the pain dissolves into an *ecstatic sensation* of *presence* and *awareness.*

Throughout the ages people have attempted to describe the experience of enlightenment, and the results have either been too simple, too complex, or too obscure. The only way to understand what is alluded to by such words as enlightenment, liberation or realisation is through personal experience.

There is no sudden breakthrough that remains forever – there are only *sudden glimpses.* But the *glimpses* encourage us to see more until, gradually, we develop the ability to integrate these experiences of *unconditioned being* with the rest of life. The process of being *total* in the moment enables us to embrace our emotions; and, through doing so, to discover our beginningless enlightened nature.

When you recognise the patterns associated with anger, and have developed sufficient confidence in view, you will be able to *stare* into your anger and experience it as *the wisdom of clarity.* When you recognise that you are becoming perceptually rigid and obdurate, you can *stare* at that need to concretise everything and experience it as *the wisdom of equanimity and equality.* When you recognise that you are becoming obsessive or somewhat frenzied with self-seduced hunger, you can *stare* into your fixation and experience it as *the wisdom of discriminating awareness,* or compassion. When you recognise that you are tightening with suspicion and jealousy, you can *stare* into your paranoia and experience it as *the wisdom of self-accomplishing action.* When you recognise that you are retracting from the sense fields, and digging yourself into depression, you can *stare* into that overwhelming bewilderment and experience it as *the wisdom of brilliant pervasive intelligence in all-encompassing space.*

So: first you familiarise yourself with the view. Then, second, you internalise the view through experience. Third, you prepare to 'catch yourself out' in the act of conforming to pre-set emotional patterns. Fourth, you *stare into the face of the arising emotion.*

This is by no means an instant cure, but it is an immediately effective method. Failure is axiomatic when it comes to attempting what is usually thought of as impossible; but so is success – right from the beginning.

241

Every time you try to stare into the face of an arising emotion, you confirm yourself in the practice of cutting through conditioning. Even wanting to start is success. Even a first failed attempt is success; because, in a very real sense, there is no such thing as a bad meditation session. We learn something, as long as we remain open to learning. So this must be our attitude if this practice is to make any difference to our lives. We are bound both to fail and to succeed many times; rather like the salmon that have to leap up waterfalls to reach their spawning grounds. Trying to change a lifetime of internal and external conditioning is a difficult task, but not an impossible one. However, your journey can be a little more joyous than the salmon's! If you begin to practise you will experience a difference in your life. The ultimate goal is always both very close and very distant; and when one day you come to realise that the path is the goal, the concepts of failure and success will no longer have any meaning.

Those who have experience of meditation may find this method easier than those who have never attempted it before. But whatever your level of experience, the existence of painful emotions is a spur to practice. This is especially the case if perception of cyclic patterns allows disenchantment with the habits of duality. Everyone has their own individual capacity, and there is no saying whether people who have sat in practice over a period of time will excel over fresh practitioners confronting their emotions directly for the first time. Motivation is absolutely necessary. Without the firm decision to embrace emotions as the path, even those who have vast meditative experience will not succeed.

It is sad to reflect on the number of people ostensibly engaged in spiritual practice, compared to the number of people who are prepared to work on themselves *as they actually are* in an everyday setting.

For some people, the inner Tantras would appear to be a quirky esoteric hobby. Practice has to make real sense. Basically, if the practice makes sense and if its purpose and function are understood, then results will be experienced and progress will ensue. In order for one to persevere in practice, it has to make sense on a real *experiential level*. If the view presented here never becomes lived-knowledge then you will not follow through and maintain the practice consistently in your life.

If you are successful in *staring* into the face of your emotions and you have become enthusiastic about the possibilities of this practice, then it is also possible to treat your pleasurable experiences in the same way. It is generally easier to learn from sorrow than from joy; so most people are content to let happiness be, rather than to risk it in any way. Real joy and well-being, however, are not threatened by the keenness of *staring*. Radiance is based on taking *insecurity as security,* so if pleasure is real, it is experienced as *complete vibrant awareness* that extends itself infinitely outward to all beings.

This is an essentialised presentation of the Dzogchen method called *trek-chod*.[2] In the practice of trek-chod emotions are deliberately generated in order to stare into them. Trek-chod is the non-symbolic correlate of the Tantric method called *zap-lam*.[3] There have been numerous bizarre theories published on this theme ranging from the idea that it constitutes a test of ultimate lack of interest in sexual arousal to the idea that it is some sort of degenerate practice that has taken the *yab-yum* (father-mother) symbolism 'too literally'.

[2] *Trek-chod* means cutting or blasting through. It can also be translated as 'exploding the confines of conventional reality'.

[3] *Zap-lam* means 'the profound path of realising the co-emergence of emptiness and ecstasy'. This includes the much misunderstood and much wondered-about practice of 'sexual Tantra'.

Sexuality is a vital part of our lives and as such is as open to transformation as any other part of life.

In Tibet there were celibate and non–celibate lineages and each structured their methods of practice according to different points of view. The celibate monastic path is based on the Sutras of the Greater Vehicle (Tib. *Theg-chen*, Skt. *Mahayana*). The Sutras stress external renunciation as the means of inner transformation. The advantage of the choiceless life–style with its many externally-applied rules and regulations is that the practitioner (nun or monk) gains a *simplicity of living* that enables her or him to avoid the otherwise almost unavoidable complications of the life of choices. The ngak'phang non-celibate path is based on the Tantras of the Thunderbolt Vehicle (Tib. *Dorje Thegpa*, Skt. *Vajrayana*). The inner Tantras stress internal renunciation as a means of transforming life circumstances into opportunities for realisation on the path. The advantage of external choice is that the practitioner opens herself or himself up to the richness of life in all its multifarious convolutions, reversals and intrigues. The Sutric path offers simplicity at the expense of richness of experiential possibilities. The Tantric path offers the wealth of life's experiences, but with it comes the wealth of complications that can sometimes be rather overwhelming. Neither path is an easy one to take, but then living a 'lay' existence is not easy either. So, sexuality is part of the experience of life. But any idea that one could approach 'Tantric sex' in the same way that one could approach ærobics is farcical. Many people could sit down and listen to a great symphony, but how many can even write music? Maybe everyone could write a great symphony, but first they would have to devote some effort to study and practice. Suffice it to say that dealing with powerful energies requires powerful abilities on the part of the practitioner.

In order to engage in the real practice of zap-lam it is vital to be able to maintain the mystic commitment to sustain *ro-chig* (the one taste of emptiness and ecstasy). The essence of this, and related practices, is to generate sensation; and, then to take that sensation as the subject/object of meditation. This sensation is then realised as the liberated energy of the self-luminous primordial state. Sexuality is part of life, so there is no harm in people learning to let go of 'themselves' a little when they enjoy each other's physicality. It is possible for people to experience an *unconstrained warmth* for each other which is not merely based on narrow self-obsession or goal-oriented technique. But if anger is deliberately aroused, and its empty nature is not realised – further unhelpful perceptual patterning is all that is accomplished. Every time life *triggers* you, and your potential for manifesting a powerful negative emotion is released, you increase the distorted power of that potentiality.

If you repeat an action many times you become 'skilled' in that action – whatever it is. Even if you repeatedly make a mistake in your action you could say that you have become 'skilled' in making that particular mistake. The term 'skill' is used here in a neutral manner and does not pertain to ideas of quality or craftsmanship. We usually find ourselves with many emotions arising on a day-to-day basis whatever we do. So it is unnecessary to arouse any emotion deliberately in addition to the ones we experience every day. In everyday life there is enough to contend with as it is. So this is an opportunity to take the raw texture of your life as a profound opportunity for realisation, and as the means of transforming pain and frustration into *delight*.

The personal pictures we have painted of the elements provide quite a narrow range. It is apparent that there is a far wider spectrum of personality types in the world than can be covered by the five elemental patterns alone.

But it should be understood that the elements interrelate to create a vast and highly sophisticated range of patterns. People often cross the boundaries of several elements in terms of the descriptions discussed. The pictures we have provided are very basic because just as space permeates every element, so the other elements permeate each other. Each element also contains the other elements within it. There are water, fire, air and space qualities of earth. There are earth, fire, air and space qualities of water, and so on. Nor do we always exist continuously in one specific mode – we fluctuate constantly. We change according to the nature of the dance between the patterns of our perception and the phantasmagorical theatre of the phenomenal world. This is a very subtle psychology and it is not intended to squeeze people into categories of any kind. People already categorise themselves in excruciatingly varied ways without assistance, so it is expressly not the legitimate activity of any spiritual practitioner to indulge in pigeonholing others as a pseudo-spiritual pastime. It is our responsibility to observe ourselves and to work with what we happen to find. It is our responsibility to discover our own clarity, in order to expose our own categories of indirect experience – our fear of emptiness and our sneaky yearning for security.

This book could have been significantly longer – maybe we could have looked at all the possible personality subdivisions: the fire /air person, the water /earth person, and so on. But really that would have been a trifle insulting. We all have the intrinsic capacity of clarity that can be awakened through the practice of shi-nè. We can discover these things for ourselves and discover our own analogies based on our own rich histories of experience. We wish everyone reading this our very warmest encouragement on their path, and hope that everyone everywhere will eventually make their journey into vastness.

Question and answer commentary

Q   Rinpoche, you said that it becomes possible to distance yourself from the 'artificial intensity' of what you feel... I'm wondering, why do you say the intensity is artificial?

Ngak'chang Rinpoche   It's artificial in the sense that it's not authentic. Intensity is an aspect of the mechanism that's attempting to maintain the illusion of duality. It's artificial because it's something that is superimposed. We have our authentic non-dual nature and then we have the structures that exist in order to attempt to prove that we are solid, separate, permanent, continuous and defined. The raw texture of the emotions we feel is not artificial, but the conceptual scaffolding in which they exist as painful experiences *is* artificial. These almost infinite forms of scaffolding are a constriction of our essential natures.

Q   When you say that operating according to the neurotic elemental patterns is impersonal... what's impersonal about it? I would have thought that the variety of forms that the 'scaffolding' took would make them very personal – they certainly *feel* very personal.

Khandro Déchen   [laughs] Yes. That's how it seems. The world we perceive seems to us to be a certain way – according to our history, culture, and social background. It's quite a shock to entertain the idea that what you think is personal actually fits into a box labelled 'another variant on the theme of samsara'. That's very sad. You might think that the enlightened state is the one that would be described as impersonal... at least from the dualistic point of view. It doesn't actually matter that there is almost infinite variety in the structures that exist within samsara.

247

They're all samsara, and hence impersonal.

NR There's nothing you can do within samsara that doesn't fit into a pre-ordained series of possibilities.

Q How are they pre-ordained?

NR They're pre-ordained by the need to maintain the illusion of duality. If you want to maintain the illusion of duality, there are only a set number of approaches to that.

KD In simple terms, there are the patterns of the five elemental neuroses. We experience these as if they were our personalities, but in actual fact, they are the method by which we avoid manifesting authentic personality. And yet from the perspective of Tantra these very patterns of impersonality are the doorways to the discovery of authentic personality.

Q Khandro Déchen, it always seems like Tantra does a backward flip on the logic of Sutra, and yet ends up saying almost the same thing... apart from the fact that it has a radically different approach to relating with the world... or am I getting hold of the wrong end of the stick completely?

KD No. You're quite right.

NR Quite. It's an entirely different paradigm. The logic of Tantra is profoundly *exciting*. The view is completely and unequivocally radical because it is not based on the logic of samsara. The view of Tantra is based on emptiness; in which all form is a fluid and unimpeded exultation!

Q Rinpoche, you mentioned the process of learning to be suspicious of our negative emotions; are we also supposed to be suspicious of our positive emotions? And I'm also wondering: what makes an emotion negative or positive?

NR   Well, it's more a matter of being suspicious of any reaction or any emotion that functions like a computer macro. That is to say – you should be suspicious of habits that perform themselves as if you were operating on auto-pilot. The terms 'positive' and 'negative' as applied to our emotions simply indicate whether we like them or not – let's not get too damn profound about this!

Q   You mentioned earlier, Rinpoche, that if you can keep the presence of your 'gaze', then your emotions become 'free energies'. I guess I still don't understand how that happens. Could you say a little more about it?

NR   There's not so much to understand, really. It's actually a matter of finding yourself there, in that condition. Some emotion arises. You feel something. It could be something very strong, or it could be the mildest kind of sensation. Then it simply occurs that you could remain present in that sensation – allowing yourself to be completely defined by the raw energy of what you feel. The words and the conceptual scaffolding fall away, and you discover something brilliant and wonderfully shocking.

KD   When your emotions become free energies this simply means that they're not under the control of the usual self-referencing systems. The energy of the emotions can free itself of conceptual manipulation by itself – we simply have to allow it.

Q   I'm thinking about what you said about realising the empty nature of the sensation of emotional pain. You said that the pain dissolves into an 'ecstatic sensation', but why, exactly, would it be ecstatic?

KD   Because you stop objecting to the pain on conceptual grounds. It's quite natural to be ecstatic, you know – I feel, at some level, that you all know this.

Q   I'd like to ask about what you said concerning recognising obsession. You said we become 'frenzied with self-seduced hunger', and I didn't quite understand what you meant by that.

NR   Hunger becomes a reference point, and seduces itself into continuing. There's nothing wrong with hunger, as long as it can be satiated. But when we feel a need for the experience of hunger to be there, simply to provide a context for the experience of feeling real... then there's always going to be something of a problem. It's called *dukkha* – unsatisfactoriness. That's the first noble truth. The truth of the experience of unsatisfactoriness.

Q   On the subject of 'staring into' my fixation and experiencing it as the wisdom of discriminating awareness, or compassion... how is compassion the same as discriminating awareness?

KD   Discriminating awareness is the traditional term for the transformed aspect of obsession. But it can be hard to understand the meaning. If you think about the word 'discriminating' – it means entering into the particular, looking at things in great detail and making very specific judgements. Awareness is broad and all-encompassing – awareness is linked with emptiness. Discriminating awareness is linked with form – because form is particular. Form is linked with compassion because in order to manifest compassionate activity you have to have infinitesimal awareness of individual forms. Discriminating awareness is compassion, or more accurately 'active-compassion', because discriminating awareness sees everything according to the extent of particular individual need.

Q   When you spoke of the feeling of being heartbroken, you said that if we were able to let go of the conceptual scaffolding, then the heartache would no longer be felt as pain. Why wouldn't it still be 'uncomfortable'?

NR   Because the word 'uncomfortable' would not exist.   Once there's no conceptual scaffolding, there are no reference points by which you could determine 'comfortable' or 'uncomfortable'; 'pleasurable' or 'painful' in the relative senses of these words.

Q   Rinpoche, you said that there's no sudden breakthrough that remains forever; only sudden glimpses.   But is there a point where more and more frequent glimpses kind of fuse together to form an unbroken continuum of enlightenment?   Or does it stay in pieces forever?

NR   Both [laughs].   You see, the idea of the fusing of sudden glimpses doesn't really work.   The idea of remaining in pieces forever doesn't work either.   It's when we realise that they are limited constructions, based on partial experiences, that both are spontaneously inseparable.   Basically, from the perspective of unenlightenment, there is no way that you can conceptualise enlightenment.   The enlightenment you could conceptualise would just be another variation of unenlightenment.

Q   Are we to take it literally when you say that everyone could write a great symphony?   Isn't there some kind of innate difference of ability in something like that, or are there just obscurations that could be dealt with through practice?

KD   Yes, you could take that literally.   But maybe you should practise and find out.

Q   This method seems terrifically useful.   But it's hard to always remember to be suspicious of myself.   It's like I need a method to remember the method!   Is there such a thing?

KD   Living the view is, in itself, the beginning and end of method.

Q   Rinpoche, you were saying the intellect is valuable within the sphere of intellect; but that outside it, it becomes increasingly useless. I don't really understand why it wouldn't always be of *some* use.

NR   Yes... There's much that can be accomplished with a spade.

Q   Pardon...?

NR   You can dig potatoes, for example.

Q   Okay...

NR   You can even carry the potatoes into the kitchen on the spade. A basket would do the job better, but a spade can still be used. Then if you want to peel the potatoes, you probably should use a knife... but, if you insist, you can use the spade. You'd have to hold it between your knees and turn the potato on its edge, and you'd lose a lot of the potato in very thick peelings... but it would still be possible. Then there's the question of cooking the potatoes. What happens then if you can't let go of the spade?

Q   I guess things would become difficult [laughs].

NR   Sure. But when has that ever stopped anyone? So... you'd have to stir the potatoes in a giant pot, just to be able to get the spade inside it. It would take a long time for the water to boil and cook the potatoes, but the task could still be accomplished. This would surely be the time to give up on the spade, but if your attachment to it has increased through continuing to use it in unlikely circumstances; you might find it a hard job to let go of it. So you may try to eat the potatoes with the spade; and even though you chip bits off your teeth, it only strengthens your belief that the spade can accomplish all ends. So you sit back after the meal and smile with satisfaction. You look admiringly at the spade. The spade glints in the candle light. The well-oiled grain of its handle looks somehow sumptuous against the white linen table cloth.

You develop romantic feelings toward the spade, you go to bed with the spade, you make love with the spade, and eventually raise a family of little trowels...

Q　You were saying that for some people, inner Tantra is just some kind of esoteric hobby... I guess this means we can convert anything into delusion?

NR　Sure. You see, if you're going to engage in this kind of practice, then it should be of some real benefit. Adopting a 'mystical outlook', can just assist us in hiding from reality. If I fill my life with oriental ritual observances, merely to avoid facing a failure to live in the world – my 'spiritual path' will accomplish nothing. If I populate my vocabulary with oriental words and spiritual catch-phrases, all I'm doing is filling time. I'd do better to involve myself in voluntary work, in order to make some real difference in the world.

Q　I'm not sure I understand the problems of becoming 'skilled' at certain things not being a good idea. Isn't anything you learn to be skilled at somehow useful?

NR　Well, in my first year at art college, I should have learned how to type; but I was excused because I was one of those people who'd already become 'skilled' at two-finger 'hunt and peck' typing, and experience had shown the instructor that it was very difficult to teach anyone to touch type once they'd taught themselves to type with two fingers. Too much 'unlearning' was required. With any skill there are bad habits you can easily learn which will inhibit you. In the *skill* of unlearning unenlightenment it's better to avoid picking up unskilful habits. Whether you're learning to drive a car, play a cello, or embrace emotions, it's fairly crucial not to develop counterproductive skills. Unlearning is arduous.

Element	Colour	Initial Reaction to Space	Distorted Energy
Earth	Yellow	Insubstantiality, hollowness, insecurity, fragility	Obduracy, arrogance, pride, fixity, wilfulness, poverty /miserliness
Water	White	Fear (of recognised threats)	Anger, aggression, hatred, violence
Fire	Red	Isolation, separation, desolation, loneliness	Indiscriminate possessiveness, obsessiveness, compulsion, consumerism
Air	Green	Vulnerability, groundless anxiety, nervousness, panic (at the feeling of susceptibility to indirect strategies)	Envy, suspicion, jealousy, paranoia
Space	Blue	Bewilderment – feeling overpowered and overwhelmed by spaciousness	Intentional ignorance, deliberate torpor, wilful stupidity, introversion, depression

Liberated Energy	Direction	Season	Time	Khandro / Pawo
Equality, equanimity, balance, harmony, wealth / generosity	South	Autumn	Mid-morning	Rinchen
Clarity, mirror-wisdom, penetrating insight	East	Winter	Dawn / sunrise	Dorje
Discriminating wisdom, compassion, pure appropriateness	West	Spring	Sunset	Pema
Self-fulfilling activity, spontaneous accomplishment, free and fluid capacity for action	North	Summer	Dusk / early night	Lékyi
Infinite unrestricted intelligence, pervasive wisdom, omniscience	Central, peripheral, pervasive, directionless	Time, continuity	Timelessness	Sang-gyé

13

Dancing in the
Space of the Earth and Sky

*Our emotions and our personal environment are
the dance of the khandros and pawos.
To know our reality as the dance of the khandros
and pawos is to fall in love with them. To fall in love with
them is to discover our beginningless enlightenment in the
endless empty nature of their dance.*

K **handro**. The word 'khandro' is a contraction of
'khandroma'. Literally it means 'sky-going lady', but
poetically it can be translated as 'sky-dancer'.[1] Khandro
pertains to the essence of the elements – to their intrinsic spatial
quality. Khandro is the *wisdom-display* quality of reality – the
emptiness aspect of phenomena as perceived through the material
form of the phenomenal world. Khandro is the inner energy
field of the elements.

---

[1] 'Sky dancer' is a term coined by Keith Dowman. It is also the name given to his
translation of the life of Yeshé Tsogyel (Routledge & Kegan Paul, 1984). Sky dancer is
used here, because it conveys a spectrum of meaning that comes closer to the essential
meaning of the term *khandro*. Keith Dowman's term seems to have entered into general
spiritual language in the West, even in contexts where there is no real understanding of
its meaning. *See also* Footnote 3, page 110.

Pawo. The word 'pawo' means 'hero' or 'warrior'. Pawo is the *method-display* quality of reality – the form aspect of the phenomenal world as perceived through the pure energy of primal space.

Dance. The idea of dance is very important in terms of the emotions. If we are to embrace the emotions as the path of inner Tantra, we have to experience this dance. Dance, in this sense, is something that we do *with* a partner. The idea is that we ourselves are dancers, and that the pawos and khandros are our dance partners. If you are a woman, your dance is with the pawo. If you are a man, your dance is with the khandro. Pawo and khandro are the male and female aspects of experience. Pawo is the form aspect of emptiness and khandro is the emptiness aspect of form. These aspects of reality, and of experience, dance with each other. They can be mistaken for duality or recognised as non-duality – but whichever is apprehended, their true nature is unchanging.

Sometimes the dance is smooth and elegant. Sometimes it is wild and furious. Sometimes you cannot quite seem to keep up – but this, in itself, is still dance. Dance never stops. So we can never say: "I'm dreadfully sorry, but I think I'll just sit this one out". That does not happen with this kind of dance. That does not happen with emotions either. We get dragged out onto the dance floor whether we like it or not – kicking and screaming if necessary. Dance is always changing. It can be stiff and graceless, when one person is always trying to lead. When both partners try to lead it becomes a war dance, or a battle. But whatever happens it always remains dance. Perceptually it can become very confusing – pleasure turns into pain, and pain turns into pleasure. In the final analysis it does not seem possible to control what is happening.

Dancing in the Space of the Earth and Sky

We may try every conceivable variation we can imagine during
the course of our lives, but we still get danced – either with our
will, or against it. Unless we have some sense of space, there is no
way out of this experience – but when there is space, dance can
become *spontaneously self-realised*. It simply needs to become
effortless, and effortless dancing can only happen through unifying
with one's dance partner. When we are unified with the pawo
or khandro, our feet hardly touch the ground. The movement
is beyond the individual dancers. We discover that being danced
is not something that has to be struggled against; or, maybe, that
dance and dancer are an indivisible phenomenon.

In the same way, our senses are danced. They are simultaneously
penetrated and engulfed by the world we perceive. The dance is a
sexual dance, but not necessarily in the ordinary sense of the word.
The dance is sexual in that we penetrate phenomenal reality and
are engulfed by it. The dance is sexual in that we are penetrated
by phenomenal reality at the same time that we engulf it. Reality
penetrates us and is engulfed by our senses.

At this point we need to investigate paradox, and to become
intimate with a style of explanation that takes rationality in and
out of seemingly endless interconnected loops. Tantric paradox, as
a means of communication, is a force that turns intellect itself into
experience. To understand paradox, one simply has to be open –
to be able to listen. One has to be able to ask questions which
invoke further paradoxes; and then to listen again. One has to
be able to continue this process as an ongoing dialogue with the
Lama, until a *breakthrough* happens. This might take days or years.

Here you will need to read very slowly. You will need to read,
and re-read – but without the frustration that might accompany
the reading of difficult material.

Everything, in its nature, is empty – everything is also characterised by infinite variety, i.e. multiplicity. This means that we are divided in terms of the multiplicity of things, but undivided (non-dual) in terms of the essence of phenomena. This is because the essence of phenomena is always the same: emptiness. Emptiness is always the same emptiness. This means that the character of our experience is that we are simultaneously divided yet undivided. We are divided yet undivided from *non-dual multiplicity*.

This is difficult material, so let us recapitulate: non-dual multiplicity is the nature of reality. Non-dual multiplicity means that the essence of all phenomena is the same – emptiness. There are no varieties of emptiness – it is always the same emptiness. Non-dual multiplicity means that although everything, in its nature, is empty – it is also characterised by infinite variety. We are simultaneously *dividedness* and *undividedness.* 2 From this point we can only continue to describe this condition in terms of paradox.

A further recapitulation: we are divided yet undivided, from non-dual multiplicity. Divided yet undivided, from the non-dual multiplicity which is the nature of reality. From this perspective there are two indistinguishable aspects to be considered – *as if* it were possible to distinguish them.

Now that we have described how emptiness and multiplicity are inseparable, we need to be able to tease these two indistinguishable aspects apart – in order to understand our own dualistic condition. We need to be able to tease them apart; but at the same time to understand that this is, in essence, an impossible operation. So, there is both the *singular non-duality of emptiness*; and, the *multiplistic appearances of form*.

2 According to the system of the five elements (from earth to space) we are: substantial and insubstantial; permanent and impermanent; divided and undivided; continuous and discontinuous; defined and undefined.

It is when we construe these forms as existing separately from emptiness that we create the illusion of becoming enmeshed in the impossible process of trying to keep them separate. This is the experience called dualism.

But how do we become enmeshed? What is this experience of being enmeshed? We become enmeshed, because we take non-dual multiplistic appearances to be separate from the non-dual singularity of the emptiness from which they arise. If we cease to identify with the singularity of the non-dual ground, and attach to non-dual appearances, as if they were separate from it – we create the illusion of duality.

The enlightened state as the ground of compassionate communication is not easy to apprehend. Enlightenment communicates with the unenlightened state as a natural reflex. The ground of this communication is described as the condition in which there is both non-duality and the appearance of duality. There is non-duality, because emptiness and form are indivisible. There is the appearance of duality – because it seems to be possible to become mistakenly identified with tangible manifestations of the intangible.

In Tibetan Tantra emptiness is understood as being female. Because of this, female imagery is very important as a symbol for the essence quality of the elements. Female symbolism arises from emptiness because of its womb-like qualities. Emptiness is creative in its essence, and continually gives rise to the world of phenomena. Emptiness is often called 'the great mother' or 'the womb of potentiality' and is understood as being the creative space from which all phenomena arise. Male Tantric practitioners hold women in very high regard, and they view women (and femaleness) as the source of inspiration. Women are the source of inchoate activity – action that defies linearity and fixed coordinates.

Women are the source of freedom to transcend the arbitrary boundaries that logic and rationality impose on spontaneity. Male tantrikas take the vow to view the phenomenal world as female – as wisdom-display, as the play of emptiness.

Female tantrikas take the vow to view the phenomenal world as male – as method-display, as the play of form. Female tantrikas hold men in very high regard, and they view men (and maleness) as the source of accomplishment. Men are the source of compassionate activity – the action that channels energy and galvanises situations for the benefit of everyone and everything everywhere.

Sky-dancing carries the meaning of having room to move, room to observe ourselves and our mechanistic mannerisms. We use expressions such as: 'take a look at yourself' or 'stand outside your situation for a moment'. In order to see clearly we need room, we need space for our natural clarity to manifest. Without recognition of our intrinsic space, we remain with our faces pressed hard up against our confusion.

The khandros are our moments of intuition, our recognition of space. As soon as we experience even the very faintest glimmer of intrinsic space, a certain clarity is present and our perception develops some translucence. We become more transparent to ourselves, and in that transparence we catch glimpses of the futility of our structured habit patterns. These glimpses develop with the experience of practice, and become a great inspiration to follow through with it. This is the khandro, the inspirational intuition that enables us to untangle our emotional jungle.

The pawos are our moments of delicious connection with definition – the precision within passion. Form, in Tibetan Tantra, is understood as being male.

262

Form is transitory in its nature. It arises out of emptiness. Emptiness gives birth to form, and form performs. Form embodies the qualities of compassionate activity.

Seen in this way, the form of our emotions (how we react to our feelings) is the pawo aspect – the form aspect of emptiness. The emptiness of our emotions is how they *feel* – this is the khandro aspect, the emptiness aspect of form. These qualities dance with each other, and also within each other. For example; when the nature of the feelings is seen as pawo, then the experiential emptiness from which they arise is seen as khandro. Then, when the reactions that arise from experiencing emotions are seen as khandro, the external causes that trigger those feelings and reactions are seen as pawo. But this is a particularly subtle perspective, and one that only develops in meaning with practice and the natural insight that arises out of the experience of emptiness.

The pawo /khandro experience can become an intellectual hall of mirrors – *if* you try to grasp its meaning with the logical mind. The only way into the pristine purity of the nature of the mirror itself is by cultivating the experience of emptiness. Tibetan Tantra is rich with anthropomorphic symbols which constitute aspects or qualities of the enlightened consciousness of an individual. The pawos and khandros are an important part of this system of symbols; but in this book we are not dealing with *visualisation* as a Tantric method. We are dealing with the practice of *embracing emotions as the path*; at the non-symbolic level of raw sensation. However, for the sake of providing visual inspiration we will give some depiction of the mystic painting of Tibet – the *awareness-imagery* of Tantra.

There are many different kinds of khandros and pawos; and, in terms of visionary methods of transformation, these are known collectively as *yidams*.

Some are *joyous,* displaying the open quality of *transmuted attraction.* Some are furiously *wrathful,* displaying the open quality of *transmuted aversion.* And some are serene or *peaceful,* displaying the open quality of *transmuted indifference.*

There is Yeshé Tsogyel; the joyous female Tantric Buddha, whose strong laughter overpowers all apparent phenomena into bliss-emptiness. Her *nakedness* displays her total lack of pretension and the nakedness of her radiant awareness. Her skin is the colour of the unified male and female essences (white and red) and displays her non-dual enjoyment of the multiplicity that plays as the energy of emptiness.

There is Seng-gé Dongma; the wrathful lion-headed khandro whose terrifying roar shatters the illusion of unenlightenment, and whose secret awareness-spell turns back the effects of black magic. She is dark blue in colour – the colour of space – and her hair is the colour of burning copper, displaying the vividness of the searing ferocity with which she out-shines all obstacles to the flow of compassion. The wildness of her dance displays her ability to overcome every aspect of illusion with unbridled energy and utter lack of nervous restraint.

There is Dorje Sempa, thunderbolt Mind-hero, the quintessence of purity, who displays complete absence of all obscurations. His serene expression and clear eyes display the utter calm and peace of having emptied every trace of referentiality. Dorje Sempa rests in the non-dual condition displaying total clarity and perfect transparence. He holds the dorje and drilbu (vajra and bell) which symbolise the indivisible qualities of compassion and wisdom.

The yidams (or awareness-beings) are unlimited in variety and function. They pervade the fabric of the phenomenal universe in the unrestricted nature of the qualities they display.

They are the dazzling active function of space. They are the key to the experience of *spacious passion in passionate space*.

All these many pawos and khandros arise out of the primary play of the elements – the khyil-khor (mandala) of phenomenal existence. This is why in Tantric terminology our entire universe (and everything that functions as part of it) is called 'the wisdom dance of the five pawos and khandros'. This dance is intimately instructive to the practitioner who is open to receiving its inspiration. This dance is our constant field of opportunity. Practitioners see the circumstances on their paths as khandros and pawos, and as such they are viewed as manifestations of the Lama. Every situation holds these inspirational qualities for accomplished practitioners because they are aware of the empty nature of themselves and the world that they perceive.

Our emotions and our personal environment are the dance of the khandros and pawos. To know reality as the dance of the khandros and pawos is to fall in love with them. To fall in love with them is to discover our beginningless enlightenment in the endless empty nature of their dance.

Question and answer commentary

Q   I'm intrigued by the fact that *khandro* and *khandroma* are familiar terms in all schools of Tibetan Buddhism, but that *pawo* is so rarely mentioned.   Why is that?

Ngak'chang Rinpoche   Well, as you may have noticed. . . Tibetan Buddhism is almost entirely represented by men, and men – especially monks – who would not be particularly interested in practices for women.

Q   But there are women practitioners too. . .

NR   Certainly.   But in the form in which the Tantric traditions have come down to the present day, the pawo practices and teachings have been largely forgotten.

Khandro Déchen   This is because the androcentric bias of Buddhism has existed right from the beginning.   But that's a product of culture, not the teaching of Padmasambhava or Yeshé Tsogyel.   The problem is that Buddhism originated in a culture that was essentially patriarchal, and this infiltrated the teachings. Initially, women were not even allowed to become nuns, and then even when they were, they were controlled by monks through the eight special rules that governed their behaviour.   This meant that male monasticism succeeded at the expense of female monasticism.

But outside of the monastic institutions there were the yogic traditions, and things there were very different.   However, many of the inspirational stories of yoginis were simply not recorded and so have been lost to us.   This has a detrimental effect on women practitioners because we have very few rôle models.

Q   It seems like there's always this tendency for men to want to dominate. . .

NR Yes... It's a problem. Unfortunately [laughs] there's no *form* of unenlightenment based on clinging to emptiness – it could not exist.

Q Rinpoche, I know there must be a very obvious answer... but *why* is there no form of unenlightenment based on clinging to emptiness?

NR Clinging requires form. From the position of emptiness, there is no conceptual framework which could be afraid of 'coming into existence'. There is no conceptual framework at all in emptiness – if there *was* it wouldn't be emptiness. It would be form, and it would be afraid of the dissolution of its form. But to get back to patriarchy... We cling to form, and our world is dominated by this form-clinging. That means as long as the world is inhabited by unenlightened beings, patriarchy is going to be the unenlightened philosophy of the beings who inhabit it. You see... patriarchy *is* form. That's why Khandro Déchen and I regard it as so important to work against the patriarchal superstructures that adhere to Tantra. And we see this as valuable not only for women, but for the enlightenment of all beings.

KD Patriarchy affects the direction of practice. With patriarchy, there's always this emphasis on emptiness – the life of the ascetic, and concentration on the path of renunciation. Renunciation is a male direction, because method, or form, has a tendency to travel in the direction of emptiness. For women things will take the opposite direction, towards form, maybe with an integration into family life. This is why pawo is very rarely mentioned; the emphasis is always on khandro. This is quite natural given the cultural bias within Tibet, and the form orientation of the world in general.

Q So where does the teaching on pawo come from, as you present it?

KD   From the Khandro-pawo-nyi-da-mélong-gyüd – part of
the gTérma cycle of Khyungchen Aro Lingma.   But it can also
be found, in essence, in the Tantras of every school of Tibetan
Buddhism.   It is also found in the Bön tradition.   It is not exactly
rare.   It's just rare to hear it presented.

Q   This is not widely known, is it?

NR   No, not the Khandro-pawo-nyi-da-mélong-gyüd.   But the
term 'pawo' can be found in many Tantric teaching cycles – there
just seems to be very little knowledge of how this is actually
practised.   For example, the three roots of Tantra are practically
always expressed as Lama, yidam and khandro, rather than Lama,
yidam and pawo / khandro – even though this arrangement is not
coherent in Tantra.

Q   What do you mean by 'not coherent'?

NR   It only reflects the practice from a male point of view.
From the female point of view it would have to be Lama, yidam
and pawo.

Q   Why is it that emptiness relates to wisdom and form relates
to compassion?

NR   Wisdom relates to emptiness because wisdom, like emptiness,
is unlimited.   Emptiness is the source of all phenomena, and
wisdom is the source of compassionate activity.   Form relates to
compassion because compassion is infinitely variegated – emptiness
is infinite but undifferentiated.

KD   You also have to remember that the wisdom that is being
described, is *primordial wisdom* – we're not talking about wisdom
in the sense of knowledge of details.   What we mean by wisdom
is *primally pure knowingness.*

NR   If specifics arise within this *primally pure knowing,* then those specifics arise as *communicative energy.* If communicative energies arise then these communications are compassion – they *are* form. Form is specific, impermanent, and inherently compassionate. Forms are impermanent because they are finite – they have a beginning and an end – they aren't emptiness-wisdom itself, but rather the *compassionate efflorescence* of primordial wisdom. Because wisdom is primordial – because it has no beginning or end – it cannot be specific. As non-specific wisdom, it is empty of specifics. Non-specific wisdom is the ground from which specific compassionate activities arise.

Q   [pause] Sorry. . . I'm a bit stunned by that. So. . . is there no wisdom in form, except as the interpenetration of emptiness?

KD   Form as compassion is always empty. Form is emptiness and emptiness is form.

NR   Emptiness and form are non-dual; so as long as we speak about them as separate from each other, they both end up sounding as if they're the same.

Q   So there's no way to make the paradox non-paradoxical. . .

NR   That would seem to be fundamental.

Q   You said that our emotions and our personal environment are the dance of the khandros and pawos. . . How can an environment and an emotion be the same thing, or have I misunderstood something?

NR   It's not that they're the same thing – it's simply that they're not different. The water element is both anger and clarity, according to who is perceiving it. This is not really something for intellectual understanding. These statements all exist as *indications.*

Q   Indications of what?

269

NR   No.

KD   Yes! [laughs] No, they're not 'indications of what' – they're indications of how to look...

NR   ... of how to feel / taste / smell / hear / cognise...

KD   What is meant by 'indication' is that something is merely *suggested*. Something is stated in order to set you up for some kind of opening. You can't really think your way around this.

NR   You see, the dance of the khandros and pawos is the existential poetry of being, and of existence. We are not separate from our environment – and yet we are. That is both tragedy and comedy. That is both samsara and nirvana. We have to go beyond separate and non-separate – that's the vision of khandro and pawo.

Q   Okay... So if to know reality as the dance of the khandros and pawos is falling in love with them and discovering enlightenment in the empty nature of their dance... I can't follow the leap from their being the play of our own energies to knowledge of beginningless enlightenment. Unless of course – [interrupted]

KD   Yes! Your energies themselves are beginningless and enlightened. Is that what you were going to say?

Q   Yeah, but then where are they hiding? Or what are they hiding as? I really don't get the whole process of unenlightenment, actually.

KD   Good!

Q   Right. But enlightenment makes so much sense these days that I can't understand how we ever got to be anywhere else. How can my energy get to be so distracted with such poor concentration over and over and over again moment by moment?

I don't get what is holding it all up. And how can we be so
stuck in this distraction when it's so bizarre, so nonsensical?

NR   Yes [laughs]. Hell isn't it? There's really no answer to
that dilemma, outside the experience of practice. But you're
absolutely right – we recreate unenlightenment in each moment
by trying to get back to enlightenment. It is not possible to get
back to an enlightenment from which we've never actually strayed.

KD   I'm afraid you're back with paradox again.

Q   If you don't happen to have a partner, is it still possible
to dance?

NR   No. But there's no situation in which you can be
without a partner. If you have no human partner, then the
whole of phenomenal reality is your partner.

KD   That's the way it has to be for a monk or a nun.

Q   In what sense are you saying that men and women are the
source of method and wisdom? In terms of personality, or what?

KD   In terms of every aspect of their being.

NR   I think the most important thing is that you have to
look for this – but not in a fixed linear way. That is the practice.
We can't really tell you what to look for, because that would be
to programme you – to condition you. You have to discover it
for yourself, from your experiential understanding of emptiness
and form. That can only come from your experience of non-
referentiality from the practice of shi-nè.

Q   I'm struck by the contrast between female 'inspirational
intuition' and male 'delicious connection'. I feel like I have some
understanding of wisdom–display and method–display, but it's
sometimes hard to distinguish which is which.

NR   That's certainly true.   It is hard to distinguish which is which – but that's actually not a problem.   In fact, it would be more of a problem if it were totally black and white.   The more you investigate wisdom-display and method-display, the more they begin to reflect each other.   It's actually not so much a question of which is which, but whether it's a man or a woman who is perceiving these displays.   Inspirational intuition. . . this for me is the essential glow of phenomena – the way in which nothing is heavy or heavy-handed.   It's the way in which everything whispers very lucidly about its perfect luminosity.   It's the way a tomato has of being red in such a luridly provocative manner.

KD   And method display or 'delicious connection'. . . this is the dynamic movement of solidity, full and strong: the heaviness and tensile strength that throbs in the muscles of reality.   It's the way that movement bursts forth in linearity and forceful direction.   It's delicious because you can taste it – it's like horseradish, it's so obviously *there*.   It almost lifts the roof off your head!   Form doesn't hint at itself.   It's a connection because that's how you perceive form.   It struts in all its nakedness for your enjoyment.   It communicates to you.   It's funny that Rinpoche and I sometimes have very opposite views of the same process because our vows mean that we perceive phenomena from opposite poles.   For instance, if we go back to the form qualities of our emotions, I see the pawo aspects in terms of their strength and solidity.   When we're caught up in them, they seem so pervasive and dense.   Their dynamic aspects display themselves by the way they follow each other with such relentless succession.

Q   If you perceive things from different viewpoints, doesn't this lead to problems sometimes?

KD   Not at all!   The practice of the different views brings us both to the same fruit and therefore enhances our relationship.

It's really fascinating to have differences between views of the world, because it provides yet another opportunity to discover the teacher in your partner.

Q   Your description of falling in love with the pawos and khandros is really very interesting. The word 'love' brings to mind a whole series of human experiences – warmth, passion, openness, appreciation, intensity. . . The possibility of relating to all phenomena in this way seems incredibly challenging. To me, there's a lot of intensity, a lot of energy associated with being in love. How would I be able to maintain that kind of openness and passion in a consistent way?

NR   Well, to start with, you wouldn't try to maintain that kind of openness and passion in a consistent way – you'd simply feel your way into the texture of the view.

KD   It's very challenging if you approach this as something you're going to launch into immediately. It's not really possible to plunge straight into a practice like this – or rather, it's not possible to plunge straight into the result of this practice. You see, this is a *practice*. If you think in terms of living the result, it's going to seem quite overwhelming – but you'll have moments in which you recognise being in love in this way, and these will increase the more you practise and the more you live the view.

Q   If practitioners see the circumstances of their paths as manifestations of the Lama, does this mean that one views all circumstances as potential teachings? Or is it that one can infuse an actual sense of the Lama into all circumstances?

NR   [laughs] I'd go for the infusion.

Q   When you use the sexual metaphor of reality penetrating us and being engulfed by our senses, it seems to suggest an incredible degree of openness. Would you say it was possible to be too open?   It seems to me that there is so much destructive energy in the world, that it's essential for survival to cut off from that sometimes.

KD   This is obviously a practice that you should enter into at times when you feel your situation to be conducive. As with any practice, there are conducive times and places. Once you understand the principle and function of any practice you can use it according to your knowledge of yourself. You have to be able to look at your own situation and make good use of your knowledge of the practices for which you've received transmission.

Glossary

Aro gTér (*A ro gTér*)   The revealed teachings of Khyungchen Aro Lingma.

attraction   *See* dö-chag.

aversion   *See* zhe-dang.

awareness-being   *See* yidam.

awareness imagery   The visionary appearances of the long-ku.
See long-ku.

Bön (*bon*)   The indigenous religion of Tibet, a non-Buddhist tradition of non-dual realisation which traces its lineages back to Buddha Shenrap Miwo.

Buddha families   *See* Sang-gyé rig-nga.

bum-pa (*bum pa*)   Jar or pot; also empowerment vase.

chagya chenpo (*cha rGya chen po*, Skt. mahamudra)   Abbreviated to chagchen.   The final phase of Tantric practice, according to the three Sarma (new translation) schools (Kagyüd, Sakya and Gélug).   The chagchen of the Kagyüd School has similarities with Dzogchen, particularly in the formless chagchen which is very similar to the Four Naljors of Dzogchen Sem-dé.   However, it should not be assumed that the chagchen of the Sarma schools are identical.

chang (*chang*)   Tibetan barley beer – and very nice too...

chö (*chos,* Skt. dharma) (i) 'As it is': reality, suchness, the way things really are; (ii) phenomena; (iii) the teachings of a Buddha.

chö-ku (*chos sKu,* Skt. dharmakaya) The sphere of unconditioned potentiality; the dimension of being; the fundamental dimension of individuated reality.

chö-nyid (*chos nyid,* Skt. dharmata) Reality; the space of being and the space of existence in which there is no distinction or differentiation between them.

chö'phen (*chos 'phan*) Banner of reality. These are cloth tails or streamers appended to drums, mélongs and also hung in shrine rooms.

chö-ying (*chos dbyings,* Skt. dharmadhatu) The space of existence.

chodpa (*spyod pa,* Skt. charya) Action, conduct, behaviour. Not to be confused with gCod, meaning 'to cut'.

chu (*chu,* Skt. jalam) Water element.

chutzpah (Yiddish) Guts, uninhibited style, 'get up and go'.

crazy wisdom *See* yeshé cholwa.

dag-ngang gTér (*dag sNang gTér*) Teachings and practices arising out of Pure Vision. Revelations that are discovered within the unoriginated space of being. This type of gTér is sometimes not included along with sa gTér and gong gTér, as it was not specifically concealed for rediscovery by Padmasambhava and Yeshé Tsogyel. Dag-ngang gTér arise from the aspect of Padmasambhava / Yeshé Tsogyel that is identical with the nature of one's own Mind. Any yogi or yogini who realises the nature of Mind can be the author of dag-ngang gTér, but usually such gTér is discovered by Lamas who are also discoverers of sa gTér and gong gTér. *See* gTérma.

Dagmèdma (*bDag med ma*) The enlightened consort of Marpa. Dagmèdma was secretly a Dzogchen yogini known as Rangtsal Ja'gyür. She appeared in visionary form to several Long-dé masters, in particular to Jomo Chhi-mèd Pema. She was the holder of the Six Yogas of Niguma, very essential Dzogchen methods, which she received in vision directly from Yeshé Tsogyel. These methods were given to Milarépa, who passed them to Réchungpa, who in turn gave them to Ling-jé Répa Pema Dorje.

Ling-jé Répa gave transmission to Jomo Menmo, the previous incarnation of Khyungchen Aro Lingma, and through her they were recalled in vision and became part of her family lineage that passed to her son, Drüpchen Aro Yeshé.

damstig (*dam tshig,* Skt. samaya) Tantric vows.

dharmadhatu *See* chö-ying.

dharmakaya *See* chö-ku.

dharmata *See* chö-nyid.

direct transmission (*dGongs brGyud*) Direct means Mind to Mind; the transmission of the nature of Mind that occurs through instantaneous sparks of awareness. The reflection of the student's beginningless enlightenment in which the nature of the teacher's mind and the nature of the student's mind are experienced as identical in that moment.

distracted-being 'Being' which is distracted from 'being as such' into fixation with 'being this' or 'being that'. Dualised being, or even 'ego'.

dö-chag (*dod chags,* Skt. raga) Attraction; the referential strategy by which duality is maintained through fixating on focuses of desire.

dorje (*rDo rJe,* Skt. vajra) Indestructible, thunderbolt, diamond, adamantine; literally 'stone lord'. Synonymous with male genitalia in Tantric twilight language, as *pema* is synonymous with female genitalia.

Dorje Legpa (*dam can rDo rJe legs pa,* Skt. Vajra Sadhu) The excellent thunderbolt. *See* ma-za-dor-sum.

Dorje Sempa (*rDo rJe sems dPa,* Skt. Vajrasattva) Thunderbolt Mind Hero. The yidam connected with purification and the Dzogchen teachings.

Dorje Thegpa (*rDo rJe theg pa,* Skt. Vajrayana) The Thunderbolt (Indestructible) Vehicle – Tantra, both at the level of yidam practice and practices of the spatial nerves, winds and essences. *See* Gyüd.

Dorje Tröllö (*rDo rJe gro lod*) Literally, 'vajra loose-hanging belly'. The most wrathful of the Eight Manifestations of Padmasambhava (guru tsen-gyé). The crazy-wisdom manifestation of Padmasambhava. *See also* yeshé cholwa.

Dorje Zampa (*rDo rJe zam pa*) The Vajra-bridge teachings (of Dzogchen Long-dé); the Thunderbolt Bridge.

Drukpa Kagyüd (*'brug pa bka' brGyud*) One of the Kagyüd schools (along with the Drigung Kagyüd and the Shangpa Kagyüd) which is closest to the Nyingma in their practice. Many Drukpa Kagyüd practitioners maintain Nyingma gTérma traditions and many monasteries of these Kagyüd traditions incorporate Nyingma practices. These are the schools of the Kagyüd tradition which have the highest proportion of ngak'phang Lamas. *See* Kagyüd; ngak'phang sangha.

Drukpa Kunlegs (*'brug pa kun legs*) A great yogi of the Drukpa Kagyüd School, sometimes described as the 'divine madman'. Drukpa Kunlegs was famous for his extraordinary behaviour and for his yogic songs of realisation, which made frequent reference to sexuality and alcohol as indispensable to achievement of realisation.

drüp-thab (*sgrub thabs*, Skt. sadhana) Tantric ritual liturgy which guides visualisation.

dug-sum (*dug gSum*) The Three Poisons, the dualistic distortions, the Three Distracted Tendencies: attraction, aversion and indifference. Any reference point or possible focus which is subject to dualistic manipulation or referential fixation. Referential fixation is the means by which we attempt to prove that we exist as solid, permanent, separate, continuous and defined entities.

Dzogchen (*rDzogs pa chen po*, Skt. Mahasandhi) Great completeness, utter totality; Rig'dzin Chögyam Trungpa Rinpoche referred to Dzogchen as 'Maha Ati' with reference to its relationship with Mahamudra.

Formless Mahamudra A special teaching of Mahamudra which was taught by the third Karmapa (Rangjung Dorje, 1284-1339) as a syncretisation of Mahamudra and Dzogchen. *See* chagya chenpo.

Four Buddha-karmas *See* lé-shi.

Four Denials Monism, dualism, eternalism, nihilism. Descriptions of reality, each of which Buddhism recognises to be only partial, and which it therefore sets out to negate.

Monism asserts that everything is one (e.g. everything is God – in the sense in which God is understood within Hinduism as defined by Buddhism). Dualism can be divided into materialist dualism and perceptualist dualism. Materialist dualism maintains that subject and object (e.g. 'I' and 'the phenomenal world') are inherently different; while perceptualist dualism maintains that form and emptiness are inherently different. Eternalism sees everything as meaningful, there are no coincidences, the soul is immortal. Nihilism asserts that there is no meaning in anything.

Four Naljors (*rNal 'byor bZhi*) The ngöndro (preliminary practices) of Dzogchen Sem-dé: shi-nè, lha-tong, nyi-'mèd, and lhun-drüp.

Gampopa (*sGam po pa*) 1079-1153. The monastic disciple of Milarépa.

Gélug (*dGe lugs*) The Gélug School was originally named the New Kadam. The old Kadam School was established by Dromdon (1008-1064), a student of Atisa (982-1054). It was reformed by Tsongkhapa (1357-1419) and as a result, the old Kadam School was superseded by the Gélug as the school of 'the virtuous ones'. It places great emphasis on monastic discipline.

gendün (*dGe 'dun,* Skt. sangha) The community of either monastic or ngak'phang practitioners. *See* Three Jewels.

geshé (*dGe shes,* Skt. kalyanamitra) Gélug qualification – a 'doctoral degree' in Sutric studies.

gö-kar-chang-lo (*gos dKar lCang lo*) Literally, 'white skirt, long (or braided) hair'; refers to the manner of dress of ordained ngak'phang practitioners. Symbolic of many aspects of Tantric practice, taking the vows to maintain the gö-kar-chang-lo is an act that commits one to one's historical place within the lineage. *See* gö-kar-chang-lo'i-dé.

gö-kar-chang-lo'i-dé (*gos dKar lCang lo'i sDe*) Those who wear, and maintain the vows relating to, the gö-kar-chang-lo – members of the ngak'phang sangha. *See* gö-kar-chang-lo.

gommèd (*bsGom med*) Literally 'non-meditation'. Gommèd is the final phase of Formless Mahamudra and equates to lhun-drüp (the final practice of the Four Naljors).

gompa (*sGom pa*, Skt. bhavana)   Meditation, to meditate; or place of meditation.

gong gTér (*dGongs gTer*)   Mind gTérma. *See* gTérma.

ground of being *See* zhi.

gTér (*gTer*) *See* gTérma.

gTérma (*gTer ma*, Skt. nidhi)   Usually abbreviated to gTér. Teachings, practices and sacred objects concealed by Padmasambhava and Yeshé Tsogyel for the benefit of future disciples, and the regeneration of the Tantric lineages.

gTértön (*gTer sTon*)   Discoverer of gTér. *See* gTérma.

gYo-wa (*gYo ba*)   Movement; 'that which moves'. The nyam (meditational experience) of gYo-wa is the experience in which one becomes completely identified with whatever arises in mind.   gYo-wa is linked with the practice of lha-tong according to the Four Naljors of Dzogchen Sem-dé.   According to other systems it is also linked with lhun-drüp.

Gyüd (*rGyud*, Skt. Tantra)   Literally 'continuity'. The teachings of Buddhism which have as their basis the principle of transformation.

indifference *See* ti-mug.

inner Tantra (*nang rGyud*)   The three inner phases of Tantric practice. In Mahayoga Tantra (Kyépachen Naljor / Nal-chen), one works primarily with the practice of envisionment.   In Anuyoga Tantra (Jé-su Naljor), a deeper experience of the awareness-being is accomplished through awakening the spatial nerves, winds and essences. Atiyoga (Shin-tu Naljor / Dzogchen) is the path beyond symbol and ritual. The principle of Atiyoga is self-liberation – there is no longer the requirement to transform anything, as everything is recognised to be pure from the very beginning. One simply remains present and aware in one's natural condition.

jinpa (*sbyin pa*, Skt. dana)   Generosity. *See* the Six Perfections.

Jung-wa nga (*'byung ba lNga*, Skt. pancha-bhuta)   The Five Elements.

Kagyüd (*bKa' brGyud*)   Literally 'word transmission'. The Kagyüd schools trace the origin of their lineages from the Mahasiddha Tilopa (988-1069) to Naropa (1016-1100) down through Marpa (1012-1097), Milarépa (1052-1135), Réchungpa (1084-1161), Gampopa (1079-1153), and Dusum Khyenpa.   In the Karma Kagyüd School, the lineage continued through the incarnation line of the Karmapas; other Kagyüd schools (Drukpa, Drigung, Shangpa, Taklung, Tro'phu, Yamzang, Shugsep, Marstang, Phagmo, Tsalpa and Baram) have their own individual incarnation lines.

Kalachakra Tantra (*dus kyi 'khor lo*)   The 'Wheel of Time' Tantra. A specific Tantric practice that exists in all schools of Tibetan Buddhism, and which has been taught extensively by the fourteenth Dalai Lama in many countries around the world.

karma   *See* lé.

Karma Kagyüd (*karma bKa' brGyud*)   The branch of the Kagyüd School headed by the incarnation line of the Karmapas.   Rig'dzin Chögyam Trungpa Rinpoche was a Lama of the Karma Kagyüd School, but also held Nyingma and Shambhala lineages.

karmic vision   The way in which dualised beings apprehend the world according to the style in which they generate duality from the ground of being.

khandro (*mKha' 'gro*)   *See* khandroma.

Khandro-pawo-nyi-da-mélong-gyüd (*mKha' 'gro dPa bo nyi zla me long rGyud*)   The Tantra of the Mirror that Reflects the Sun and Moon of the Khandros and Pawos.   A teaching from the Aro gTér cycle of Khyungchen Aro Lingma, that relates to romance as spiritual practice.

khandroma (*mKha' 'gro ma*, Skt. dakini)   Literally 'sky-going woman' or more poetically 'sky-dancer'.   Often abbreviated to khandro.   Awareness-beings who manifest the functions of the buddha-karmas, i.e. who fulfil enlightened activity.   The khandro is the Lama manifesting as circumstances of the path.

khatvangha (*khat wan ga*)   The Tantric trident carried by Padmasambhava and Yeshé Tsogyel, representing the presence of the yum or yab respectively.

The three points of the khatvangha pierce the fabric of attraction, aversion and indifference at a single thrust.

khor-wa *('khor ba,* Skt. samsara) Cyclic experience of existence; going round in circles. The vicious circle of dualistically conditioned births and deaths; the state of unenlightened beings constricted by dualistic perception – a self-defeating waste of time and energy. The state in which every activity undermines itself in terms of our attempt to establish ourselves as being: solid, permanent, separate, continuous and defined.

khorlo *('khor lo,* Skt. chakra) Wheel, circle, cycle.

khyil-khor *(dKhil 'khor,* Skt. mandala) Literally, 'centre and periphery'. The term 'mandala' should be understood according to context. Usually it means an awareness-being along with his or her retinue of minions (surrounding display of active quality aspects, in terms of the manifest functional parameters of the awareness-being – the interactive environment in which the awareness-being communicates his or her method display). Also, the retinue of vajra disciples of a vajra master. The atmosphere in which something takes place – the entire field of events and meaning.

Khyungchen Aro Lingma *(khyung chen A ro gLing ma)* The 19th / 20th century female gTértön who received the Aro gTér in Pure Vision directly from Yeshé Tsogyel.

Könchog Sum *(dKon mChog gSum)* The Three Precious Ones or Three Jewels: Buddha (Sang-gyé), Dharma (Chö), and Sangha (Gendün Gen-kar and Gendün Gen-mar – the white ngak'phang and red monastic sanghas).

ku-sum *(sKu gSum)* The three spheres of being: the sphere of realised emptiness, the sphere of realised energy, and the sphere of realised form.

Lama *(bLa ma,* Skt. guru) Teacher of Tantra, vajra master. The Lama's function is to mirror our intrinsic enlightenment. The Lama also mirrors our neuroses, obsessions and fixed psychological patterns.

lé *(las,* Skt. karma) The word commonly used to mean 'cause and effect'. More essentially it means perception and response. We react to what we perceive according to our conditioning.

Karmic vision is the totality of how we experience reality, unless our beginningless enlightenment sparkles through the fabric of our conditioning and illuminates a glimpse of non-duality.

lé-shi (*las bZhi*)   The Four Buddha-karmas, or kinds of enlightened activity, namely: enriching (*gyé-pa*), pacifying (*shi-wa*), magnetising (*wang*), and destroying (*drakpo ngön-gCod*).

lha-tong *(lhag mThong*, Skt. vipashyana)   Clear or further vision, one of the two main aspects of meditation practice (the other is shi-nè).   It is important to remember that the words 'shi-nè' and 'lha-tong', when used in the context of Dzogchen, do not mean exactly the same as the words 'shamatha' and 'vipashyana' in other Buddhist contexts.   This has been the subject of considerable confusion.   See *Roaring Silence,* by Ngakpa Chögyam (Aro Books, 1998).

lhun-drüp (*lhun grub*)   Spontaneity / spontaneously accomplished.

living the view   Refers to a way of seeing that is applied within Tantra and Dzogchen teachings.   It is utterly profound and natural, and has no connection with 'applied philosophy'.   Living the view involves being open to the teachings or instructions that are given at the level of 'mere indication' (*see* mere indication), such as regarding every scalp hair as a khandro or pawo.   Living the view is also an openness to seeing the world as the play of emptiness and form;   or, as manifestations of the Lama's transmission.

long-ku (*longs sKu,* Skt. sambhogakaya)   The sphere of intangible appearance, the sphere of vision, or the sphere of realised energy.

lotsawa (*lo tsa ba*)   Spiritual translator – one who not only translates the words, but is aware of the experiential meaning.

lung (*lung*)   Transmission through sound.

ma-za-dor-sum (*ma gza' rDor gSum*)   The three main Protectors of the Nyingma school;   Mamo Ekajati, Za Rahula, and Damchan Dorje Legpa.

Mahamudra   *See* chagya chenpo.

Mamo Ekajati (*ma mo e ka dza ti*)   The single-braid mother.   One of the ma-za-dor-sum.

mandala *See* khyil-khor.

Marpa (*mar pa*) 1012-1097. The disciple of Naropa, and teacher of Milarépa.

mDo (*mDo,* Skt. Sutra) Discourses and teachings by Shakyamuni Buddha, which adhere to the principle of renunciation.

mé (*me,* Skt. agni) Fire element.

mélong (*me long*) Mirror – an important symbol of Dzogchen.

mensch (Yiddish) A reliable person who has integrity, courage and honesty.

mere indication (*man ngag,* Skt. upadesha) The most essential directions, in which the meaning is implicit within the instruction. There is no possible explanation or commentary beyond the mere indication. If one needs clarification, then one has not understood. If one has not understood, then there is nothing to be done: one is not ready for the practice.

method display (*thabs rol pa'i ngang*) Method display refers to a man's externally manifested quality in which his internal sensitivity gives rise to external power. It refers to a woman's internal compassion from which her external sensitivity arises. 'Method' is linked with compassion, or that which moves within wisdom space. The divisionless experience of method and wisdom constitutes the goal of Tantra. *See* wisdom display.

Milarépa (*mi la ras pa*) A great yogi famous for his songs of realisation and his accomplishment of the practice of tu-mo. Although Milarépa is most commonly known as a lineal link in a line that has become primarily monastic, he had many realised ngak'phang disciples. Of his 'eight great disciples' only one was a monk. His ngak'phang disciples were: Réchung Dorje Drakpa from Gung-tang; Shi-wa 'ö-Répa from Tsang; Se'ang Répa from Do-ta; Ngang-dzon Gyalpo from Chhim-ung; Khri-la Répa from Nyi-shang; Dri-gom Répa from Mu; and Sang-gyé Répa from Rag-ma.

Mount Meru A visionary method of relating to the mandala principle through the mytho-symbolic geography of ancient Indian cosmology.

In terms of Inner Tantra it relates to the central channel.

myong pa / ma (*sMyon pa/ma*) Wisdom eccentrics. 'Crazy' yogis
or yoginis who wander from place to place. Their 'wandering' can be
either external / geographical or internal / attentional. Wisdom eccentrics
are often given to interest in unlikely subject matter, as opposed to the
concerns of religious convention. They are often given to writing and
speaking poetry.

naljorpa / ma (*rnal 'byor pa/ma*, Skt. yogi / yogini) Practitioners of
the spatial yogas. Either ordained Tantric practitioners or non-ordained
Dzogchen practitioners.

namkha (*nam mKha'*, Skt. akasha) Space element.

namthar (*rNam thar*) A spiritual biography.

ngak'phang (*sNgags 'phang*) Literally 'mantra wielding'. *See* gö-kar-
chang-lo; gö-kar-chang-lo'i-dé.

ngak'phang sangha (*sNgags 'phang gi dGe 'dun*) *See* gö-kar-chang-lo'i-dé.

ngakpa / ma (*sNgags pa/ma*, Skt. mantrin / mantrini) Ordained members
of the Tantric sangha. *See* ngak'phang; gö-kar-chang-lo; gö-kar-chang-
lo'i-dé.

ngö-drüp (*dNgos grub*, Skt. siddhi) Accomplishment; usually refers to
the 'ultimate siddhi' of complete enlightenment but can also mean the
'relative siddhis' – Eight Mundane Accomplishments.

nirmanakaya *See* trül-ku.

nyi-mèd (*gNyis med*, Skt. advaya) Non-dual; without duality.

Nyingma (*rNying ma*) The 'Ancient' school of Buddhist Tantra brought
to Tibet in the eighth century. The Nyingma tradition is actually a school
by default, as it only developed as a separate 'school' in response to the
introduction of new schools (Sarma) from the eleventh century onwards.
Whilst it represents the Buddhism brought to Tibet at the time of
Padmasambhava and Yeshé Tsogyel, it is fundamentally heterodox – a
collection of lineages that are unique in their character and independent
in their functioning.

This is due to the fact that its lineages were maintained by isolated ngak'phang masters during the period of King Langdarma's persecution of Buddhism in Tibet. Apart from the six major lineages, there are also many minor lineages and innumerable family lineages. The continuing gTérma tradition also assures this individuality. *See* gTérma.

oral transmission (*sNyan brGyud*) The possibility of transmission that occurs when an explanation of the nature of Mind is being given.

outer Tantras (*phyi rGyud*) The three introductory phases of Tantra, comprising Kriya Tantra (Cha-wa Gyüd), Upa Tantra (Cho Gyüd), and Yoga Tantra (Naljor Gyüd). They represent increasing levels of purification that lead to the state in which 'pure' and 'impure' cease to have any spiritual meaning.

Padmakara *See* Padmasambhava.

Padmasambhava (*padma 'byung gnas*) The male Tantric Buddha, and consort of Khandro Chenmo Yeshé Tsogyel. Invited to Tibet in the eighth century by King Trisong Détsen, he introduced and established the tradition of the nine Buddhist vehicles in Tibet.

pawo (*dPa' bo,* Skt. daka / vira) Hero or warrior; the aspect of the experience of being as form – which is experienced as undivided from emptiness. The male reflection of khandroma.

pema (*padma*) Lotus; symbol of the fire element.

phung-po (*phung po,* Skt. skandha) Aggregate or heap; the psycho-physical constituents that make up an individual.

Protector (*chos sKyong*) Literally, 'reality-protector'. Beings bound by oath to protect the knowledge of reality, i.e. Buddhist teachings and practice.

Réchungpa (*ras chung pa*) 1084-1161. The ngak'phang disciple of Milarépa.

Ri-mèd (*ris med*) Literally 'without bias'. Ri-mèd is an activity or realisation related to the fruit rather than the path. The Ri-mèd Lamas realised the fruit of their own traditions, then proceeded to master the practices of other traditions, whilst holding them as distinct (i.e. not mixing them).

Ri-mèd is often misunderstood to be a path in which various traditions can be followed at the same time.

rig'dzin (*rig pa dzin pa,* Skt. vidyadhara)   Holder of non-dual awareness.

Rig'dzin Chögyam Trungpa Rinpoche   The great 20th century Mahasiddha whose incarnation stems from the Mahasiddha Trung Masé, who lived at the time of the fifth Karmapa (Dézhin Shegpa, 1384-1415). These incarnations were: Kunga Gyaltsen, Kunga Zangpo, Kunga 'ö-Sel, Kunga Namgyal, Ten'dzin Chögyal, Lodrö Ten'phel, Jampal Chögyal, Gyür'mèd Ten'phel, Karma Ten'phel, Chökyi Nyingjé, and the eleventh incarnation, Chökyi Gyamtso – Chögyam Trungpa Rinpoche.   His current incarnation lives in Tibet and is called Karma Ngedon Chökyi Seng-gé Pal Zangpo (Gloriously Good Lion of Dharma of the True Meaning), usually shortened to Chökyi Seng-gé Rinpoche.

rigpa (*rig pa,* Skt. vidya)   Instantaneous presence; non-dual awareness.

rinchen (*rin chen,* Skt. ratna)   Jewel; symbol of the earth element.

rLung (*rLung,* Skt. prana)   Air element.

ro-chig (*ro gCig,* Skt. ekarasa)   The experience of emptiness and form as non-dual – having the same taste.   The word taste (*ro*) relates to the experiential quality in which emptiness and form are realised as inseparable.

Root Teacher   *See* Tsa-wa'i Lama.

sa (*sa,* Skt. bhumi)   Earth element.

sa gTér (*sa gTer*)   Earth gTérma.   *See* gTérma.

sadhana   *See* drüp-thab.

Sakya (*sa sKya*)   One of the Sarma (new translation) schools.   It takes its name from the monastery founded by Könchog Gyalpo in southwestern Tibet in 1073 at Sakya (the 'place of grey earth').   The Khon family, of which he was a member, had formerly owed allegiance to the Nyingma School.   The Sakya School is divided into two principal sub-sects: the Ngor, founded by Ngorchen Kunga Zangpo (1382-1457); and the Tshar, founded by Tsharchen Losal Gyamtso (1502-1556).

sambhogakaya   *See* long-ku.

samsara *See* khor-wa.

samten (*bSam gTan,* Skt. dhyana) Meditation. *See* the Six Perfections.

sang-yab (*gSang yab*) Male spiritual partner or consort. The male aspect of a female awareness-being.

sang-yum (*gSang yum*) Female spiritual partner or consort. The female aspect of a male awareness-being.

sangha *See* gendün.

Sang-gyé Rig-nga (*sangs rGyas rigs lNga,* Skt. pancha-tathagata) The Five Buddha Families; the anthropomorphic symbols of the Five Elements. The word 'families' refers to the range of the quality spheres of the elements in terms of the khyil-khor or mandala principle, in which a vast range of experiential attributes are assigned to visionary appearances which can be experienced through Tantric practice.

schlemazl (Yiddish) A useless, clumsy individual who is also unfortunate and accident-prone.

schlemiel (Yiddish) Foolish, rather pathetic person, often the victim of the schlemazl's clumsiness.

sem (*sems,* Skt. citta) The small 'm' mind; the mind which can stray into dualism and engage in interminable attempts to prove itself to be solid, separate, permanent, continuous and defined.

sem-nyid (*sems nyid,* Skt. cittata) The nature of Mind; the empty quality of Mind – the awareness-space in which sem arises and enters into either compassionate communication or dualistic contrivances.

Seng-gé Dongma (*seng ge mDong ma,* Skt. Simhamukha) The lion-headed female sky-dancer.

Shakya Shri (*sha kya shri*) A great 19th century gTértön of the Drukpa Kagyüd School who received dag-ngang gTérma of Pure Vision from Milarépa. Shakya Shri was a ngak'phang Lama and a contemporary of 'a-Shul Pema Legden (the previous incarnation of Drüpchen Aro Yeshé, the son of Khyungchen Aro Lingma). He began his spiritual life as a monastery cook who was foolishly derided by the monks, who thought they were the 'real practitioners'. *See* Milarépa; dag-ngang gTér.

shérab (*shes rab,* Skt. prajna)   Discriminative awareness.   *See* the Six Perfections.

shi-nè (*zhi gNas,* Skt. shamatha)   Remaining uninvolved with the thought process.   Usually translated as 'calm abiding' or 'peacefully remaining'. The practice of silent sitting.

siddhi   *See* ngödrüp.

Six Perfections (*pha rol tu phyin pa drug,* Skt. satparamita)   The Six Transcendental Perfections or Six Paramitas: generosity, discipline, patience, vigour, meditation and discriminative awareness.

skandha   *See* phung-po.

sKu-mNyé (*sKu mNye*)   Massage of the spatial nerves.   A system of psycho-physical exercises.   These practices are found in medical Tantras, the inner Tantras and Dzogchen Long-dé, the Series of Space.   In Long-dé, they are a method by which the spatial nerves are galvanised, producing psycho-physical effects in the energetic atmosphere of the body.

sphere of intangible appearance   *See* long-ku.

sphere of realised manifestation   *See* trül-ku.

sphere of unconditioned potentiality   *See* chö-ku.

Sutra   *See* mDo.

symbolic transmission (*brDa brGyud*)   Exists in two forms, according to the Dzogchen teachings: formal symbolic transmission occurs when the teacher holds up a symbolic object as an indication of the nature of Mind, perhaps saying something cryptic relating to the state being expressed; informal symbolic transmission occurs when the teacher does anything that expresses the nature of Mind through symbolic means – for example, when Tilopa hit Naropa on the head with his shoe.

Tantra   *See* Gyüd.

tantrika   Practitioner of Tantra.

Tashi Chhi-'dren (*bkra shis khyi 'dren*)   One of the consorts of Padmasambhava.   She is the tigress who accompanies Dorje Tröllö, the most wrathful of Padmasambhava's eight manifestations.

tawa (*lTa ba*, Skt. drishti)   View, in terms of understanding or knowledge of reality.

The Five Elements   *See* Jung-wa nga.

Thegchen (*theg pa chen po*, Skt. Mahayana)   The Greater Vehicle.

Three Distracted Tendencies   *See* dug-sum.

Three Poisons   *See* dug sum.

Three Precious Ones   *See* Könchog sum.

three spheres of being   *See* ku sum.

Thunderbolt Bridge   *See* Dorje Zampa.

Thunderbolt Vehicle   *See* Dorje Thegpa.

ti-mug (*gTi mug*, Skt. moha)   Indifference; the referential strategy by which duality is maintained through obliviating – retracting from focuses which contain no possibility for referential manipulation.

tirthika (*mu sTegs pa*)   One who adheres to any combination of the Four Denials (four philosophical extremes): monism, dualism, eternalism and nihilism.   *See* Four Denials.

tong-pa-nyid (*sTong pa nyid*, Skt. shunyata)   Emptiness.

trek-chod (*khregs gCod*)   Exploding the confines of conventional reality. The practices of Dzogchen where one 'finds the presence of awareness in the dimension of' some specified focus.

tri (*khrid*)   Transmission through explanation.

trül-ku / tulku (*sprul sKu*, Skt. nirmanakaya)   The sphere of realised manifestation or realised form.   'Emanation body', the human body aspect of enlightenment.   'Trül' should not be confused with the syllable 'trul' (*'krul* – delusion); or 'trul' (*'phrul* – appearances').

Tsa-wa'i Lama (*rTsa ba'i bLa ma*, Skt. Mulaguru)   Root Teacher. There are two types of Root Teacher: there is the vajra master from whom one receives empowerment and explanation of the Tantric teachings, and there is the specific Root Teacher who points out the nature of Mind.

tsül-trim (*tshul khrims,* Skt. shila) Discipline. *See* the Six Perfections.

Tsogyel Tröllö (*mTsho rGyal gro lod*) Yeshé Tsogyel manifesting as Dorje Tröllö, who displays the unpredictable quality of yeshé cholwa – wisdom gone wild. *See also* yeshé cholwa.

tsöndrü (*brTson 'grus,* Skt. virya) Vigour. *See* the Six Perfections.

tu-mo (*gTum mo,* Skt. chandali) Literally, 'fierce woman'. The yoga of 'spatial heat', an important practice of Milarépa, Réchungpa and Khandro Yeshé Réma (Khyungchen Aro Lingma).

vajra *See* dorje.

vajra pride (*lha'i nga rGyal*) The sense in which practitioners realise themselves to be inseparable from the awareness-being.

Vajrayana *See* Dorje Thegpa.

wang (*dbang,* Skt. abhisheka) Tantric empowerment; transmission through employing symbol.

wisdom display (*ye shes rol pa'i ngang*) Wisdom display refers to a woman's externally manifested quality, in which her internal compassion moves in external wisdom space. It refers to a man's internal sensitivity from which external power arises. Wisdom here means the 'state of knowingness' – the capacity to comprehend whatever presents itself through feeling its emptiness rather than by analysing its content. The divisionless experience of wisdom and method constitutes the goal of Tantra. *See* method display.

wisdom-being *See* yidam.

yab-yum (*yab yum*) Father-mother. The male-female imagery and practices of inner Tantra.

yeshé cholwa (*ye shes 'chol ba*) Crazy wisdom; wisdom gone wild; wisdom that is unpredictably unpredictable. Wild style of behaviour connected with wrathful practice in charnel grounds. (See *Crazy Wisdom* by Chögyam Trungpa, Shambhala, 1991). Wisdom that has no referential coordinates with regard to spiritual formulas. Wisdom that gives rise to activities that cannot be understood in terms of religious conservatism.

A type of realisation often manifested by Mahasiddhas, and one which is often criticised by those who adhere to conventional religious propriety. To this day puritanical fundamentalists attempt to discredit this manifestation of enlightened activity.

Yeshé Tsogyel (*ye shes mTsho rGyal*)   The female Tantric Buddha. The spiritual consort of Padmasambhava.   She is the origin of the Mother Essence Lineage, and the most important figure in the Aro gTér. Khyungchen Aro Lingma, a great female gTértön of the late 19th and early 20th centuries, received the Aro gTér directly from Yeshé Tsogyel, and transmitted it to her son Aro Yeshé.   This is the lineage now held by Ngak'chang Rinpoche and Khandro Déchen.

yidag (*yi dvags,* Skt. preta)   One who starves for anything but is unable to derive any nutrition from that for which it starves.   This can apply to intellectuals, spiritual materialists, spiritual imperialists, or to anyone who feels empty of things that are external.   A class of mytho-symbolic beings with thin necks and very wide mouths.   Whatever they eat turns to fire or poison.   Offerings can be made to them symbolically by practitioners, and by this means they are able to derive a sense of being nurtured.

yidam (*yi dam,* Skt. ishtadevata)   A personal practice of awareness-being.

yogi / yogini   *See* naljorpa / ma.

Za Rahula (*gZa' ra hu la*)   *See* ma-za-dor-sum.

zap-lam (*zap lam*)   Literally, the profound path.   The method by which one unifies bliss and emptiness.   In terms of this book, it refers to the practice of arising as the yidam in order to transmute an emotion.

zhé-dang (*zhe sDang,* Skt. dvesha)   Aversion; the referential strategy by which duality is maintained through fixating on focuses of friction that exist when threats are projected on to the world.

zhi (*gZhi*)   The ground of being, the base.

zopa (*bZod pa,* Skt. kshanti)   Patience.   *See* the Six Perfections.

Ngak'chang Rinpoche executing a calligraphy

Appendix A

Sky Signatures

The calligraphies in this book are the work of Ngak'chang Rinpoche. They are a new set of calligraphies, rather than the ones initially executed for *Rainbow of Liberated Energy*. Ngak'chang Rinpoche was keen to replace the original calligraphies, as he felt that they represented a phase of the craft in which his brush work was very young and inexperienced. These new calligraphies speak for themselves, but we have decided to include something about the background of the images.

Ngak'chang Rinpoche describes the form of words in the Tibetan scripts as: 'script-symbols from the sky-expanse'. He sometimes calls them 'sky signatures'. To introduce readers to the meaning that lies behind the appearance of these calligraphies, here is what Rinpoche has said about this art:

> If a calligraphy is authentically executed; the 'sky' signs itself, within itself and out of itself, in its own dimension. The nature of Mind is like the sky, an expanse without limit. The ideas and images that arise within it, are like clouds in the sky. Clouds appear and disappear, but the nature of the sky is unchanged. When a spontaneous calligraphy can arise as freely as the play of clouds, then maybe the sky has signed its signature.

The script Rinpoche uses is called *u-mèd*. It originates from the ancient script *lha-bab-yig-gé*, meaning: 'script-symbol from the sky-expanse'. In Tibetan culture the written word is regarded as sacred, because it carries the knowledge of liberation. The form of these 'sky signatures' is both very ancient and very modern. Their spontaneous style was first evolved by the late venerable Rig'dzin Chögyam Trungpa Rinpoche, as a consequence of the influence of Shunryu Suzuki Roshi. Shunryu Suzuki Roshi was a close friend of Trungpa Rinpoche, and a master calligrapher. Variants of this spontaneous style were later taken up by other Lamas, including H. H. Ta'i Situ Rinpoche. Spontaneous calligraphy is very new to the Tibetan tradition and as yet has no rules. This means that Lamas tend to work rather individually.

Rinpoche works with Chinese brushes but uses traditional Indian ink. The Indian ink is reduced by heating to increase the shellac content, which gives the images their characteristic crispness. As distinct from the Chinese and Japanese styles, Rinpoche works with a heavily-loaded brush, rather than with a 'dry' or sparsely-loaded brush. Due to the speed at which the calligraphies are executed, droplets of ink explode onto the paper, causing the characteristic splatters. The paper is hand-made rag paper from Sikkim. During production, it is pressed between thread-bare blankets, which gives it its unique heavily-ridged texture. It has many unusual qualities, such as inconsistent texture and a sporadically non-absorbent surface. It is this texture which causes the characteristic ragged edges of the brush strokes.

The following vignettes of the history of Rinpoche's calligraphy were originally included in *Rainbow of Liberated Energy*. Rinpoche had intended this material to be omitted from *Spectrum of Ecstasy* but we requested that certain passages be retained and included here as they provide a delightful insight into his personal history.

I often worked by candlelight in the evenings. The candles guttered and were occasionally prone to minor explosions. Writing by candlelight was an eventful procedure. McLeod Ganj in the winter was a long series of power cuts. Often the only constant source of light emanated from Yeshé Khandro's kerosene stove[1] – a warm glow that betokened fried noodle *tsè-cho-cho*.[2] The intermittent lightning was a better light source than the sputtering candles that dribbled on my notebook, continually threatening to set fire to the paper. Amji Pema la[3] would be sitting with his last patient of the day, taking pulses and asking diagnostic questions, which were periodically obliterated by dramatic rolls of thunder. Thunder is so much louder in the mountains than elsewhere. Tibetans call thunder 'the voice of the dragon', and when you live in those high places the image is highly evocative.

During the time I was with them, they taught me the *u-chen tsugs*, the great-headed script which is used in the carving of texts onto wooden printing blocks. Writing these characters became such a pleasure and fascination to me that I filled many rolls of paper with thousands of awareness-spells (*ngak* or mantra). I used to make presents of these to fill the mani-khorlos, the 'wish-path wheels' that the older Tibetans especially love to spin as they walk to and from the market.

---

1 Electricity is a strictly erratic commodity in the Himalayas.

2 *Tsè-cho-cho* is a Tibetan variant of vegetable chow mein.

3 Amji (Doctor) Pema la and his wife Yeshé Khandro were the people Ngak'chang Rinpoche stayed with while living in McLeod Ganj and Kathmandu.

Later, my friend and vajra brother, Lama Sonam Sangpo Rinpoche, showed me how to write in the *u-mèd tsugs*, the cursive without-head style. This almost entirely separate alphabet was difficult to learn, especially as there are several different forms of it. He had endless patience, checking the new shapes that were unfamiliar to my hand. Sonam Sangpo Rinpoche is one of the saintliest people I have ever known, and I am always deeply moved by his genuineness and supreme good heart. When my writing was obviously utterly appalling he'd say: "Yes, good, from this you start and become excellent". And when my writing was passable he'd say: "Oh, this is very wonderful!" He always seemed so pleased by every minor improvement that I made.

A calligraphy is an act of self-disclosure –
it hides nothing of what we are – so showing people your
calligraphies is a bit like taking off your clothes. It's a naked
presentation of what you are. The blank sheet of paper is an
empty mirror in which we have the opportunity of seeing
ourselves through the brush and ink.

– Ngak'chang Rinpoche

NGAKMA SHARDRÖL RANG-TSAL JA'GYÜR CHHI-MÈD WANGMO

Appendix B

The Confederate Sanghas of Aro

The Confederate Sanghas of Aro are linked groups of White Tradition practitioners in the U.K., Europe, and North America; under the guidance of Ngak'chang Rinpoche and Khandro Déchen, the Lineage Holders of the Aro gTér; and under the spiritual direction of Ngakpa Rig'dzin Dorje, Naljorpa Mingyür Dorje, Ngakma Nor'dzin Pamo, and Ngakpa 'ö-Dzin Tridral.

The White Lineages of the Nyingma School are sometimes known as the house-holder or non-monastic traditions. The colour white has an array of meanings that apply to those whose practice is primarily based within the Tantras. In Tibet, white is commonly regarded as a colour worn by lay people, and therefore connotes that the wearers are not monks or nuns (who wear red or maroon), although they are ordained practitioners. White is also the colour of purity – the colour of undyed cloth. As a Tantric symbol, white relates to the aspect of practice in which nothing has to be renounced at the outer level, because everything is regarded as intrinsically pure – pure from beginninglessness.

The lineages of the White Tradition owe their inspiration to Padmasambhava and Yeshé Tsogyel (the Tantric Buddhas) and teach, more than any other, integration of practice with everyday life.

Appendix B

Many great siddhas and accomplished masters in these lineages have been nomads, farmers or crafts-people. Some have lived as hidden yogis and yoginis, with nobody knowing who they were. There have been great teachers who have been illiterate, yet whose teachings that have occupied scholars for centuries. Many important Lamas of this tradition, both men and women, have been family people, whose family lives have demonstrated the essence of the teaching in its most profound respects. The teachings and practice style of the White Tradition can obviously be of immense benefit to us in the West today. The Confederate Sanghas of Aro have been established to make this tradition more accessible.

Sang-ngak-chö-dzong, the first of the Aro sanghas, was established in 1977, and became a Registered Tibetan Buddhist Charity in 1993. It was given its name by H. H. Jigdral Yeshé Dorje Dudjom Rinpoche, as an inspiration for the establishment of a ngak'phang or White Tradition sangha in the West. Since then, other Aro sanghas have been established as charitable organisations in North America (Aro Gar), Austria (Aro Gesellschaft), Germany (Aro Gemeinschaft), and the Netherlands (Aro Stichting).

We publish a quarterly magazine called *vision*, which provides information on the ngak'phang tradition of the Nyingma School and occasionally also on the White Lineages of the Kagyüd and Sakya Schools. The Confederate Sanghas of Aro hold retreats and open teachings at various locations throughout the year.

Ngak'chang Rinpoche and Khandro Déchen teach regularly in Britain and the U.S.A. (New York and California), where they have personal students (apprentices and disciples). They also occasionally teach in Germany, Austria and Switzerland in conjunction with their senior disciples, such as Ngakpa Rig'dzin Dorje, who have apprentices in these countries.

The Confederate Sanghas of Aro are engaged in raising funds to establish a retreat place in Britain. It will be called Aro Gar, after the valley in the Himalayas where Khyungchen Aro Lingma established the yogic encampment in which the Aro gTér cycles of teachings were first given. This will become the permanent home for the style of teaching and practice for which Ngak'chang Rinpoche and Khandro Déchen have become known. Once Aro Gar has been established, annual summer open teaching retreats will be held in the style of yogic encampments, where it will be possible to study a wide variety of Tantric arts and crafts, as well as the meditative practices of the inner Tantras.

We have already acquired a collection of Nyingma texts of the Khordong gTér and Dudjom gTér, plus an extensive library of English-language books. We have assembled a collection of statues and thangkas of the major Nyingma awareness-beings. Among the sa gTér (earth gTér that are physical objects, as well as actual texts) that are the treasures of the Aro Tradition, Aro Gar will house the shrine of three fabulous spiritual heirlooms: the sacred meteorite-iron nine-pronged gTér vajra of Padmasambhava which was discovered by Guru Chöwang; the bell and dorje of Jomo Menmo; and, the empowerment vase of Ratna Lingpa.

Ngak'chang Rinpoche and Khandro Déchen wish to establish Aro Gar as a happy, creative environment in which the qualities of human warmth and friendliness are paramount, and extended to all who wish to participate in the enactment of vision. We hope to be able to encourage the creative talents of the individual, to pass on skills, and to provide a rich variety of supports for practice. As a house-holding tradition, we stress the importance of enabling people to establish their contexts of practice in their own homes.

Once the land is acquired, other Lamas of the Nyingma tradition will be invited to teach, as well as Lamas of other Tibetan schools who have specialised in art and craft skills of the inner Tantras. Although there will be a strong emphasis on the art, music and dance aspects of the ngak'phang tradition, Ngak'chang Rinpoche and Khandro Déchen also wish to establish a training course in Buddhist counselling and psychotherapeutic skills. Any contributions toward these exciting endeavours are warmly welcomed – however small.

For further information on open teachings and retreats, and the charitable aims and objectives of the Confederate Sanghas of Aro; the Apprenticeship Programme with Ngak'chang Rinpoche and Khandro Déchen; Ngakpa Rig'dzin Dorje; Naljorpa Mingyür Dorje; Ngakma Nor'dzin Pamo and 'ö-Dzin Tridral please write to:

Sang-ngak-chö-dzong (U.K.)
The Administrative Secretary
P.O. Box 65, Penarth
South Glamorgan CF64 1XY
U.K.

Aro Gar (U.S. & Canada)
The Administrative Secretary
P.O. Box 247, Chelsea Station
New York NY 10113-0247
U.S.A.

Aro Gesellschaft (Austria)
c/o Renate & Dr. Lukas Gallei
Am Forst 17
A-7212 Forchtenstein
Austria

Aro Gemeinschaft (Germany)
c / o Jürgen Pfundt
An den Hueren 99
D-41066 Moenchengladbach
Germany

Aro Stichting (Netherlands)
c / o Marinus Lazaroms
Asterstraat 2
6301-WZ
Valkenburg a / d Geul
Netherlands

Please include a large stamped self-addressed envelope (or International Reply Coupons).

We can also be contacted via the International Aro Tradition website at http://www.aroter.org

Index

Abandonment, 29, 49-51
Active-compassion, 82, 159, 252
Adzom Dorje, 148
Anticipation, 89, 157, 189, 192
A-rig Shé-zér Khandro, 148
Aro Yeshe, 148
Attraction, 154; as one of the distracted tendencies, 22-3, 44-5, 51-2, 63, 154, 189, 209, 266
Aversion, as one of the distracted tendencies, 22, 44-5, 51-2, 63, 101, 189, 266
Awareness-being, 20, 117, 177, 267; envisionment practice of, 160; wrathful, 117; see also Wisdom being; Yidam
Awareness-spell, 114, 176, 266

Bön, 113, 115, 177, 270
Buddha, 64, 80; Tantric, 266
Buddha families, 21
Buddha-karmas, 175
Buddhism, 27, 38, 57, 187; androcentric bias of, 268; as belief system, 10-11; trap of, 202;
Buddhist, 18, 33, 39-41, 68, 144; artificial personality, 79; centres, 20, 109; concept of 'sin', 45;

point of view, 200; practice, 16, 201; texts, 44

Chang, 176
Chhi-'mèd Rig'dzin Rinpoche, 63, 90, 177
Chö-phen, 149
Chögyam Trungpa Rinpoche, 53, 151
Clarity, 89-90, 92, 98, 119, 143, 174, 243, 248, 264, 266; association with anger, 140, 147, 203, 272; dreams of, 27; of undisturbed water, 147; result of shi-nè, 195, 248
Compassion, 114, 117, 151, 158-60, 201, 205, 264, 266, 270-1; as cummunication, 19, 263, 271; as discriminating awareness, 243, 252; as form, 82; desireless desire of, 158; idiot, 160; intention of, 202; of Yeshé Tsogyel, 59, 63; and cynicism, 172; see also Discriminating awareness; Form
Compassionate activity, 201, 252, 264-5; men as source of, 264, 270
Consolidating, 189, 192
Counselling, 56-8; see also Therapy; Psychotherapy
Crazy-wisdom, 176, 177, 178;

of Drukpa Kunlegs, 176-7
Creativity, 29, 173, 233-4; primal, 17

Dagmèdma, 179
Dalai Lama, 113
Dance, 36, 95, 116, 185, 194, 248, 260-7; of pawos and khandros, 187, 259-60, 267, 271-3; of Sengé Dongma, 266; performance, 14; spontaneous, 74, 80
Death, 8, 40, 43, 69, 134, 138, 186, 211; as opposite of life, 187; instant, 211; of spiritual culture, 115; Row, 94
Desire, 30, 94, 101, 151-60, 193; as lust, 44; connection with compassion, 205; for comfort, 9; for security, 210
Dharmadhatu, 202
Dharmakaya, 121
Direct transmission, 148
Discriminating awareness, 151, 159, 243; as compassion, 252; *see also* Compassion
Distracted-being, 24, 33, 36, 38, 95, 98, 195; *see also* Unenlightenment
Dorje, 149, 266
Dorje Legpa, 146
Dorje Sempa, 266
Dorje Thegpa, 246; *see also* Thunderbolt Vehicle; Vajrayana
Dorje Tröllö, 177, 206
Dreams of clarity, 27
Drub-thab, 114
Drukpa Kagyüd; lineage, 61
Drukpa Kunlegs, 176-7; *see also* Crazy-wisdom
Duality, 16-17, 22-3, 27, 31, 33, 41, 48, 52-4, 76, 128, 151, 168, 195, 237, 239, 249-50, 260; appearance of, 263; as indirect experience, 75; as inspiration for practice, 17; association with human body, 64; constrictions of, 160; desire-fulfillment machine of, 159; disenchantment with, 244; entering into, 67; illusion of, 39, 43, 249-50, 263; *see also* Ego
Dukkha, 252
Dzogchen, 50, 63, 147, 177, 197, 245; practice of, 80; Protectors of, 146; transmission, 148; view, 51

Ego, 33-4, 66-7
Ekajati, 146
Empowerment, 114, 178
Emptiness, 41, 51, 53-4, 70, 132; allowing humour, 156; as ecstasy, 247, 266; as equivalent to form, 54, 59, 195, 271; as essence of being, 13-16, 187, 262-3; as female, 263-5; as source, 17, 18, 88, 91, 174, 265, 270; as security, 209; avoidance (fear) of, 158, 186, 210, 248; clinging to, 269; experience of, 24, 119, 121, 145, 195, 212, 239-40, 265, 273; form and, 65, 69, 77, 108, 151, 160, 197, 252, 263, 270-1; getting used to, 16, 23, 194-5; in relation to view, 81-2, 250; of rationality, 55; of Yeshé Tsogyel, 59; qualities, 42-3, 259-60; *see also* Tong-pa-nyid
Energy; constricted, 27, 47, 103-4, 125, 188, 204-5, 273; ecstatic, 194; emotional, 9, 107, 112, 117, 203, 239, 251; destructive, 276; liberated, 28, 103-4, 143, 158, 174, 242, 247; nature of, 6, 130; negative, 105; of emptiness, 266; play of, 13, 15; sphere of, 17-18, 23; *see also* Khyil-khor

Index

Enlightenment, 22, 27-8, 32, 73, 152, 194, 203, 242; avoidance of, 69-70; beginningless, 17, 28, 48-9, 146, 259, 267, 272; energetic aspect of, 176; imitation of, 78; non-conceptual nature of, 253; non-duality with unenlightenment, 33, 40, 67, 195-7, 209; difficulty in recognising, 29; symbols of, 112, 118; *see also* Liberation; Realisation

Failure, 132, 243, 244; as ornament, 91-2, 99-100; *see also* Success

Fantasising, 189-90

Form, 194; as active-compassion, 82, 252, 270-1; as discriminating awareness, 252; as male, 265; clinging to, 50, 69, 195, 197, 269; emptiness and, 17, 53-4, 65, 69, 108, 151, 160, 263, 271; emptiness of, 59; multiplicity of, 249-50, 262; of the irrational, 55-6; play of, 13, 15, 77, 264; qualities, 42, 53-4, 274, 260; transient nature of, 41-3, 271; *see also* Compassion

Formless Mahamudra, 80

Four Denials, 48

Four Naljors, 38, 80

Freezing, 189-92

Gélug, 115

Gampopa, 179

Géshe, 176

Geshé Damchö Yönten, 115

God, 48-9, 108, 200; and Devil, 33

Gommèd, 80

Ground of being, 13, 15, 88

gTér, 19, 177, 270

gTérma, 270

gTértön, 19

gYo-wa, 51

Heart Sutra, 54

Indications, 271-2

Indifference; as one of the three distracted tendencies, 22, 44-5, 51-2, 63, 101, 189; transmuted, 266

Infinite variety, 250, 262; *see also* Form

Insecurity, 140-1, 143, 159, 167, 169, 212, 240; as security, 40-1, 132, 209-10, 245

Intellect, 141-2, 203; abandoning, 23, 88, 241; as aggression, 142; as experience, 30, 261; as obstacle, 48, 62-3, 173-4; limitations of, 16, 29, 33-4, 74, 81, 104, 213, 241, 254, 265, 272

Intensity, 9, 92, 205, 275; artificial, 47, 191, 240, 249; leading to obsession, 189; seeking, 6, 8-9, 49, 51

Jamyang Khyentsé Wangpo, 114

Justification, 89, 95, 105, 143; as righteous indignation, 200; letting go of, 94, 146-7

Kagyüd, 80; Drukpa, 61; Karma, 179

Kalachakra Tantra, 113

Karma, 105, 118; *see also* Karmic vision

Karma Kagyüd, 179

Karmic vision, 201-2

Khandro-pawo-nyi-da-mélong-gyüd, 222, 270

Khandro Ten'dzin Drölkar, 178

Khatvangha, 63

Khor-wa, 77

Khyil-khor, 20, 126; energy of, 110; experience of, 108-11, 118-19; mirroring, 116; of inner elements, 107, 112; of phenomenal existence, 267

Khyungchen Aro Lingma, 148, 149, 177, 270

Kunzang Dorje Rinpoche, 178-9

Lama, 68; activities of, 176; as one of the Three Roots of Tantra, 270; as projection, 61-2; Bönpo, 115; crazy-wisdom activity of, 178; devotion to, 59, 267, 276; relating to, 58, 261; services, 189; Tibetan, 113; transmission of, 148

Lé-shi, 175

Lha-tong, 50

Lhun-drüp, 80

Liberated-being, 17, 24, 33, 73, 239; see also Enlightenment

Liberation, 19, 22, 28, 41, 45, 63, 91, 242; fear of, 47; nature of, 14; see also Enlightenment, Realisation

Lineage; celibate and non-celibate, 246; Karma Kagyüd, 179; of Padmasambhava, 161; of Shakya Shri, 61

Living the view, 8, 178, 254

Long-process, 58-60; bypassing, 58; see also Counselling; Short-process; Therapy

Lotus; as symbol, 160-1; position, 85-7

Love, 64, 110; being in, 32, 110, 275, 116-17; for pawos and khandros, 259, 267, 272, 275; for self, 110; for spade, 255; need for, 158; of emptiness and form, 151, 160

Lung, 114

Magic Dance, 113

Mantra, 114

Medicine Wheel, 119

Mahamudra; Formless, 80

Mahayana, 246

Mandala; see Khyil-khor

Manic-depression, 204

Manipulation, 45, 46, 101, 102, 251

Mantra, see Awareness-spell

Marpa, 179

Maslow, Abraham, 39

Ma-za-dor-sum, 146

Meditation, 81, 103, 247; 'bad', 244; emotion as subject/object of, 241; encouraging view, 74; practice of silent sitting, 15, 23, 74-6, 87; see also Shi-nè

Meditational deity, 20; see also Awareness-being; Yidam

Mé-long; as ornament, 148-9; as symbol, 147-8; see also Mirror

Method display, 274; see also Wisdom display

Milarépa, 179-81; secret namthar of, 61

Mirror; as symbol, 143, 265; of Mind, 32, 147-8, 265; -wisdom, 143; see also Mé-long

Monks, 115, 156, 176-7, 268

Mount Meru, 68, 113

Multiplicity, 262, 266; see also Form

Naljorpa, 179

Namkha'i Mélong Dorje, 149

Namkha'i Norbu Rinpoche, 177

Namthar, 61

Naropa, 179

Natural condition, 16, 33, 55, 125, 137, 165, 185, 194

Nature of Mind, 148, 177, 180

New Age, 207

Ngakpa/ngakma, 176, 178

Ngak'phang, 133, 246

Nirmanakaya, 23, 121

Nirvana, 272

Non-dual, 28, 65, 69, 80, 237, 262-3, 271; conceptualising, 54; experience, 16, 25, 34, 59, 99, 104, 237, 249, 260; expression,

17; qualities of elements, 125, 137, 147, 151, 165, 182, 185; *see also* Enlightenment; Liberation

Nuns, 268

Nyi-mèd, 50

Nyingma, 114, 147, 239

Obliterating, 166, 189, 191; *see also* Freezing; Fantasising

One taste, 51, 247

Oral transmission 148

Padmasambhava, 19, 24, 118, 160, 161, 218-19, 268

Paradox, 29, 67, 69, 271, 273; as heart of Tantra, 41-2, 261-2; of duality / non-duality, 14; of language, 23, 54

Paranoia, 165-7, 169, 171, 172-5, 243

Passion, 151, 275

Patriarchy, 269

Pema, 160; *see also* Lotus

Personality, 247-8, 273; artificial, 79; authentic, 250; of khandros, 117, 200; of Yeshé Tsogyel, 60-1

Play, 46-7, 85, 92, 99, 156, 160, 162; of elements, 267; of emptiness and form, 77, 266; of energy, 13, 15, 272; of form, 15; primal, 187

Prana, *see* rLung

Projection; as basis for devotion, 61; as problem, 61; of anger, 143; paranoid, 166-7

Protectors, 146

Psychotherapy, 56, 58; *see also* Counselling; Therapy

Psychosis, 23, 59, 65, 171

Pure elements, 202

Rahula, 146

Rationality, 55, 261, 264; letting go of, 55-6

Realisation, 40, 61, 74, 160, 176, 179, 242; approach to, 202; experience of, 32, 198; extending to everyone, 151; opportunities for, 63, 246, 247; practices for, 7; taking on appearance of, 79-80; *see also* Enlightenment; Liberation

Realised manifestation, 18-19, 23

Rebirth, 121

Réchungpa, 179

Reference point, 9, 22, 42-7, 51, 73, 75, 252; freedom from, 151, 160, 253; non-attachment to, 100; impermanent nature of, 43, 65-6; pain as, 47; securing, 44, 46, 91, 155

Ri-mèd, 114

Rigpa, 51; *see also* Non-duality

Rinchen, 134

rLung, 114

Ro-chig, 247; *see also* One taste

Root Teacher, 59, 178

Séra Jé, 115

Sakya, 114

Sambhogakaya, 23, 155; *see also* Sphere of energy

Samsara, 52, 64, 69, 70, 77, 78, 101-3, 249, 250, 272; *see also* Khor-wa

Sang-yum, 61, 179

Sang-yab, 61

Security; as insecurity, 40, 132, 209-10, 245; claustrophobia of, 69, 77; impermanence of, 126, 170; of control, 9; of pain, 47; seeking, 40-1, 47, 128, 137, 142, 157, 169, 248; total, 69

Seng-gé Dongma, 266

Sense fields, 18, 23, 243

Sexual Tantra, 245-6

Index

Sexuality, 152, 261,246-7

Shakya Shri, 61

Shi-nè; as facilitating view, 81, 110; as method of discovering space, 16, 38, 156; practice of, 15-16, 23, 74-5, 85-9, 144, 148, 166, 174, 184-5, 248, 274; *see also* Meditation

Short-process, 58; *see also* Long-process

Siddhi, 63

Sin, 44

Skandhas, 21

sKu-mNyé, 226

Sky Dancer, 60, 259

Spacious passion, 267

Sphere of energy, 17, 18, 23, 73; *see also* Sambhogakaya

Sphere of realised manifestation, 18, 73

Sphere of relative manifestation, 18, 73; *see also* Nirmanakaya

Sphere of unconditioned potentiality, 15, 18; *see also* Dharmakaya

Success; and failure, 91-2, 99-101, 132, 244; as ornament, 99-100, 244; *see also* Failure

Sulking, 232-3

Sutra, 60, 246, 250

Symbolism, 18, 265; as compassionate communication, 19-21; contradictions in, 113, 115, 118-19; cultural, 112-13, 120-1; imagery, 18, 23; meaning of, 63; of dorje and drilbu, 266; of elements, 110-11; of enlightenment, 112, 118; of lotus, 161; of tiger, 177; of yab-yum, 245; of Yeshé Tsogyel, 62

Symbolic transmission, 148, 180

Tashi Chhi-'dren, 177

Therapy, 56-8, 212; *see also*

Counselling; Psychotherapy

Thig-lé, 203

Three Poisons, 44

Three Terrible Oaths, 177-8, 206-7, 210-12

Thunderbolt Bridge, 121

Thunderbolt Vehicle, *see* Dorje Thegpa; Vajrayana

Tibet, 113-15, 132, 179, 246, 270

Tibetan; cosmologies, 113-14; culture, 10, 60-2, 86, 133, 181; language, 113

Tirthika, 48

Tong-pa-nyid, 88; *see also* Emptiness

Transmission, 114, 148, 180, 276

Trek-chod, 245

Tri, 114

Tsogyel Tröllö, 206

Tu-mo, 181

Unenlightenment, 40, 253, 269, 272-3; as unreal, 80, 266; non-duality with enlightenment, 33, 64, 67, 197, 203, 209; unlearning, 256; *see also* Enlightenment

Vajra master, 59

Vajra pride, 59, 64

View, 73-5, 275; as emptiness, 82, 250; as result of shi-nè, 81, 110, 156, 176, 195; of Dzogchen, 51; of Tantra, 250; working with, 238-45; *see also* Living the view; Meditation

Visualisation, 59-60, 62-3, 160, 265; of Yeshé Tsogyel, 62-3

Wang, 114; *see also* Empowerment

Wisdom; and compassion, 114, 172, 243, 252, 266, 274; as emptiness, 82, 270-1; mirror-, 143;

primordial, 135, 140, 271; *see also* Compassion
Wisdom-activities, 175
Wisdom-display, 259, 264; *see also* Method-display
Wisdom being, 20, 59; *see also* Yidam, Awareness-being
Wisdom-fire, 151, 160
Wrathful, 63, 117, 206, 266

Yab-yum, 245
Yeshé Tsogyel, 19, 24, 59-64, 146, 177, 206, 259, 266, 268
Yidag, 201
Yidam, 20, 59, 118, 146, 266, 267, 270; *see also* Awareness-being; Wisdom-being

Zap-lam, 245, 247